DIS

FUKUSHIMA. -JAPAN- NUCLEAR DISASTER.

DISASTERS IN THE AIR

Andrew Brookes

IAN ALLAN
Publishing

*To Teresa, Charles
and Katherine
The best reasons one
pilot has for coming
back alive*

CONTENTS

First published 1992

ISBN 0 7110 2037 X

Published by Ian Allan Ltd, Shepperton, Surrey; and printed by Ian Allan Printing Ltd at their works at Coombelands in Runnymede, England.

ABBREVIATIONS AND GLOSSARY

ATC	Air Traffic Control
CVR	Cockpit Voice Recorder
DME	Distance Measuring Equipment. Equipment used to measure, in nautical miles, an aircraft's slant range from the beacon.
FDR	Flight Data Recorder
FL	Flight Level. A level of constant atmospheric pressure related to a specific pressure datum (1013.2mb). Each level is stated in three digits, eg FL250 represents a barometric altimeter indication of 25,000ft; FL255, an indication of 25,500ft.
GCA	Ground Controlled Approach
GPWS	Ground Proximity Warning System
ILS	Instrument Landing System
MDA	Minimum Descent Altitude. The lowest altitude, expressed in feet above mean sea level, to which descent is authorised on final approach during a standard instrument procedure where no electronic glideslope is provided.
NDB	Non-Directional Beacon. Enables the pilot of an aircraft equipped with direction finding equipment to determine his bearing to or from the transmitting radio beacon. He can then 'home' on, or track to or from, the station.
nm	nautical mile
NOTAM	Notices to Airmen. NOTAMs contain information (not known sufficiently in advance to publicise by other means), the timely knowledge of which is essential to personnel concerned with flight operations.
RT	Radio Telephony
TACAN	TACtical Air Navigation. A UHF air navigation aid which provides suitably equipped aircraft with a continuous indication of bearing and distance to the TACAN station.
Transponder	Otherwise known as Secondary Surveillance Radar (SSR). Enables each suitably equipped aircraft to superimpose its individual designator on the radar return painted on a ground controller's screen. In enabling controllers to differentiate between 'blips' with accuracy, it confers a higher degree of safety in a crowded and high-speed environment such as an airway. If an emergency occurs, the pilot of an aircraft fitted with a transponder 'squawks' Emergency Code 7700 to alert the ground agency.
VOR	VHF Omnidirectional Range. A ground-based electronic nav aid transmitting VHF signals 360° in azimuth, orientated from magnetic north.
VORTAC	VOR/Tacan. A navigational aid which provides VOR azimuth, Tacan azimuth and Tacan DME at one site.

INTRODUCTION

The English word 'travel' has its origins in the French *travail*, meaning 'work' or 'torment'. And *travail*, in turn, was derived from the Latin *tripalium*, a three-staked instrument of torture. Travel in the old days was obviously not meant to be fun.

The nature of travel altered fundamentally once a significant number of people travelled for other than purposeful reasons. That was not until relatively recently; it took until 1972 before more than one in two Americans had ever flown. Perhaps people were slow to find the spare time, cash or imagination to fly to their land of dreams, but it is far more likely that aircraft were long perceived to be not very safe or reliable. An advert issued in 1927 by Bill Boeing's Seattle-based company certainly offered little immediate reassurance: 'The Boeing policy is to so develop airplane design and construction that today's spectacular feat of bravery will become tomorrow's accepted mode of speedy transportation — inexpensive, dependable, safe!'

To illustrate the magnitude of change over the last half century, there were only 26 flights across the North Atlantic during the whole of 1940, whereas about 450 million passengers now board airliners each year in the US alone. While annual world airline departures over the last decade increased by 30% and total passenger numbers by 50%, many flight safety initiatives, such as the fitment of ground proximity warning devices, were being made in parallel. Consequently, the statistic that an annual average of 1,056 fatalities during the 1980s must be set in context. The aviation insurance group AISL has calculated that if airlines were still killing people at the 1950 rate, the annual death toll would be around 15,000. Current accident rates seem proof, not of danger and irresponsibility, but that the vast majority of airlines and their flight crews are operating with commendable skill and care.

We have reached the stage therefore where it is now nearly 20 times safer to get airborne in an airliner than to travel by car. More people die in England and Wales from falling downstairs (568 in a typical year) than from air crashes. Yet there is no denying that the sky can still be an unfriendly place. If an airliner's engines fail while flying down an airway, there is no pulling into the kerb and calling a garage. This explains why the words of Capt A. G. Lamplugh, written over 60 years ago, remain just as relevant today: 'Aviation is itself not inherently dangerous, but to an even greater extent than the sea, it is terribly unforgiving of any carelessness, incapacity or neglect'.

Despite the advent of super new airliners, the human dimension of flying remains constant though this may not be immediately apparent from US Government Flying Regulations issued in 1920:

'Pilots will not wear spurs while flying.
'Don't take the machine into the air unless you are satisfied that it will fly.
'In taking off, look at the ground and the air.
'Pilots should carry hankies in a handy position to wipe off goggles.

'Riding on the steps, wings or tails of a machine is prohibited.

'Learn to gauge altitude, especially on landing.

'If you see another machine near you, get out of the way.

'Do not trust altitude instruments.

'Before you begin a landing glide, see that no machines are under you.

'If flying against the wind and you wish to fly with the wind, don't make sharp turns near the ground. You may crash.

'Do not use aeronautical gasoline in cars or motorcycles.

'Never take a machine into the air unless you are familiar with its controls and instruments.

'If an emergency occurs while flying, land as soon as possible.'

If these Regulations emanated from a government department today, they would likely fill a tome instead of a page and be far more verbose and jargon-ridden. Yet despite their quaintness, these exhortations are in most instances just as valid today as they were 70 years ago.

Consequently, although *Disaster in the Air* deals with transport flying accidents spread over more than half a century, the basic flight safety lessons remain relevant notwithstanding the changing technological background against which they are set. This may explain why my 'air disasters' are not confined simply to those that result in mega-deaths. A 'disaster' can be described as 'something which strikes with calamity', and that does not necessarily involve large numbers. If you are a Buddy Holly fan, the loss of your idol in a flying accident northwest of Mason City, Iowa, on 3 February 1959 will always be a calamity, irrespective of how many died with him. Similarly, the loss of a fully-laden DC-3 in 1940 could make just as big a 'disaster' headline as the loss of a wide body with 400 on board today. Suffice to say that I regard a flying disaster as an accident that might have been prevented.

When dealing with past accidents I have tried to pass on food for thought rather than pious platitudes. It is also worth making the point, via the following extract from a 1962 Flight Safety Foundation Bulletin, that post-accident investigation is no sinecure:

'An inspection lamp was left on at the top of a pair of steps. A person passing knocked the steps, causing the lamp to roll off. On falling, the lamp struck and shattered on a tin containing a fluid which burst into flames. On investigation it was confirmed that the tin contained a highly flammable fluid unauthorised for cleaning purposes. The inspection lamp did not have a protective guard fitted.

(1) What was the cause of the accident?

(2) Whom do we blame?

    a. The person who knocked the steps causing the lamp to fall?

    b. The man who brought the highly flammable liquid into a restricted area for cleaning purposes contrary to regulations?

    c. The person who wilfully or otherwise removed the protective guard from the lamp?

    d. The last person to use the lamp for not reporting the missing guard?

    e. The operator for not ensuring that the lamp was in a sound condition before using it, and for not securing it properly at the top of the steps?

    f. The supervisors who permitted the use of a lamp that did not conform to safety standards, or inappropriate use of highly flammable liquids?'

And that incident was relatively straightforward. How much more complicated is the crash of a US-manufactured jumbo, powered by British engines, owned by a Swedish company and operated by a German airline which crashed while under Australian air traffic control after last being serviced at a Far East airport? If flying was once much simpler, so too was accident investigation.

Finally, as it is so easy to be clever with hindsight, I hope that I do not give any offence to aviators involved in tragic accidents, or to their friends and relatives. I regard all those who have had the misfortune to be part of any flying accident as colleagues who would wish successive generations to learn from their experiences. *Disaster in the Air* is certainly not written to point the finger at anyone — I have enough pilot flying hours under my belt to admit that, sometimes, there but for the Grace of God went I. If this book just stops anyone from thinking that aircraft cannot bite, and stimulates thought as to what to do should that awful moment occur, it will have done its job.

The last aircraft to be launched under the Avro name was the Type 748 short/medium haul airliner. On 8 April 1972, at an airfield near Sienna in Italy, one of the Rolls-Royce Dart turboprop engines on this 748 failed just after take-off. The aircraft was allowed to roll and yaw such that the starboard wing tip struck the ground. As the tip ran along the ground, the aircraft pivoted around it and pitched nose-down. When the 748 finally came to rest, the impact caused the fuselage to break aft of the cabin and the fin tailplane to break rearwards. Fire then broke out, spreading rapidly from front to back. All of which showed how quickly an aircraft can come to grief but modern aircraft are built so well that although four people died on the 748, the flight crew and 14 passengers survived.

THE HINDENBURG

It was not until 1887 that the electrolytic production of aluminium enabled a very lightweight rigid structure of girders to be built around hydrogen-filled gas bags. Once Count von Zeppelin, initially derided as 'the crazy inventor', mated this combination with Daimler engines, the first practical airship was born. Zeppelin's creation was soon to come of age as a weapon of war, but by the time the Count died in 1917, he had become equally convinced that the big airship was ideally suited to transoceanic passenger carriage.

Dr Hugo Eckener, a man of equally massive personality and intellect, succeeded the old Count in control of Luftschiffbau Zeppelin at Friedrichshafen on Lake Constance. But it was not long before the terms of the Versailles Treaty threatened to raze Eckener's airship works to the ground. He saved the day by securing a contract to provide a large airship for the US Navy, and the eventual delivery of the USS *Los Angeles* to the Lakehurst Naval Air Station, New Jersey in 1924 was a personal triumph for Eckener. The good doctor was now given the freedom, if he could raise the money, to build the airship he felt sure would entice German and American financiers to back a transatlantic line.

Although constrained by both lack of money and size of assembly shed at Friedrichshafen, Eckener created what was probably the most successful airship ever built — the *Graf Zeppelin*. Christened by the Count's only child on what would have been his 90th birthday, the *Graf* made a series of spectacular flights to North and South America as well as Siberia. Yet for all its pioneering achievements, *Graf Zeppelin* was really just a demonstration craft that was too small and too slow for regular North Atlantic service. Once a new hangar was completed at Friedrichshafen, the way was clear for Eckener to go for the big one.

LZ (Luftschiff Zeppelin) 129 was the 118th dirigible of the Zeppelin line. Initial design called for an airship 811.1ft long (subsequently reduced to 803.8ft to squeeze inside the 804ft shed at Lakehurst), 135.1ft in diameter and with a gas volume of 7,062,000cu ft. A thousand cubic feet of pure hydrogen under standard conditions weighs 5.61lb; as the same volume of air weighs 80.72lb, the net lift is therefore 75.11lb per 1,000cu ft. With a gross lifting capacity of 236 tons, after allowing for its own weight and fuel LZ 129 could still carry more than 20 tons. This capacity was double that of the *Graf Zeppelin*, and translated into 50 passengers plus a crew of 40-45. Powered by four Daimler-Benz 16-cylinder high speed diesels, newly-developed by a rearming Reich for use in motor torpedo boats, LZ 129 was to be capable of a cruising speed of 77mph and a range of 8,420 miles.

The hull comprised 15 transverse main frames or rings. Each was a 14-storey high 36-sided polygon made from a light alloy of copper and aluminium called duralumin. Joined together by 36 longitudinal duralumin girders, the 15 main frames compartmentalised the ship like an ocean liner and separated the ship's gas cells. Eckener's original intention was to inflate the 16 gas cells with non-inflammable helium. In addition, 14 of them were each to contain a smaller hydrogen filled inner

Above:
Looking forward in the Hindenburg's *control room nose. The elevator wheel on the left controlled the huge horizontal flippers aft which raised or lowered the nose. In front of the elevator man was an altimeter, a variometer showing rate of climb or descent, an inclinometer showing nose-up or nose-down angle, and thermometers recording gas and outside air temperatures. On orders from the captain or officer of the watch, the elevator man also handled the toggles which operated the manoeuvring valves in the middle of the gas cells, and the ballast tanks. On the right of the picture is the rudder wheel for steering, together with gyro and magnetic compasses.*

Below:
The narrow lower walkway leading from bow to stern inside the great airship's belly.

cell. Hydrogen would be valved off to keep the ship balanced as engine fuel was burned, thereby preserving the much more expensive helium. Both automatic and manually operated valves were therefore positioned right in the centre of the hull. Access to them was via an axial walkway running through the exact centre of the airship, and gas was valved up through long 'chimneys' to the top of the envelope.

Unfortunately for the Germans, about 90% of the world's supply of helium was concentrated in a small area around Amarillo, Texas and the US Congress had forbidden the export of this precious resource. Eckener hoped that four Zeppelins would eventually provide a weekly service across the North Atlantic, two built and flown by Germans and the other pair by Americans, and that such a joint venture would persuade Congress to release subsidised helium. This was to prove wishful thinking and the inner cells were never installed. In an effort to safeguard the cells that now had to be filled with flammable hydrogen, six coats of a gelatin solution resembling latex were brushed on to the cotton fabric to render the bags gastight.

LZ 129's maiden flight lasted just over three hours on 4 March 1936, after which Dr Eckener observed, 'gentlemen, at last we have built a real airship'. LZ 129 was still nameless during her early flights but on 31 March she was scheduled to depart across the South Atlantic for Rio. By then she had been christened *Hindenburg* after the late German President and World War 1 hero whose victory over the Russians at the Tannenburg Lakes meant as much to the Germans as Trafalgar did to the British.

That the *Hindenburg* represented Dr Eckener's ideal inter-continental airship was best exemplified by its magnificent and spacious passenger accommodation contained, not in an underslung gondola, but on two decks entirely within the ship's hull. Embarking passengers entered either port or starboard up a pair of stairlike gangways lowered to the ground by a winch. They arrived on the upper 'A' deck to be greeted by a bronze bust of Field Marshal Hindenburg in a niche on the front bulkhead. Leading off two corridors in the centre of 'A' deck were 25 staterooms. Stateroom sounds very grand for a cabin measuring 6ft 6in by 5ft 6in and lacking even a porthole because it was inside the hull. Nevertheless, it far surpassed the cramped conditions of modern long-haul airliners. Each *Hindenburg* cabin had an upper and lower berth, tip-up wash basin with hot and cold running water, collapsible writing table and call facility for the steward. The walls were decorated in pearl grey linen and during the day, the upper berth was folded away and the lower made into a settee to turn the cabin into a comfortable sitting room.

Moreover, there was plenty to see and do outside the cabins. Outboard of the staterooms on the port side was the dining room where all 50 passengers could eat at one sitting. Tablecloths were of quality linen on which were fresh flowers and solid silver cutlery. Fine china sporting the Zeppelin company crest (a white airship outlined in gold superimposed on a blue globe with longitude meridians and latitude parallels in gold) acted as a fitting backdrop to superlative meals prepared by Chef Maier and his four cooks. Chief Steward Kubis and his six stewards, plus a stewardess to care for the children and help lady passengers with their hair, served both tables and cabins. On top of it all the best of German wines were available from a 'cellar' in the keel.

The corresponding space on the starboard side was divided into a lounge and library/writing room; like all public rooms, they were decorated with mural paintings. The comfortable chairs were so light that they could be lifted with two fingers and there was even a 112lb duralumin Bluthner grand piano. Promenade decks outboard of the public rooms were connected by a cross-passage at the after-end of 'A' deck. Passengers spent hours gazing through Plexiglas windows at the land or sea passing underneath — the Hindenburg usually cruised at an altitude of around 800ft.

On the lower 'B' deck were more prosaic features such as crews' quarters, galley serving the dining room above by dumbwaiter and toilets. There was even a shower, the first such luxury aboard any aerial conveyance, which passengers signed up to use. Waste water from both shower and washbasins was collected for use as ballast. There was also a tiny bar which doubled as the only entrance to the smoking room. The latter was pressurised to prevent the admission of any leaking hydrogen, and yellow pigskin leather on the walls further minimised the fire risk. As a final safety measure, a bar steward was on duty night and day to ensure that all smoking materials were extinguished before anyone left his domain. All this, and passage to America, from as little as $400.

The streamlined control car, 28ft long and 9ft across surrounded by glass windows, hung underneath at the front of the airship. Its most important feature was the control room housing the duty officer of the watch, his navigator and the rudder and elevator men. There were servo motors for both elevators and rudders, and a rudimentary autopilot slaved the rudder to the gyro compass. However, in turbulence the automatics were disconnected and the elevators and rudders controlled manually. The elevator man faced a pressure board with indicators for each of the main gas cells, and there was also a ballast board which showed at a glance how much water was in the seven ballast tanks (each of 4,400lb capacity) spaced along the keel. If the sun came out and heated the hydrogen, gas was valved to keep the ship in trim: when it got cooler at night water ballast was let out to increase the lift. The control room had telephone connections to 14 locations around the ship. Orders to the sailmakers on the axial gangway running through the middle of the ship were via a speaking tube, thereby obviating the need for electrical equipment which might have posed a fire risk. Finally, on the starboard side of the control room were the engine telegraphs which, as on a seagoing vessel, summoned power changes from the engineers' room in the keel.

It has to be said that completion of LZ 129 owed much to Adolf Hitler's accession to power. The Nazi Party saw propaganda value in giant airships with swastikas emblazoned on great vertical fins, and in March 1935 Air Minister Goering went so far as to take control formally of the Zeppelin operating company. Resentment at this government interference in his operations, together with a tendency to express loud anti-Nazi opinions, made Dr Eckener no friends in high places. When Goebbels insisted that the *Graf Zeppelin* and *Hindenburg* make a three-day flag waving flight just prior to the referendum on annexation of the Rhineland at the end of March 1936, Eckener did not hide his disapproval. 'If the airships were to be used for political purposes,' he declared, 'it would be the end of the airship.' Goebbels eventually forbade German newspapers to mention Eckener's name or publish his photograph.

On the other hand, Capt Ernst Lehmann, Eckener's most senior captain and a man not averse to entertaining passengers on the concertina, was much more pragmatic and politically adept. The government took advantage of their controlling interest in the operating company to move Eckener upstairs to be chairman of the board, leaving the way clear for Lehmann to take his place as director. It was Lehmann who commanded LZ 129 on its maiden flight and stood on the *Hindenburg's* bridge as she and her stablemate flew in formation over every town and city in the Reich with populations of 100,000 or more. From now on, Eckener found himself increasingly denied any formal say in the operation of the ship.

Hindenburg's first crossing of the South Atlantic at the end of March was a spectacular undertaking given that the new craft had only 128hr 8min flying time. There was the odd engine problem but nothing untoward and on 6 May *Hindenburg* began her first flight to Lakehurst carrying 50 passengers. Lehmann commanded, though Eckener was on board as a passenger, and the trip was a great success. On its return to Europe, the *Hindenburg* landed at the new Rhein-Main international airship base eight miles south of Frankfurt; being 1,000ft nearer to sea level than Friedrichshafen, Frankfurt operations allowed the *Hindenburg* to lift 13,500lb more on take off.

The distance from Frankfurt am Main to Lakehurst is 3,597 miles and the first *Hindenburg* flight time west to east was 49hr 3min. During 1936 she made 10 round trips to the US and on all went very well with minimum maintenance problems. By the end of the operating season in October, the *Hindenburg* was enjoying enormous amounts of favourable publicity around the world, both in the press and from very satisfied customers. Optimism was everywhere. The *Hindenburg's* sister ship, LZ 130, was expected to be completed in September and the first of a new breed — longer and capable of lifting 100 passengers — was scheduled to leave an even bigger Friedrichshafen building shed in the summer of 1938.

On the last three trips of 1936 to South America, Capt Max Pruss, who had commanded *Graf Zeppelin* 16 times across the Atlantic, took over the *Hindenburg*. The great craft was then laid up over winter for inspection and cleaning. As it was now clear that helium would not become available for the foreseeable future, cabin space for 22 more passengers was added to take advantage of the greater lift generated by hydrogen.

At 20.00hrs on 3 May, set against a spectacular searchlight backdrop, the *Hindenburg* departed Frankfurt on her first North American flight of 1937. There were 239lb of mail, 326lb of freight, 1,938lb of luggage and two baskets of dogs on board, but only 36 passengers. The crew numbered 61 including 20 young trainee airshipmen. To mark the new season, the public relations department arranged to fly Herbert Morrison, a radio announcer from WLS Chicago, the 'Prairie Farmer Station', to Lakehurst where he could describe the landing and interview passengers — especially those going on to Chicago — for his Saturday night prime time programme. With everyone embarked, Capt Pruss gave the command, 'Up ship'. A brass band, which had been entertaining all and sundry during loading, struck up 'Deutschland, Deutschland Uber Alles'. Mooring lines were cast off, the nose cone disconnected by Chief Rigger Knorr, and the great ship began to rise. At about 300ft, telegraphs from the command gondola signalled Chief Engineer Sauter and his men to start the diesels. At 20.15hrs, the *Hindenburg* set course 281° to join the Rhine at Koblenz.

Capt Lehmann had boarded the *Hindenburg* at the last moment, but Capt Pruss, late of the Kaiser's Navy and Lehmann's elevator man 20 years earlier, was in command. Given that the Zeppelin company had more ships on the drawing board than in the air, three more captains — Sammt, Bauer and Ziegler — served as watch officers and another — Witteman — travelled as an observer. If the *Hindenburg* was short of anything on that flight, it was not airship expertise.

The French having denied overflying rights, the *Hindenburg* set course down the Rhine to Holland, out to sea over Flushing, a quick jink through the English Channel and then out into the North Atlantic. Facing forward at the rudder wheel reading his compass was the steersman, while on the port side the helmsman stood sideways at the elevator wheel monitoring altitude and inclination. Behind the

Left:
Capt Max Pruss in the
Hindenburg's *control car. To the end*
of his life, Pruss maintained that, 'If
you want to travel quickly, take an
aeroplane; if you want to travel
comfortably, take an airship.'

Below:
Manhattan gets its last look at the
Hindenburg *as Capt Pruss brings her*
down Broadway at 15.00hrs on 6 May
1937 before the sunshine gave way to
thunderstorms. The starboard pair of
engine gondolas, streamlined like 20ft-
long eggs, is visible. Besides a full-time
mechanic, each gondola housed a
1,200hp diesel engine connected to a
four-bladed 20ft diameter wooden
'pusher' propeller to drive the great
cathedral through the sky. Right at the
back of the airship were four huge fins,
each 105ft long, 49ft wide and 12ft
thick at the root.

bridge, the watch and navigating officers bent over the maps and weather charts. Up the stairs and into the hull, Chief Radio Operator Speck and his crew worked the 900-meter band until clear of Ireland and then the 600-meter band over the sea. Position reports were passed back to Hamburg on short wave every 15min and there was an on-board radio service including English and German news broadcasts picked up twice daily. In between there was a brisk traffic in personal telegrams to inform waiting friends and relatives that the *Hindenburg* would arrive at New York on 6 May at 06.00hrs.

Hamburg radioed DEKKA, *Hindenburg's* callsign, to warn of a squall line over the North Sea as the airship crossed Holland. Pruss ordered a turn north to get behind the front, and in this fashion the airship moved down the Channel before turning WSW for mid-Atlantic.

Sunrise on 4 May found her south of the Old Head of Kinsale circling to the north of a small depression. Breakfast started the leisurely round of gracious living for which the Zeppelin line was famous. 5,500lb of fresh meat and chicken, 220lb of fish, 330lb of delicatessen items including caviar, 440lb of dairy products plus 33gall of milk and 800 eggs were just some of the stores loaded at Frankfurt. By the time anyone had space left for a late night snack, the *Hindenburg* was 400 miles north of the Azores steering the great circle route for Cape Race on the tip of Newfoundland.

The ground crew waiting in New Jersey numbered 92 Navy personnel and 139 civilians, the latter paid $1 an hour each. To save money, it was agreed that the Lakehurst landings would take place either at 06.00hrs or 18.00hrs and that ground crews need only be called an hour beforehand. By the evening of 5 May, it was clear that 50mph headwinds had so delayed the ship that it stood no chance of meeting the original arrival time of 06.00hrs the following day. On Pruss' instructions, a signal was sent from DEKKA informing NEL (Lakehurst's callsign) that the landing would be postponed until 18.00hrs.

At dawn on 6 May after a pretty uneventful crossing, the *Hindenburg* was at 700ft over the sea west of Yarmouth, Nova Scotia. She was eight hours behind schedule but on course for Boston 350 miles away. Navigating officer Max Zabel knew that a low pressure area had moved rapidly out of the Mississippi Valley into central Pennsylvania but there was no cause for concern.

North of Boston Lightship, Capt Pruss took his ship down to 600ft and then 500ft. The sun had burnt through the fog by the time the *Hindenburg* crossed the harbour and suburbs of Boston to the joy of spectators below. Then it was over Providence and New Haven, before running down Long Island Sound while everyone grabbed an early lunch so as not to miss the first sight of New York. Packed luggage was piled up under the watchful gaze of the Field Marshal's bust as all was made ready for a quick turn round at Lakehurst. Return bookings had been so good — many passengers were heading for the coronation of King George VI — that even the 112lb aluminium piano had been left at Frankfurt to free maximum weight for paying payload. The *Hindenburg* would refuel and reload in record time, and the signal sent to NEL at 14.55hr set the tone: RETURN OF LAUNDRY IS NOT NECESSARY STOP WILL SAIL AS SOON AS POSSIBLE PRUSS.

But the public relations drum still had to be beaten and as New York hove into sight, Capt Pruss steered *Hindenburg* towards Times Square, passing directly over sightseers on the West Side of Broadway. From every available vantage point, thousands craned their necks to see the great shape slide past gleaming in the sunlight. After rounding the Statue of Liberty, Pruss wowed them over Ebbet's Field in Brooklyn where the Dodgers were playing Pittsburgh Pirates. Then he turned north again to cross Wall Street and the Hudson before turning south for New Jersey.

After requesting Lakehurst weather at 15.30hrs, NEL replied: BROKEN CUMULUS CLOUDS SURFACE WIND SOUTHEAST ELEVEN KNOTS GUSTS TWENTY KNOTS SURFACE TEMPERATURE SEVENTY FOUR PRESSURE TWENTY NINE SIXTY THREE FALLING SLOWLY. Off to the west, the men in the gondola could see black summer thunderstorm clouds gathering and at 15.47hrs NEL sent: GUSTS NOW TWENTY FIVE. As the *Hindenburg* passed over Lakehurst Air Station just after 16.00hrs, Capt Pruss dropped a weighted message stating: 'Riding out the storm'.

Capt Heinrich Bauer relieved Capt Sammt as duty watch officer at 16.00hrs in time to implement Pruss' instructions to ride south along the storm wall towards Atlantic City. The beaches looked bright in the sunlight but it was all dark and gloomy to the west. At 17.12hrs NEL sent: 'THUNDERSTORM MOVING FROM WEST OVER STATION SURFACE TEMPERATURE 70 FALLING SURFACE WIND WEST SIXTEEN KNOTS GUSTS TWENTY ONE WIND SHIFTED FROM NORTH AT 1600 EST PRESSURE TWENTY NINE SIXTY FOUR RISING'. Twenty minutes later the station recommended 'DELAY LANDING UNTIL FURTHER WORD'. Pruss answered: 'WE WILL WAIT YOUR REPORT THAT LANDING CONDITIONS ARE BETTER'. Then he told a steward to get some sandwiches ready for the passengers while they waited; no-one could be hungry after all they had eaten recently, but it would keep people occupied.

The officer with ultimate responsibility on the ground at Lakehurst was Cdr Charles E. Rosendahl USN. He knew all about airships and weather having commanded USS *Los Angeles* and served as navigating officer on board the USS *Shenandoah* when that ill-fated craft broke up in a severe thunderstorm over Ohio in 1925. At 18.12hrs NEL signalled: 'CONDITIONS NOW CONSIDERED SUITABLE FOR LANDING' followed 10min later by: 'RECOMMEND LANDING NOW COMMANDING OFFICER'. Assuming that the thunderstorm had just about cleared, Pruss wired Rosendahl: 'POSITION FORKED RIVER COURSE LAKEHURST'. Watch officer Bauer told the elevator man that they should be over the field in about 15min.

Cdr Rosendahl called his soaked ground crew out to their stations once more at 18.45hrs. Six men were detailed to the mooring mast with two lieutenants working atop. The ship would drop its yaw guys first: four men were in each yaw guy coupling party and 10 men worked the yaw guy capstans. The main wire coupling party comprised six men. They took the main wire in hand as it touched the ground and then shackled it to a lead from the main wire winch on the mooring mast; the mast's diesel would then crank her down. Another 68 men were assigned to the forward landing lines, 43 to the forward car, 37 to the stern car and 46 to the stern landing lines. All these groups of men, working under the command of their respective bosuns, lined up into wind in port and starboard rows parallel to the ship as she approached the mast. Herb Morrison stood ready to record for the 'Prairie Farm Station'.

In the control car, Helmsman Schoenherr steered approximately northeast from about Whitings to the south edge of the field while Chief Radio Operator Speck was winding in his trailing aerials and closing down the radios. At around 18.55hrs the section chiefs reported to Capt Pruss. Chief Electrician Lenz declared the electrics to be fine — his men had not needed to change so much as a fuse all trip. Chief

Engineer Sauter reported all engines serviceable. Chief Rigger Knorr mentioned in passing that something about Gas Cell 4 near the tail made him think that it might be leaking, but he would look at it after landing.

Just before 19.00hrs, a steam whistle summoned Chief Knorr and the rest of *Hindenburg's* crew to their berthing stations and duties including lowering the front and rear landing wheels. Sunset was officially 19.55hrs but twilight was early that evening. As the showers dragged off east towards the Atlantic, the weather began clearing to the west though a light drizzle was still falling over Lakehurst. Wind had become light and variable.

Hindenburg still steered northeast as she crossed the Air Station fence at 19.04hrs, flying at 600ft and 73kt to enable Pruss to look at the surface conditions. He saw the ground crew drawn up for an east wind and therefore took the airship about five miles beyond the field before swinging her round for an approach towards the mast from the west. In the interim, the wind shifted southerly, so a second turn was needed to approach the mast from a northerly direction.

At 19.11hrs Pruss ordered gas to be valved for 15sec and 'All engines idle, ahead'. The ship was still tail heavy so more gas was valved from the forward cells for another 15sec. Now down at 350ft, the aft engines were set to idle astern. The ship remained aft heavy so six men from the off watch were sent forward to the bow to provide an extra moment of about 180 tons.

At 19.19hrs *Hindenburg* appeared to be dead level and in perfect balance. Pruss ordered 'All engines full astern' and heading just about south, his great airship drifted to a dead stop just short of the mooring mast. She was now at 200ft and a minute later the captain ordered 'Forward engines idle ahead; aft engines idle astern' to ensure that he had power immediately available should the need arise. At 19.21hrs the forward starboard yaw line was dropped in a coil, followed by the port: both were made fast to the capstan lines by the men below.

Crew members at their landing stations on the lower gangway between Gas Cells 4 and 5 suddenly saw a bright blue-white flash on the front bulkhead of Cell 4 in front of the tail fin. They also heard a 'frump' similar to a giant gas kitchen range being lit. In the command gondola they felt the ship lurch. For a moment someone thought a rope might have broken but then there was a tremendous second detonation as flames burst through the top of the ship. Girders, molten aluminium, wires, struts and burning fabric began to fall around people jumping for their lives. Capt Bauer was ordered to drop the water ballast. He tried to pass the instruction by telephone and voice tube, but no-one answered.

Within a few seconds the whole after part of the ship was a mass of flames. Down on the ground the illuminated landing parties froze in their tracks, their arms transfixed upwards reaching for the landing lines, until suddenly they realised what was happening and started to flee. Herb Morrison's recording for WLS, Chicago, entered media history: 'It is practically standing still now. The ropes have been dropped and they have been taken hold of by a number of men on the field. It is starting to rain again. The back motors of the ship are holding it just enough to keep....It's burst into flames! Get out of the way! Get this, Charley, get out of the way, please! It's bursting into flames...This is terrible! This is one of the worst catastrophes in the world! The flames are 500ft into the sky. It is a terrific crash, ladies and gentlemen. It is in smoke and flames now. Oh the humanity! Those passengers! I can't talk, ladies and gentlemen. Honest, it's a mass of smoking wreckage. Lady, I am sorry. Honestly, I can hardly...I am going to step inside where I can't see it. Charley, this is terrible. Listen, folks, I am going to have to stop for a minute because I have lost my voice.'

A great ball of fire rose above the ship. As burning hydrogen escaped from ruptured gas cells, the *Hindenburg* rose to about 500ft, but as the fire swept forward she came down again slowly to the ground in a tail-down attitude. Flames poured from the nose 'like fire out of a volcano'. Given that only 32sec elapsed from the time the first tiny flame was seen from Cell 4 until the *Hindenburg* lay a smoking ruin on the ground, it is amazing that 62 of the 97 people on board survived the holocaust.

Of the 36 passengers, 13 died on the field, in the infirmary or at nearby hospitals. Chief Knorr, plus 21 others from the *Hindenburg's* crew and one groundcrew man, also perished. Capt Lehmann came out of the wreckage alive. The charred flesh fell off his back in chunks but he sat quietly in hospital, a large piece of gauze in one hand and a bottle of picric acid in the other, swabbing his burns. From time to time he would look out of the window and repeat, 'I don't understand'. The following day, he just seemed to give up and died.

The aftermath of the *Hindenburg* tragedy highlighted many features common to major aircraft accidents. First there was the need to safeguard other machines of a similar type, which in this case led Dr Eckener to signal the skipper of the *Graf Zeppelin*, 'All further flights are to be suspended until the cause of the *Hindenburg* catastrophe has been determined.'

To this end, the US Navy Dept ordered a board of inquiry to convene on Saturday 8 May, but it backed off when the Dept of Commerce declared this to be a civilian air matter. The Secretary of Commerce then appointed a lawyer and two members of the Bureau of Air Commerce to inquire into the accident, and they began deliberations on Monday by meeting in the empty hangar that had previously served as the *Hindenburg* waiting room and then mortuary for its victims. Six technical advisers, including Cdr Rosendahl, were detailed to assist the board. The Germans set up a parallel commission of inquiry led by Dr Eckener. He was assisted by five specialists, two of whom — Dr Ludwig Durr, Zeppelin's chief designer since 1901, and Professor Max Diekmann, a noted authority on atmospheric electricity — flew with Eckener to Cherbourg, caught the liner *Europa*, and attended the US hearings from the fourth day onward.

Eighteen days of testimony were taken from 97 ground witnesses and surviving crew members, including a badly burned Capt Pruss. Once the inquiries were complete, the Commerce Dept's Chief of Air Transport married some 1,200 pages of US and German reports together to produce a reasonable degree of consensus. Remarkably, several crew members stationed for landing in the *Hindenburg's* tail section saw the start of the fire and lived to tell the tail. Between Gas Cells 4 and 5 were both a ventilation chimney upwards and a ladder down to the keel. From witnesses' testimony it was clear that a fire had roared up the chimney. Once gas burned away, the tail — already slightly heavy — dropped, enabling some of those aboard to scramble out. As the nose tilted steeply upwards, the axial walkway through the centre of the ship became another chimney, and a long jet of flame now appeared out of the airship's nose. The whole front section then collapsed back to earth, crushing the accommodation decks under a tangle of flaming wreckage.

This then was the result of the accident, but it was not the cause. All agreed that the 'Great Floating Palace' would never have burned if it had been inflated with helium. Nevertheless, over its entire history up to 3 May, the Zeppelin company could boast that not one of 50,000 farepaying passengers had been killed or injured on any of its airships. To find the cause of the accident, the inquirers had to determine why the hydrogen within the *Hindenburg* burst into flames that day.

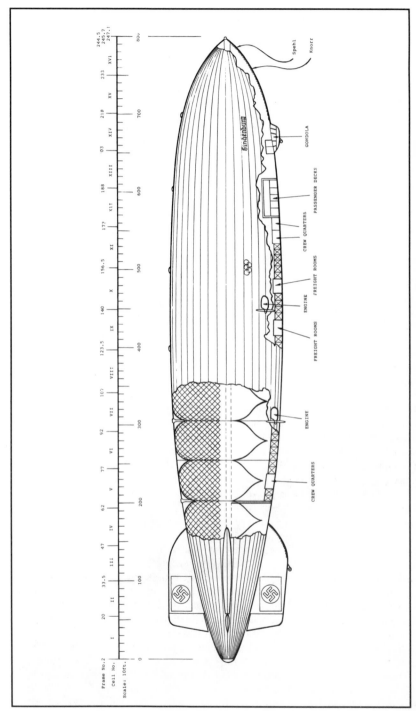

Partial cutaway drawing of the German dirigible LZ 129, Hindenburg, showing the landing stations of Rigger Eric Spehl and Chief Rigger Knorr.

19

Above:
At 19.21hrs, just as the landing lines were being dropped, Hindenburg *burst into flames.*

Below:
Hindenburg *starts to settle tail-down while a Lakehurst mooring mast looks impassively on.*

20

Sabotage was a prime suspect, not least because it got quite a lot of people off the hook. Another trait that recurs after most major accidents is the very human one of ducking to avoid any blame that might be going round, and the *Hindenburg* inquest was no exception. Capt Pruss for a start must have resented any implication that he handled the *Hindenburg* badly, and over the years he became increasingly convinced that a passenger he remembered acting suspiciously was the saboteur who caused the loss of his ship. When others postulated a leak from the gas cells, he remained convinced that he had seen nothing wrong with any of the remote reading instruments in the control gondola. Similarly, Cdr Rosendahl had made the decision to recall the *Hindenburg* for landing. Perhaps the fear that he might be blamed for an error of judgement helped convince him that a small incendiary device, concealed adjacent to Gas Cell 4, caused the catastrophe. Rosendahl argued that it might have been pre-set and had the airship arrived on time instead of 13hr late, a great symbol of Nazi Germany would have been destroyed without the horrific casualties.

Many years later, a new school of thought postulated that one of the three riggers, Eric Spehl, set an incendiary device based on a flashbulb, flashlight battery and photographic timer. Spehl was an amateur photographer with some anti-Nazi friends, and being a rigger he was one of the very few allowed to use the axial gangway above which the bomb was supposed to have been placed.

Unfortunately there is not a shred of evidence to support any of these spectacular hypotheses. None of the photographs or newsreels taken of the disaster show any flame starting other than that at the top of the fin, and no flashbulbs or batteries were found among the charred remains. As for poor Eric Spehl, his landing station was in the airship's bow. As the stern crashed to the ground, and the axial gangway became a chimney, the searing heat and flame roared up to where he and 11 other crewmen clung to the girders. One by one they lost their grip and fell into the burning inferno below, so Spehl was never able to refute his accusers.

The German inquiry went further than its US counterpart when it stated that, 'the possibility of deliberate destruction must be admitted.' However, apart from the lack of any firm evidence, the balance of probabilities argues against such a finding. First, all passenger baggage was X-rayed as it was checked in. The authorities were relentless in the cause of safety; matches, lighters and camera flashbulbs were confiscated and checks were so thorough that a passenger carrying a gift-wrapped Dresden doll had to remove the packaging and the inspector went as far as to examine under the skirt. Given Teutonic thoroughness in such matters, it is difficult to believe that any passenger could have smuggled an incendiary device on board.

As for the crew, not only were many of them ardent supporters of the government but they were also handpicked for their compatibility with others. Impartial observers commented on the excellent esprit de corps on board, so it is difficult to believe that any one would kill himself and his mates to make a symbolic gesture. It is also misleading to view German politics in 1936 through post-1945 eyes. Dr Eckener may well have objected to his precious *Hindenburg* cruising over German cities during the referendum on reoccupying the Rhineland, but the distinguished US commentator William Shirer, who covered the 'election' from one corner of the Reich to the other, had no doubt that the vote of approval for Hitler's action was overwhelming. To have blown up the *Hindenburg*, like voting against marching back into the Rhineland, would have been to strike against the nation as much as the governing party.

The inquirers had therefore to seek some other cause that provided both leaking hydrogen and the means to ignite it. A host of possibilities were considered such as major structural failure, propeller wreckage or a stuck-open automatic valve, combined with lightning strikes, spontaneous combustion or hot sparks from the engine. Yet despite 'thorough questioning of all witnesses, inspection and search of the wreckage, and evaluation of all pictorial documents,' the German commission's report had to admit that, 'no completely certain proof can be found for any of the possibilities'.

However, although both inquiries noted that the actual cause of the fire 'still remains unknown', they agreed that 'the following explanation of the accident appears to be the most probable'. During the landing approach, the ship had made a very sharp turn to port in order to head into the wind which had suddenly shifted southerly. In Dr Eckener's view, and he was perhaps the greatest airship expert, it is possible that this sharp turn overstressed the hull; certainly, tension gauges salvaged from the wreck showed that the 'bicycle spoke' wires bracing the main frame rings had been at very high tension. This in turn snapped a bracing wire, which slashed open Gas Cell 4 or 5 like a razor. Leaking hydrogen then entered the space between the cell and outer cover, causing an inflammable mixture of hydrogen and air to gather in the upper portion of the airship. It was also possible that gas valved prior to landing had not been completely dispersed while the airship flew at low speed.

The gas could have ignited from one of two reasons. First, for several minutes after the *Hindenburg* dropped her landing ropes, there would have been an equalisation of the static charges between ship and ground. The result would have been electricity discharged into the atmosphere as St Elmo's Fire. Second, a spark could have been caused by a discharge of electricity from the moist outer skin to the ship's framework, the latter being better earthed or grounded after deposition of the manila landing ropes. Yet it is a measure of the uncertainty surrounding the whole investigation that the Americans preferred the first theory and the Germans the second.

To this day there are those that believe that the German and US governments conspired to agree on the snapped bracing wire and electrical discharge combination in order to hush up some great crime or scandal that would have embarrassed them both. Yet the Nazis, who had already destroyed their own Reichstag to pin the blame onto their opponents, could surely have derived much benefit from the destruction of the *Hindenburg* had they believed its loss to be caused by sabotage. Since they did not, or saw no benefit from 'fixing' the evidence or 'framing' anyone, it would appear that they found the inquiry findings acceptable. Suffice to say that when the outer cover of the LZ 130 was applied, the dope through which its lacing cord was run contained graphite to make it conductive. Furthermore, when LZ 130 was making its early test flights, efforts were made to determine the static charge on the ship which would be discharged when ground contact was made. These developments were not publicised and would have been unnecessary if the static discharge theory had been merely a cover-up.

It has to be said that there was no firm evidence that a bracing wire broke. Surviving crew members were confident that there could have been no substantial escape of gas without their knowledge, and although Chief Rigger Knorr died without saying what he thought was wrong with Cell 4, it cannot have been anything very serious or he would have raised the alarm instead of merely making a casual remark about the matter. In an earlier, less secular age we might be more willing to agree with Hermann Goering's assessment that the loss of the *Hindenburg* was 'an act of God'. Yet the result would have been the same — a loss of public faith in airships as passenger transports. No Zeppelin ever made another commercial flight, and the blackened framework of the *Hindenburg* was sold for $4,000 and shipped back to Germany to be reforged into Luftwaffe heavier-than-air craft.

It was an ironic end to a great dream, but a dream was what it was and herein lies the great flight safety lesson. The *Hindenburg* was the biggest flying machine the world has known: a Boeing 707 could shelter under its tailplane. Moreover, she could lift around 240 tons and carry over 100 people at a time when the DC-3 could only carry 21 passengers and two tons. But even though no aircraft carried a paying passenger across the Atlantic until two years after the Lakehurst conflagration, the future still lay with the DC-3 and its progeny. They had the advantage of speed, could operate more flexibly in all weathers, and needed much less manpower support.

But the most crucial reason why the *Hindenburg* was a dinosaur heading down a dead-end street was its lack of inbuilt safety. All forms of transport involve elements of risk, but most people accept those associated with cars or trains because they are far outweighed by the benefits of getting somewhere quickly and efficiently. Back in 1908, Hugo Eckener told a chemist friend of his decision to join the Zeppelin enterprise. The reaction was one of horror: 'That's terrible! Hydrogen and petrol, the two most treacherous substances in existence! How can you meddle with these explosive substances?' The friend had a point. Lethal quantities of hydrogen were manageable on a relatively small vessel manned by professionals wearing antistatic coveralls and hemp-soled shoes, but something as huge as the *Hindenburg* offered endless opportunities for danger. Apart from faults going unnoticed in a ship of that size, how could any human organisation offer a long-term guarantee to counter every thoughtless cigarette smoker, child with sparking wind-up toy or screwball desperate to make a gesture?

There is no getting away from the fact that the Hindenburg was designed to be flown with helium. Once it became clear that helium was not to be immediately forthcoming, the great craft should have been mothballed or at least restricted to proving flights until the situation changed. In pushing the *Hindenburg* into commercial service without the crucial design feature necessary to operate it with a sufficient margin of safety bordered on irresponsibility. Consequently, it is relatively unimportant why the *Hindenburg* burned at Lakehurst. If the tragedy had not happened on 6 May 1937, almost certainly it would have happened sometime later. Anyone who stood in the axial corridor that ran through the airship's centre, and saw the 65ft of hydrogen on all sides without any means of getting out, knew that the *Hindenburg* was a death trap waiting to happen. Gambling all to prove a capability point before it is safe to do so can rapidly turn a dream into a nightmare.

DON'T PUSH YOUR LUCK

Back in August 1929, as the *Graf Zeppelin* was proving the feasibility of long-range airship travel, former Democratic presidential candidate Al Smith announced that a Zeppelin mooring mast would crown the top of the Empire State Building that his company was then constructing. The Depression, plus the greater practicability of operating out of Lakehurst, soon killed the idea of an air terminal 1,250ft above Fifth Avenue and 34th Street, but after it opened in May 1931 the Empire State Building became every bit as prominent a feature of the New York skyline as feisty Al intended.

At dawn on the morning of Saturday 28 July 1945, a summer storm that began life in the far-off Caribbean began to make itself felt when the Empire State's 102nd-floor observation platform disappeared in lowering cloud. Two hundred miles north in a suburb of Boston, Lt-Col Bill Smith left for Bedford Field. Late of Latham, Al and West Point, Smith had only been back in the USA for a month after his squadron had exchanged England for South Dakota. Two days previously his CO had put together a 'furlough' party of men whose families all lived around New York. Smith had ferried them from Sioux Falls to Newark, NJ in a B-25 Mitchell, before flying on to Boston to see his wife. He was now scheduled for an 08.30hrs take-off to return the way he came. It promised to be no big deal; despite being only 27 years old, Smith had over 50 European combat missions to his name and was one of the youngest Lt-Cols in the Army Air Force.

'Looks to me like I'll be goin' Instrument,' he declared after getting a weather update at Bedford. Alongside him now was the B-25's crew chief, Sgt Christopher Domitrovich. He had only met Smith for the first time two days earlier, and although both men had served with distinction in Europe, their backgrounds had been very different — one, the deputy commander of a famed bomber group, the other a crew chief on lumbering C-47 transports. As Smith scowled at the weather map with its squall line moving in from the Atlantic, pushing dense clouds and rain against the coastline, the Airdrome Officer put down the 'phone and reported that Boston Control could not approve an 08.30hrs 'Instrument' direct to Newark. There was too much instrument traffic booked in there already; the earliest take-off slot on offer was 11.00hrs.

Smith was not best pleased because he had promised to pick up his CO and the rest of the party by 10.00hrs at the latest. He glanced back to the weather map and peered at La Guardia Field, about 15 miles northeast and less than five minutes flying time across Manhattan from Newark. 'What's it like at La Guardia?' he asked. Running down his weather teletype the Airdrome Officer replied, 'As of 10min ago, La Guardia reported Contact, 1,500ft ceiling, lifting to 6,000ft, local fog and light rain.' 'Contact' meant that Smith would have to fly below the cloud base, keeping in

Lt Col William Franklin Smith, highly decorated combat veteran of the war in Europe.

visual contact with the ground at all times. If the cloud base dropped below 1,000ft, Smith knew that the regulations called for the flight to be terminated and his aircraft brought back to Bedford Field. 'What the heck,' he must have thought as he beat a restless tattoo on the desk top with the swagger stick he had bought in an expensively reckless moment in London: 'this is a milk-run compared to bombing the Ruhr.' Turning back to the lieutenant he ordered, 'Have Boston clear me Contact to La Guardia.'

A new order had come in the previous week to the effect that only fliers having official business with the base could land at La Guardia. 'No problem there, lieutenant,' declared Smith when reminded of the fact, though in signing the declaration that he had official business with the 1338th Base Unit he was also tacitly acknowledging the section stating, 'I am familiar with the danger areas in my line of flight.'

Smith's aircraft, with the serial 0577 on the tail, had once been a bomber and the name *Old John Feather Merchant* was still emblazoned under the cockpit. However, the machine guns and top turret had been removed and the B-25 converted into a rudimentary transport by the simple expedient of fitting wooden benches on either side of the area where once had been compartments for the radio operator and navigator. The aircraft was fuelled up and ready to go by the time Smith and Domitrovich drove out to the flight line. They swung up into 0577 through the open belly hatch and a moment later were putting on headsets and strapping in. As the second Cyclone engine burst into life, a jeep hove into view to disgorge a young sailor, Albert Perna. He waved a piece of paper at the pilot, the hatch was opened again, and Perna swung inside, happy that he had managed to hitch a ride to console his parents who had just learned that his brother had been killed in the Pacific.

Out along the taxiway towards Runway 18, Domitrovich read down the check-list. Although he was buckled into the right-hand seat, Domitrovich was no pilot. His job, to ensure that the B-25 was fit to fly, was complete before they left the ground. Bill Smith in the left-hand seat was effectively flying solo as both pilot and navigator.

'Army 0577, you're cleared for take-off.' Smith acknowledged, opened the throttles and released the brakes. It was 08.55hrs as the aluminium-clad *Old John Feather Merchant* rolled forward and on passing the 3,000ft marker, Smith lifted the B-25 smoothly into the sky. The Mitchell was much lighter and faster than the giant four-engined B-17 Flying Fortress he had flown operationally during the previous two years. Smith's climbing left turn over the outer airfield did not last long because even at low altitude, scattered patches of fog and low cloud partially obscured the ground. Yet what was a bit of bad weather to someone just back from rainy England? It was certainly no time to dwell on the fact that this was only the second time he had ever flown a B-25.

As they flew on at 1,000ft and 230mph, Bill Smith mentally put Bedford Tower behind him as he reached over the control column to dial up the first en-route radio frequency. In and out of the scudding clouds, he navigated initially by the Providence radio compass beacon. As the city of Providence came into view under the left wing, he could see darker storm clouds ahead over Narrangansett Bay. If the weather held, they would reach New York in 50min — then he would decide whether to land at La Guardia or Newark.

Old John Feather Merchant maintained 1,000ft and a SSW heading above northern Connecticut as more and more rain splattered the windscreen. A particularly heavy cloudburst over Hartford buffeted the B-25 more than somewhat, forcing Smith to throttle back to lessen the turbulence. Up ahead lay New Haven and Long Island

26

Sound; glancing down at his map, Smith reaffirmed that once past New Haven, a touch of right rudder would allow him to follow the coast round to Stamford. A hard left sweep across open water would then take the B-25 into La Guardia, but it would be a race against the weather.

By Bridgeport the B-25 was down around 900ft and 225mph but even though forward visibility had reduced to three miles, Smith could still see the sweeping arc of the Sound. He tried to raise New York Center but they were busy with instrument traffic and asked him to stay off the air until approaching La Guardia.

Four minutes later it was time to swing left towards La Guardia, but unfortunately not direct. The flight planning authorities back in Boston had been insistent; once the B-25 reached the New York area, it was to steer clear of all Instrument traffic operating into or out off any of the four major metropolitan airports. So Smith had to head 130° across the Sound to the jutting promontory of Kings Point. From there he would head due south before swinging west towards the airport in Astoria, Queens, named after the onetime bomber pilot and long-time mayor of New York, Fiorello La Guardia.

As Smith coasted in over Kings Point, the controllers' and pilots' cross-talk from La Guardia, Mitchell Field, Floyd Bennett Field and Newark came through his earphones in growing intensity. Concentrating on flying and navigating under solid cloud whose base continued to lower, he could not keep mental track of all the arriving and departing aircraft that seemed to be being controlled all around him. They in turn did not know he was there and to crown it all, ground now lost radio contact with one of the aircraft in the melee, Navy 2171.

To keep clear of cloud, Smith crossed Little Neck Bay at 650ft. Glancing up from his map, Domitrovich tapped his pilot's shoulder and pointed to the Bronx Whitestone Bridge off the right wing. Peering through the windscreen wipers valiantly trying to sweep away the large drops, Smith caught sight of the blurred twin towers of the suspension bridge. It was 09.45hrs as he edged his aircraft over Bayside at 600ft. With approximately 15 miles to run to La Guardia, it was time to give those good ol' boys a call.

Unfortunately, La Guardia tower controller Victor Barden was not in a very receptive mood. Seven commercial airliners were stacked at 1,000ft intervals awaiting landing clearance, and others were holding on the ground pending re-contact with Navy 2171 and clarification of its position.

'La Guardia Tower, this is Army 0577.'

'Army 0577, this is La Guardia Tower. What is your position and altitude?'

'About 15 miles southeast of you at six fifty, Contact. I'd like the current Newark weather.'

La Guardia was ahead of Smith's starboard wing and Newark 30 miles ahead to port of the nose. New Jersey was hidden under a sullen overcast sky but it was where his boss and passengers for South Dakota were waiting. Life would be so much easier if the B-25 could fly direct to Newark — all Smith needed was a bit of co-operation from the weather and the ground.

But Barden had no spare capacity to provide a flight watch as well as local air traffic service. 'Army 0577,' he replied tersely, 'contact Newark Tower on 341k/c for Newark weather or Army Flight Service Center. Over.'

Smith was now in a bit of a quandary. He knew that he could not just pitch up at Newark without being in direct violation of his flight plan. But at 650ft he was legal for an approach to La Guardia — best to aim there and then try and smooth-talk them into feeding him into the Newark circuit.

La Guardia Airport just after midday on 24 May 1956. Its proximity to Manhattan in general, and the Empire State Building in particular, is clear. The Port of New York Authority

Victor Barden's load was eased when Navy 2171 appeared over Newark Field with radio failure. American 750 was cleared to carry out an approach and Barden was given clearance to release United 1820 and Colonial 740 for take-off. *Old John Feather Merchant* crossed La Guardia's outer perimeter fence as the United Airlines DC-3 lifted off and disappeared into the low cloud hovering over the East River. Barden turned his gaze back towards the taxying Colonial 740 when a great silver shape arced past.

'Tower, this is Army 0577.'

Barden's initial reaction was unprintable, but he recovered like a good professional. 'Tower to 0577. Wind northeast at 12. Use runway 36. Are you familiar with the traffic pattern?'

The undertone of command was lost on Smith. 'I'd like to land at Newark, Tower. What is the weather over there, please?'

'Tower to 0577, you are out of bounds. Move to the extreme southeast of the field and fly a left holding position, Contact.'

Smith was not to be overawed by any of this. 'Tower, I have official business at Newark at 10.00hrs. I would appreciate as little delay here as possible.' He probably reasoned that La Guardia would be so busy that it would be more than happy to hand him on to an instrument clearance into Newark, but he was only half correct. Barden was certainly preoccupied with American 750 due on southwest finals, but he was also fed up with arrogant Army air types fresh back from Europe behaving as if they still ruled the skies. The Chief Controller at the New York Airway Traffic Control Center was also adamant that Smith should not sneak into the Newark instrument pattern which was fully booked until 13.00hrs. Airways therefore contacted the Army Flight Service Center – a console board less than 20ft away – asking for authority to order the B-25 pilot to land at La Guardia in response to his violation of controlled airspace. Capt Esterlein of the Army Flight Service Center was then in the process of trying to placate a 5-star general who insisted on being given landing clearance into Mitchell Field ahead of an emergency Air Evacuation aircraft.

'It's up to them if they wish to file a violation,' snapped Esterlein, who had no authority to order any aircraft down. 'Give the pilot the latest Newark weather and ask him to advise his intentions to Airways.'

The ball bounced back into Barden's court as he was trying to separate a loitering Army 0577 from American 750, a DC-3 passing 2,500ft on final descent. After giving the 09.30hrs Newark weather, New York Center confirmed that Barden was being given every assistance short of actual help: 'The decision's yours, Tower.'

Realising that he had little choice, Barden reached for the microphone and passed the Newark weather — 'Ceiling 1000, variable, lower broken, visibility two and one quarter miles. Advise intentions.' Smith must have smiled to himself as he bulldozed through the regulations for the second time that day. Rolling *Old John Feather Merchant* out of the turn and on to a southwest heading towards the East River he declared, 'I'll go Contact to Newark, Tower.'

'0577, maintain three miles – repeat three miles – visibility. If unable to maintain, return to La Guardia.'

'Roger, will do,' replied the southern drawl without conviction.

'Oh, 0577, at the present time I can't see the top of the Empire State Building. Over.'

A delay of a few seconds elapsed on the wire-recorder that taped all air traffic transmissions before an almost bored voice responded: 'Roger, Tower, thank you.'

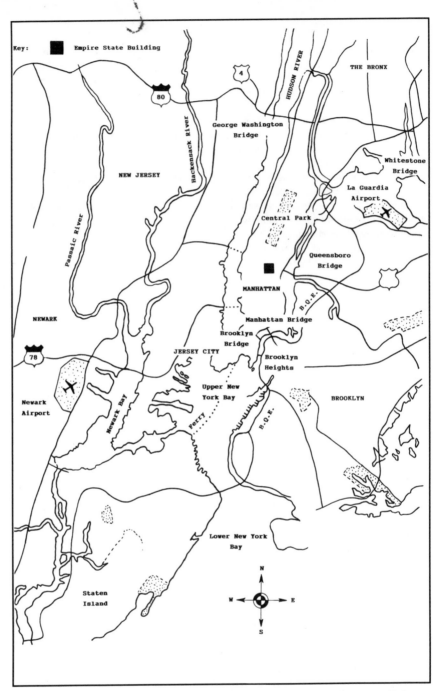

New York landmarks relating to Lt-Col Bill Smith's fateful attempt to fly across the city visually from La Guardia to Newark Airport.

After watching the B-25 disappear from view, Barden turned to more pressing matters as American 750 burst through the overcast.

Leaving Bowery Bay heading west, Smith aimed for Ward's Island. Once there he would run down the East River until clear of Manhattan, then turn to cross the Hudson River, Jersey City, Newark Bay and into Newark Field. The clock on the instrument panel read 09.53hrs — when he said he would get to somewhere by 10.00hrs, he meant it.

The only trouble was that lowering cloud and distorting rain finally combined to confuse and disorientate Smith at the last hurdle. Overestimating the time he had flown down the East River, he mistook the Queensboro Bridge for either the Brooklyn or Manhattan. Turning right at 500ft over what he assumed to be the final approach over clear water, he lowered the landing gear. Only six or seven miles to go now — in a minute he would see Jersey City.

But it could not have been long before Smith and Domitrovich realised that the buildings emerging from the gloom were far too high and massed together to be the same flat Jersey City they had flown out over two days earlier. Finding to his horror that they were over Manhattan around Madison Avenue, Smith pulled the B-25 into a left hand climbing turn and pushed the throttles as far forward as they would go. Despite raising the undercarriage lever, there would have been a frustrating 20sec delay before the retraction sequence was completed and the B-25 fully freed from drag. It did not help the rate of climb that the fuel gauge needles were still not reading much below full. Being a good crew chief, Domitrovich had filled the four wing tanks to their 974gall capacity so that his pilot could land, pick up passengers and fly on to Sioux Falls with the minimum of delay.

The B-25 would have been hauling itself through 700ft as the wheels were half up. Down below, Manhattans inured to the noise of urban bustle became aware of the Cyclone engines striving for height and safety. Pivoting over 51st Street, the B-25 cleared the Rockefeller Center rooftop garden by about 25ft and came back over Fifth Avenue. Stopped at a red light at Fifth and 45th Street, a radio sports announcer felt his car shake as the aircraft's closeness reverberated through the concrete canyons. He willed the B-25 to clear the 700ft Salmon Tower on the corner of Fifth and 42nd Street.

Smith was heading back to the East River, perhaps even to return to La Guardia, but fate had placed the Chrysler Building in his path: as the stone edifice emerged from the cloud, he had to break off right to find another escape path. In an office on 39th Street, James Jagger was dictating letters into his Sound Scriber machine. He had just started one to the Dean of Michigan University when his concentration was shattered by a loud din. He crossed to the window in time to see an aircraft teeter down Fifth Avenue: other witnesses watched it continue to climb agonisingly slowly crossing 38th and 37th Streets. Approaching 35th Street the B-25 turned east as if trying to break out of Manhattan once more. Passing 975ft above 34th Street, Army 0577 flew into the 79th floor of the Empire State Building!

Chunks of stone and pieces of *Old John Feather Merchant*, including a 109lb section of undercarriage, cascaded down in all directions; remarkably, none of the hundreds of pedestrians and motorists then moving about down below were killed. Inside the Empire State Building, the results were less pleasant. The 12ton bomber, moving at around four miles per minute, hit the Building at an upward angle. The right wing scythed through the 79th floor offices of the Catholic War Relief Services agency. Three workers sitting at their desks nearest the north-facing windows were crushed

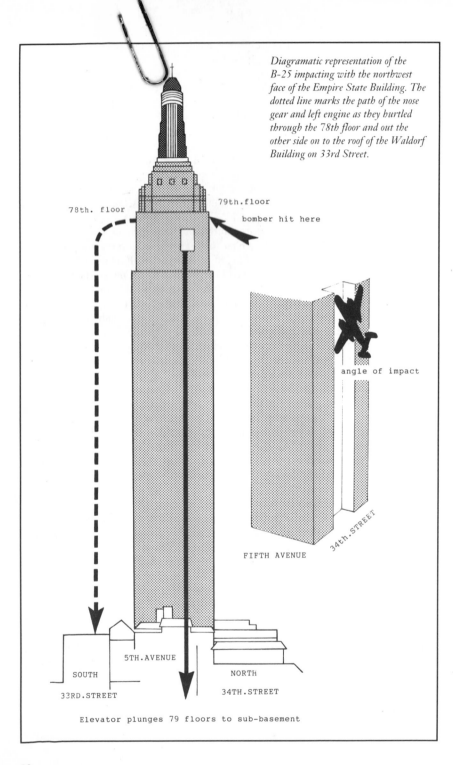

Diagramatic representation of the B-25 impacting with the northwest face of the Empire State Building. The dotted line marks the path of the nose gear and left engine as they hurtled through the 78th floor and out the other side on to the roof of the Waldorf Building on 33rd Street.

78th. floor

79th.floor

bomber hit here

angle of impact

FIFTH AVENUE

34th.STREET

5TH.AVENUE

SOUTH

NORTH

33RD.STREET

34TH.STREET

Elevator plunges 79 floors to sub-basement

Shattered pieces of Old John Feather Merchant *hang precariously over 34th Street. The aircraft made an 18ft x 12ft gash in the Empire State Building on impact.*

instantly, as were the aircraft occupants when their raised cockpit was flattened on contact with a 16in beam embedded in the ceiling just behind the windows.

As the B-25 tore into the heart of the largely open-plan office, the right wing sheared off in sections and its fuel tanks burst open. The wing's progress was then halted as it slammed into a vertical steel column, but the bad news was that its engine catapulted from its mounting through the office. Drenched in fuel, several ladies were racing for the foyer when the blazing engine caught up with them. The resulting fire, which became so intense that it melted the glass and metal partition, now spread back into the office where other people were stumbling about in a daze. At this moment, three of the B-25's six oxygen tanks erupted: the explosion was heard out into the harbour and mistaken by some for a Japanese air raid on New York.

The B-25's left wing tore into the 78th floor which, very fortunately, was unoccupied. The outer wing section sheared off but the partially raised nose gear rocketed down the centre corridor, blasted through the south wall and plunged down on to the roof of the Waldorf Building on 33rd Street. The 2,700lb engine took off on its own diagonally towards a bank of elevators, passing through two 8in brick walls and skipping a 4ft-wide drop before entering the shaft enclosing elevators Nos 6 and 7. Betty Lou Oliver, the elevator operator inside car No 6, was working the last day of her summer job. She had just started down from the 79th floor when the white-hot engine severed the car's cables, plunging her 1,000ft into the basement.

Within three months the Empire State Building had been completely repaired and the Army had agreed to pay $288,901.90 in damages. However, lost lives could not be redressed so easily. Thirteen people died in the catastrophe that day, including three in the aircraft, plus another 26 injured. Having said that, it is amazing that the death toll was not much worse after so much uncontrolled destruction was showered over a quarter of a mile in the heart of a major city in mid-morning. Amazingly, Betty Lou Oliver survived. Giant springs in the basement cushioned her plummeting fall, and the lift continued to bounce for several minutes. But while she soon recovered physically, her mind was beyond repair.

The Army Air Corps inquiry immediately set out to find out what caused one of their aircraft, flown by a highly decorated pilot, to end up in the wrong place with a vengeance. Major technical in-flight distractions such as engine failure were rejected by evidence from an unexpected quarter. When James Jagger's dictating machine was played back, it was found to have recorded the unfaltering hum becoming a roar of approaching serviceable engines that only ceased at the moment of impact.

The basic cause of the accident was that Lt-Col Smith became transfixed with reaching Newark by 10.00hrs to the detriment of every other consideration including flight safety. But that is the easy part — it is far harder to identify why this experienced aircraft commander behaved as he did rather than wait just a few hours until he could fly a legal and safe instrument approach into Newark.

There was no denying that the rank badges and combat ribbons on Smith's tunic testified to the high standards he had set and achieved in combat. Yet humans have many facets and certainly when Bill Smith flew his B-17 back from England, a changed character emerged from that which his subordinates were used to. Exuberantly announcing on crossing the coast of Maine that he could locate Bradley Field, Ct 'with my eyes closed', Smith whooped and hollered his way over New England at full throttle and tree-top height. Disregarding his flight plan and barnstorming over civil as well as military airfields, Smith raised hell. Perhaps it was an understandable reaction after being released from the strain of continual combat, but maybe it signified how he would react in a non-combat zone where the rules were significantly different.

Smith, with his swagger stick, Brooks Brothers custom-tailored uniform and reputation for trimming his moustache to look like Clark Gable, could have been preoccupied with maintaining an image. Perhaps that image thrived over Europe where the military ruled the skies, and having survived the natural winnowing process of a bombing tour in Europe, Smith possibly thought that US civilian air traffic constraints only applied to lesser mortals. But it is easy to make too much of the different operating regime. Smith had not operated his B-17 during 1944 and 1945 like some independent buccaneer. Bomber operations at that time involved great massed formations forming up, running into and out of dropping zones and returning to a host of bases with pinpoint precision and timing. Smith would have lived and breathed flying regulations as a bomber group senior executive, so why did he ignore or bend all the orders and instructions on 28 July 1945?

Was the answer at Newark where the CO of the 457th Bomb Group was waiting? This man had a good record as a pilot and administrator, but being aloof and lacking the common touch, he would have won no popularity contests. Yet that should not have bothered someone as senior as Smith, especially as the CO delegated a great deal of responsibility to his deputy. If anything the CO was a stickler for the book, so he would have understood had Smith reported that the rules forced him to delay until he could get an instrument slot into Newark.

Although we can never know what went on inside Smith's mind that day, it seems most likely that the only pressure he was under was self-imposed. Psychiatrists can argue as to whether he was a 'can-do' type who pushed his luck once too often, or if he missed the excitement of combat and needed his 'fix' of danger. The thing to bear in mind is that most rules of the air have come into being because a previous generation of fliers felt them to be necessary to save lives. Irrespective of rank or experience, any pilot ignores or bends these rules at his peril.

Bill Smith was not the first pilot, nor will he be the last, to succumb to the disease of 'press-on-itis'. With hindsight it is easy to say that he had enough flying experience to know that he was cutting it too fine, but knowing when to draw the line becomes that much harder when tunnel vision takes over and you just *have* to meet that deadline, pick up those passengers on time, or whatever. Pressure on pilots, placed there by their operating authority or themselves, should never become so great that it becomes impossible to say 'No'.

Finally, the B-25 accident demonstrated how quickly a major accident can occur after a pilot becomes disorientated. Given that Lt-Col Smith was well over Manhattan before he tried to escape, he must have remained unaware of his true situation for some time. It may even have been Domitrovich who eventually put him back in touch with reality. Flying on instruments is not easy. Doing so while switching back and forth to seek visual clues against a backdrop of constant air traffic control chatter is a sure recipe for toppling the brain. Know the limits of your aircraft, but just as importantly, know your own as well.

HIGH JINX?

Not withstanding wartime priorities, there was sufficient optimism around in late-1943 for the British Air Ministry to set about identifying postwar long-range airliner requirements. Modified bombers seemed a natural interim solution but by the middle of 1944, A. V. Roe & Co, the company that sired the great Lancaster bomber, had decided to go for an entirely new four-engined pressurised-type. After the war years of the Lancaster and its derived transport, the York, it seemed only right that this child of the new age of peaceful co-existence should be christened Tudor.

Heavy military commitments forced Roy Chadwick, Avro's chief designer, to dedicate only a small team to the Tudor. However, work progressed sufficiently for two Tudor 1 prototypes to be ordered in September 1944. Finished in silver, the first prototype was flying next June, by which time 20 were on order for the British Overseas Airways Corporation (BOAC).

The Tudor 1 was the first British pressurised transport, capable of carrying 12 passengers in new standards of comfort across the Atlantic. Yet despite the hype, initial flight trials revealed directional and longitudinal instability and pre-stall wing buffeting. Larger fins, rudders, tailplanes and wing root fillets were incorporated, but they decreased the Tudor 1's range to the point where it became a doubtful prospect for the trans-Atlantic market.

Despite being given a cleaner airframe and more efficient engines, BOAC called for no fewer than 343 further changes at the final Tudor 1 design conference. Some put this down to the extremely high standards being set for the Corporation's first postwar airliner. More likely, BOAC had already decided that it preferred the tried and tested Lockheed Constellation which made the first scheduled postwar trans-Atlantic flight from La Guardia to Hurn via Gander and Shannon at the beginning of 1946.

Gambling everything on the greatly enlarged Tudor 2, which like the Tudor 1 was fully pressurised, Avro had the first prototype (G-AGSU) built and ready for flying in just six months. Such was Chadwick's reputation that BOAC placed a contract for 30 Tudor 2s each capable of carrying 60 passengers, and Qantas and South African Airways followed suit to raise the total order to 79. Unfortunately, Chadwick's test pilots told him that, although the aircraft was quite pleasant to fly, there were signs of defects similar to those on the Tudor 1.

Avro was concurrently tackling the problems of the Tudor 1 — the process seemed to drag on because only one structural change could be made at a time to assess its effect — and the company appeared to have made it reasonably viable by April 1946. Further good news was forthcoming when British South American Airways (BSAA) ordered four Tudor 4s — revised Tudor 1s with the front fuselage lengthened by six feet and seat pitch decreased to carry 32 passengers.

The second Tudor 1 prototype flew in May but BOAC's nagging criticisms continued. The airline even ordered five Constellations as an insurance measure and

Above:
Avro Chief Test Pilot Bill Thorn (left) shakes hands with Chief Designer Roy Chadwick in the cabin entrance of the first British pressurised transport, the Avro Tudor. BAe

Below:
Tudor 2 prototype, G-AGSU, in May 1947. The Tudor 2 was a stretched version of the Tudor 1 designed to carry up to 60 passengers on BOAC's Commonwealth routes. This new fuselage made it the largest aircraft produced in the UK up to that time. BAe

used them to mount a London-New York service from 1 July, but Lockheed did not have an entirely clear field. Almost immediately afterwards, a TWA Constellation crashed near Reading, Pa, and the whole fleet was grounded for 30 days until the cause was identified and remedial action taken.

Although BOAC's lack of confidence in the Tudor was further underlined by the announcement in August that it had ordered six Boeing Stratocruisers, on 5 September the airline at last received the first of its 20 Tudor 1s. To a grossly overworked Roy Chadwick, striving to cope with everything from bread and butter Lincoln and Anson work through new assignments such as the Athena trainer, the maritime reconnaissance Shackleton and a shiny new delta winged bomber, it must have come as a great relief when the Tudor 1 was awarded a Certificate of Airworthiness. To crown it all, the fourth production aircraft was christened *Elizabeth of England* by the heir to the throne on 21 January 1947.

Yet the euphoria was short lived. Although *Star Panther*, first of BSAA's Tudor 4s, was flown by test pilot Bill Thorn on 9 April 1947, two days later BOAC finally rejected the Tudor 1 as incapable of meeting its requirements. The Tudor 2 was still in the running, but weight increases resulting from modifications such as enlarged fin and rudder had reduced performance to a point where the airliner could no longer operate east of Calcutta or south of Nairobi. As this constraint compelled Qantas and South African Airways to look elsewhere, the Tudor 2 order was reduced to 50.

Not that the Tudor was wholly unloved. *Star Panther* inaugurated a service from London to Bermuda at the hands of BSAA chief executive, AVM Don 'Pathfinder' Bennett, on 28 May 1947. A twice weekly experimental service continued for the next three months, by which time the second Tudor 4, *Star Lion*, was ready to undertake a 16,500 mile demonstration and route proving flight to South America and back. After staging through Lisbon, Dakar, Natal, Rio, Buenos Aires and Santiago before returning on schedule and without incident on 9 October, Bennett, a pilot's pilot if ever there was one, found *Star Lion* entirely satisfactory under a wide variety of conditions. As soon as other Tudors became available, he intended to establish a regular service beyond Bermuda to Cuba as well.

Improvements to the Tudor 2 continued in Avro's experimental workshops at Woodford, where the edge of the Cheshire Plain meets the moors of the High Peak. The latest batch, which reduced tailplane incidence and increased elevator control stiffness, necessitated removal and modification of the flying control system. By using the night shift to complete the task, a proving flight was scheduled for Saturday 23 August. After tossing a coin, the task fell to chief test pilot Bill Thorn assisted by Sqn Ldr David Wilson DFC as co-pilot/technical observer, senior radio operator John Webster and flight engineer E. Talbot.

It reflected the Tudor 2's importance to Avro fortunes that Thorn's crew was joined that Saturday by none other than Sir Roy Dobson (Avro's managing director), Roy Chadwick (now technical director) and his replacement as chief designer, Stuart Davies. But before the Merlin engines could be started, Dobson was summoned to the telephone. Instead of being back in a few minutes as promised, he was away for so long that Chadwick finally declared, 'Shut the door and let's get on with the flight'.

G-AGSU had just taken off at 10.58hrs in brilliant sunshine when it was suddenly seen to falter, skim over Shirfold Farm on the northeast boundary of Woodford aerodrome, and strike the ground. After ploughing uncontrollably across two fields, the fuselage split behind the centre section, catapulting Roy Chadwick 60yd into a tree and fatally fracturing his skull. The Tudor's silver wings ripped through a high wall of trees, scattering wreckage over 400yd in all directions before its nose came to rest in a pond. Both pilots were injured and as a result were drowned in the pond, while radio operator Webster died from a fractured skull. The flight engineer was pulled from the wreckage with multiple injuries. Only a blood stained Stu Davies managed to climb out under his own steam.

On Monday every newspaper in the land paid tribute to the memory and achievements of one of the world's greatest aircraft designers. Chadwick was still only 54 and full of futuristic ideas when he died, but none of his obiturists knew what an avoidable accident this had been. Stated baldly, when the night shift completed modification work, the ailerons were reconnected incorrectly. Thus, although the elevators got the Tudor airborne, when Bill Thorn applied aileron to compensate for crosswind over the runway, the wing responded in the wrong direction. He would instinctively have applied more aileron to try and pick up the wing, and the flight engineer last saw Thorn holding the control spectacle hard over to port. If only he had had more height to play with, Bill Thorn was a good enough pilot to have realised what was wrong, but being so low the starboard wing tip touched the runway. Once that happened, the largest aircraft produced in the UK up to that time rapidly went outside any human control.

In defence of the fitter who removed the old cables and assembled new ones, he had no drawings to work to and had to rely entirely on memory. When he completed his task, it 'looked the same' as it did before he dismantled it. Two inspectors also checked his work and were sure that they had carried out a full check that the controls operated correctly. All of which goes to show that no-one involved in aviation should ever be hurried so much that corners risk being cut to a dangerous extent. Furthermore, irrespective of experience or qualifications, and no matter how blessed with good fortune a pilot might think himself to be — DON'T ASSUME, CHECK.

Despite Roy Chadwick's belief that he could have seen off the Constellation or any other competition if only he had been given the time, the Tudor was still no mean achievement. G-AHNP *Star Tiger* had joined *Panther* and *Lion* by November 1947, and these all-metal machines with their 120ft wing spans and weighing over 37 tonnes at take-off settled down quite nicely on BSAA's Caribbean runs. The 2,250-mile stretch between Santa Maria in the Azores and Bermuda was the longest ocean crossing plied by any commercial airline at the time. Notwithstanding the Tudor 4's ample range, BSAA commanders found the flight to be very demanding because, despite carrying all the latest navaids, there was nothing to tune them into until the last 200 miles or so.

Occasionally, headwinds were strong enough to prevent a Tudor from reaching Bermuda. When such winds were forecast, aircraft simply waited in the Azores for better weather. Problems arose only when strong winds were not discovered until an aircraft got airborne, a not uncommon occurrence because the Portuguese forecaster at Santa Maria had no weather ships and few commercial vessels to provide him with reliable data about this stretch of the Atlantic. BSAA therefore built in safety margins by dividing westbound crossings over the featureless sea into three phases. The first step was to calculate the Point of No Return (PNR), beyond which the aircraft could not return to Santa Maria if it lost one engine. However, although committed to going on after PNR, the Tudor could still divert to Newfoundland. BSAA rules insisted that captains arrive at Bermuda with not less than two hours of fuel in hand in case sudden squalls forced them to stand off. If increased headwinds cut this safety margin below limits, the Tudor had to divert to Newfoundland. Once Canada passed out of reach, an aircraft entering the third phase was irrevocably committed to flying on to Bermuda; there was no other land within reach.

All this was well known when *Star Tiger* took-off from London on 27 January 1948 for another round trip to Cuba. The commander was Capt Brian McMillan, one of many ex-Pathfinders who had followed Bennett into BSAA. His crew consisted of co-pilot David Colby, radio officer Robert Tuck, navigator Cyril Ellison and two stewardesses. These 'Star Girls', Lynn Clayton and Sheila Nicholls, had 25 passengers to look after including AM Sir Arthur Coningham, Commander of the 2nd Tactical Air Force during the invasion of Europe.

The first leg, from London to Lisbon, was uneventful except that the cabin heater failed. Although some BSAA pilots like Capt Geoffrey Womersley described the Tudor as 'the best civil airliner flying', others regarded it as a bag of nails. Capt Gordon Store, a veteran airline man who became BSAA's Operations Manager, did not mince words:

> 'The Tudor was built like a battleship. It was noisy, I had no confidence in its engines and its systems were hopeless. The Americans were 50 years ahead of us in systems engineering. All the hydraulics, the air conditioning equipment and the recircling fans were crammed together underneath the floor without any thought. There were fuel burning heaters that would never work; we had the floor boards up in flight again and again.'

On landing at Lisbon after a freezing journey at 21,000ft, the heater was snagged together with one of the compasses. These defects were mended during the night-stop but trouble with the port inner engine delayed departure by two and a half hours. Almost at once after lifting off, the heating circuit failed again as did the compass.

Waiting in the Azores was another ex-Pathfinder pilot, Capt Frank Griffin. His Lancastrian was carrying freight to Bermuda where it would be trans-shipped to *Star Tiger* once some passengers got off. On arrival at Santa Maria, McMillan and Colby joined Griffin in the met office. Departures westbound were always timed for middle or late afternoon because crews could only find their way to Bermuda by astro-navigation. The three conferring pilots were briefed that strong winds, increasing with height, were expected along the route. The best winds for *Star Tiger* were down at low level, but thick cloud cover could then obscure the skies for 1,000 miles or more, making an astro position check impossible before PNR. As there was no point in the Lancastrian going ahead of the Tudor, both captains decided on a 24hr delay to let the winds drop.

Normally a Tudor would have flown across the great bowl of the Atlantic at around 20,000ft, but although the next day's forecast showed a slight abatement, headwinds at height were still persistent enough for McMillan to elect to fly *Star Tiger* at 2,000ft where the component was forecast to be lightest. There would still be heavy overcast along the first part of the route, but star shots looked to be obtainable well before half way.

The Lancastrian took off first on Tuesday 29 January, followed around an hour later at 15.34hrs by *Star Tiger*. Second officer Ellison had calculated that the trip should take just under 12.5 hours, and as a Tudor filled to the gills with fuel had a 16hr endurance, *Star Tiger* levelled at 2,000ft and set course for Bermuda with apparently ample margin for the unexpected.

At 16.11hrs, radio officer Tuck made first contact with the Lancastrian ahead. Griffin's crew reported good weather while experiencing a wind 15kt stronger than forecast. In addition to keeping contact with the Lancastrian, Tuck also sent back half-hourly position reports in morse. It is interesting to note from the Santa Maria logs that although the crew had flight planned to fly at 2,000ft, every message from the aircraft mentioned 20,000ft.

After five hours flying, Tuck established contact with Bermuda, but it was not until *Star Tiger* was almost half way, more than an hour later, that a clearance in the overcast enabled Ellison to shoot the stars. On the basis of his astro fix plus forecasts from Bermuda, he estimated flight duration to be still under 14hr. An hour or so later, *Star Tiger* passed PNR.

Shortly after midnight the Tudor reached 50° west or 750 miles from Bermuda. Around 01.30hrs, Griffin's navigator got his first fix for some time and found that the Lancastrian had been blown 68 miles north of intended track during the past hour. This indicated an unforecast southwesterly wind change just as *Star Tiger*, 150 miles behind, passed her point of no alternative. Capt McMillan was committed to Bermuda.

At 02.00hrs Ellison managed to get an astro fix which indicated that the Tudor had been crabbing away from Bermuda towards New York. The new course turned *Star Tiger* right into wind. At 03.15hrs, she was close enough to get a 'Class l' radio bearing from Kindley Field, Bermuda ('Class l' meant within an accuracy of 2°). McMillan was satisfied that he was on course and that his safety margin, though reduced, was still adequate. After Tuck acknowledged the bearing, nothing more was heard from *Star Tiger*.

It was not until 04.35hrs that the controller in Bermuda raised the alarm. As time went on, it became clear that the problem was bigger than simple radio failure. Capt Rees, commander of the relief crew waiting for *Star Tiger* in Bermuda, assumed command of Griffin's Lancastrian and took off on a search after dawn. Twenty five other aircraft, mostly US military based at Kindley, took part in the search that day. Nearly 1,000hr of further searching were undertaken over the following five days, but not a trace of *Star Tiger* or those on board was ever found.

Capt Griffin would testify before the subsequent inquiry that he had experienced no turbulence, icing, fog or electrical storms that could account for the loss of the

Tracks followed by Star Tiger *and* Star Ariel *before their disappearance.*

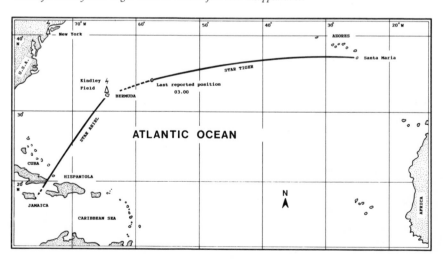

Above and above right:
Wreckage of the Tudor 2 prototype after it crashed in a pond off the northeast boundary of Woodford aerodrome on 23 August 1947. Rescuers who plunged into the pond had to swim through fuming petrol and thick oil, but their bravery could not prevent the deaths of Roy Chadwick, Bill Thorn, co-pilot David Wilson and senior radio operator John Webster. BAe

Tudor following close behind him. Although the Minister of Civil Aviation personally grounded the Tudor fleet, the most searching analysis failed to find any design or construction weakness which might account for the disaster and so the Tudor had to be 'ungrounded'. A mass of evidence was presented on fuel starvation caused by faulty fuel cock settings, together with other possible reasons for loss of control, but none were really credible unless McMillan and Colby behaved extremely negligently.

It must have been a major catastrophe if Robert Tuck, whose experience as a radio operator went back a couple of decades, had been unable to send at least part of a distress message. Don Bennett believed that *Star Tiger* had been sabotaged on the orders of those who felt threatened by his independent airline, but no evidence has ever been found to substantiate this view and it has to be said that Bennett, for all his brilliance, did tend to subscribe to conspiracy theories more readily than most.

A more credible alternative was that the crew lost the use of all radio equipment so that they could not ask for further radio bearings. They then stumbled about the Atlantic looking fruitlessly for the spot of land that is Bermuda until the aircraft ran out of fuel. Yet this does not really compute because Capt McMillan already had an accurate wind finding and bearing from Bermuda. All he needed to do was fly down the reciprocal having applied the right drift and he would not have been too far out.

Above:
The first Tudor 4 to fly, Star Panther, in British South American Airways livery. Tudor 4s were modified Tudor 1s with a 6ft longer forward fuselage and the flight engineer's position removed to accommodate 32 passengers with reduced seat pitch. BAe

Even if his crew could not see Bermuda visually, and the weather was good enough for them to do so, they would surely have climbed and homed in using one of their navaids. For the running-out-of-fuel theory to be credible, every radio and piece of nav kit would have needed to fail simultaneously, whilst at the same time Ellison forget all he had ever learned about dead reckoning navigation.

Capt Womersley did not entirely rule out sabotage, but he thought it more likely that a propeller broke away, cut through the fuselage and severed the control cables. But there might have been a simpler explanation. It has been postulated that *Star Tiger* may have been lost because the crew delayed in dealing with an outboard engine failure at comparatively low altitude. Again this presumes more than one failure — engine fault followed by crew error — but it might point in the right direction. Returning to the flightdeck, *Star Tiger's* crew are confident from the 'Class 1' bearing that they are nearing Bermuda and heading in the right direction. Everyone is tired after a long and busy flight, and brains are at their least efficient in the early hours, so it is not beyond the bounds of probability that crew members forget that they are not flying at their usual 20,000ft. Radio officer Tuck has certainly given that impression in his position reports.

Let-down then commences at the allotted point, but after descending through only 2,000ft they hit the sea. No-one sees the threat looming up because it is still night; having 'driven' into the sea, the Tudor is lost without trace.

This explanation may sound unlikely but the altimeters of those days, which relied on three clock-like hands with a very small one indicating tens of thousands of feet, could easily be misread, particularly if a pilot was weary or hard pressed. In fact, Capt McMillan had had to deal with one problem after another since leaving London and he was heard to complain of feeling very tired at Santa Maria. If McMillan had been in control and his co-pilot had been dozing (or the other way around), the navigator had been concentrating on his calculations and the radio operator writing up his log, a margin of error of only 2,000ft could well have been used up before anyone noticed. Forget the failed engines, navaids or whatever; if we assume that nothing was wrong up to the point of impact, it would explain why no distress message was ever sent.

Of course, there are many today who would like to believe that *Star Tiger* simply disappeared, like other craft before and since, into the dreaded 'Bermuda triangle'. It was perhaps just as well that this phenomenon had not become popularised when BSAA's fourth Tudor, G-AGRE *Star Ariel*, departed Kindley Field, Bermuda at 12.42hrs on 17 January 1949. *Star Ariel* had left London four days earlier for Jamaica via Gander, Bermuda, and Nassau. After reaching Kingston without incident, it set off back home only to meet up in Bermuda with *Star Lion*, originally bound for Santiago but now grounded by engine failure. It was decided to transfer *Star Lion's* passengers and crew to *Star Ariel*, which would be turned round and sent back direct to Kingston and then on to Chile.

Although the Tudor 4 cabin was arranged to seat 32 passengers in two compartments, there were only 13 fare-payers on *Star Ariel* as it headed to Jamaica under the command of Capt J. C. McPhee. He elected to transit at 18,000ft where there was a slight tailwind component, and his aircraft had a 10hr endurance for a flight that navigator V. D. J. Shapley estimated would take 5hr 28min. Given the good en route weather forecast, it promised to be a simple, routine flight with plenty of safety margins.

Flight plan track was a straight 216° until reaching Morant Point at the southeast corner of Jamaica. PNR was 575 miles from the start, but critical points seemed irrelevant once it became apparent that the skies were completely clear above 10,000ft. At 13.32hrs, the first in-flight report from radio operator G. C. Rettie stated that *Star Ariel* was 150nm southwest of Bermuda at 18,000ft. Another position update at 13.42hrs reported passing 30° north at 13.37hrs and changing to Kingston frequency: this was the last thing ever heard of *Star Ariel*, its crew or its passengers.

Star Ariel's ETA in Kingston was 18.10hrs and at 18.54 the company ordered another of its aircraft, then at Nassau, to start a search. At 21.08hrs an all-out search was ordered. As *Star Ariel* was manned by an experienced crew, and carried normal radios, Loran, Rebecca, astro-navigation equipment and a drift indicator, the search was organised on the assumption that the Tudor had been on course when it came down. Yet despite the efforts of some 80 aircraft searching over six days, no trace was or ever has been found of *Star Ariel*.

The inevitable inquiry was mystified. Not only were the crew fit, fully qualified and in possession of all the latest nav kit, but also C-AGRE took-off over two tons below maximum permissible weight. From all the evidence, it flew well above the freezing level in almost perfect weather with no clear air turbulence around, and endurance was almost twice estimated flight time.

Some years later, structural failure would become known to the public largely through experiences with the early Comets. However, *Star Ariel* had flown less than 350hr and cabin pressure differential at 18,000ft would have been too small to cause disintegration had decompression occurred. Moreover, the Comet sagas showed that if an aircraft broke up in the air, some parts of the wreckage descended comparatively slowly and remained visible to searching eyes for many hours.

As for sabotage the inquiry stated: 'While the possibility of the planting of an infernal machine cannot be entirely eliminated, it can be said that no evidence has been found to suggest that sabotage had anything to do with the loss of this aircraft.' Again, if a bomb had gone off while the airliner was on course, parts of the wreckage should have floated for some time and therefore been noticed.

Yet if the aircraft had been under control when it ditched, there should have been time to send a distress message during the descent from 18,000ft. Why were there no signs of life saving equipment, especially as the sea was not rough and the two rafts in the centre section were designed to inflate automatically? At the request of the Minister of Civil Aviation, the distinguished aviation pioneer Lord Brabazon undertook an investigation into the design and construction of the Tudor 4 in relation to its airworthiness and safety. He was assisted by a number of technical experts who carried out a carefully co-ordinated research programme into the aircraft structure, materials used, defect history, auxiliary systems, possibility of fire and explosion, presence of noxious gases and effects of lightning and static discharge. At the end of all this labour, Lord Brabazon's study could shed no further light and the inquiry was forced to conclude that, 'Through lack of evidence due to no wreckage having been found, the cause of the accident is unknown.'

Fleet Air Arm experience during World War 2 indicated that, if an aircraft hit the sea in a dive, it could go completely under water. Unless the crew flew into the sea while in the descent, a much less likely event than in the case of *Star Tiger*, the only credible way this could happen would have been for the controls to fail dramatically. Given that *Star Ariel* had been flying perfectly for at least an hour, something sudden and terrible must have occurred like Capt Womersley's theory of the exploding propeller which cut through the fuselage, severed all the essential control cables and put the radio operator out of action at the same time. That was a very tall order so,

Tudor interior which, for its day, set new standards of passenger comfort. BAe

while the best hypothesis must be that *Star Ariel*, like *Star Tiger*, flew into the sea, we are never likely to confirm the reason why.

The loss of *Star Ariel* finally damned the Tudor 2 in BOAC's eyes and ensured that only 18 of the type were ever built. The second inexplicable loss of one of their airliners also finished BSAA as an independent operator, though Don Bennett took some Tudor 2s and proved them to be very useful freighters during the Berlin Airlift. Once that was over, Bennett set up a new company called Fairflight Ltd with two Tudors restored for passenger work. Among Fairflight's many and varied commissions was a contract to take a party of Welsh rugby supporters to Dublin on 10 March 1950. They were to fly there in G-AKBY, a Tudor 2 which just two days previously had had its Certificate of Airworthiness amended to raise the maximum number of people (including crew) that could be carried from 77 to 83.

G-AKBY, commanded by Capt Dennis Parsons, uplifted 78 passengers and five crew from Llandow airport near Cardiff. After an uneventful flight they landed at

Collinstown airfield, Dublin, whereupon the supporters travelled on to see the Wales-Ireland international in Belfast. Two days later the party reassembled for the return trip. After crossing the Irish Sea, the Tudor's crew called Llandow at 14.50hrs to be told to join the circuit at 1,000ft for Runway 28, wind straight down the runway at 10-15kt, visibility 15 miles. G-AKBY joined downwind, flew a left hand circuit on to finals and was lined up for landing at about two miles and 500ft with gear and flaps down.

From the Tower, the approach looked a little low. The shallow glide angle continued, giving eye witnesses the impression that if it was maintained the landing would occur well short of the runway. When G-AKBY was about half a mile out at 100-150ft, a small increase in power was heard. The rate of descent seemed to slightly reduce, but almost immediately afterwards there was the roar of engines increasing suddenly up to full power. Concurrently the nose started to rise, slowly at first but then developing into a steep and rapid climb such that the Tudor lifted rapidly to around 350ft. When the angle was 60-70°, all engine noise ceased abruptly, the airliner stalled and then struck the ground starboard wing down. There was no fire but only three passengers out of the 83 souls on board survived.

After excluding such remote possibilities as a deranged passenger deliberately interfering with the controls, the subsequent inquiry found no evidence to indicate that both pilots became incapacitated simultaneously or that the flying pilot's seat suddenly slipped back. The elevator control system was in no way defective, the autopilot could not have become inadvertently engaged because its master valve was found in the 'off' position, and an Auster pilot in the Llandow circuit at the same time experienced no undue gusting or turbulence. Landing on the 1,600yd-long Llandow runway should have been no problem to Capt Parsons; he had brought the Tudor to rest in 1,300yd in less headwind at Dublin. This left only one likely cause — that the aircraft's centre of gravity had become substantially aft of the permitted limit.

When G-AKBY's Certificate of Airworthiness had been amended on 8 March to allow six more people to be carried, it was stipulated that the centre of gravity with gear and flaps down must be within 85-100in aft of the datum point. Yet the inquiry found that Fairflight's policy on load distribution in response to the new passenger limit was far from clear. Their Chief Engineer and Chief Inspector gave conflicting evidence on precise seating fits for the final flight, and when G-AKBY's load sheets were recovered, they showed that Capt Parsons had adopted an erroneous mean passenger arm of 43ft. The true figure should have been 46ft 7in, but not content with incorrectly assessing the aircraft's overall centre of gravity, Capt Parson's miscalculation would only have been permissable providing around 2,000lb of baggage was stowed in the main forward hold. As rugby enthusiasts returning from an away match tend to carry only hand baggage, it was not surprising that no portions of heavy luggage were recovered from the wreck.

With all passengers strapped into their seats on the final approach, and the weight of overhead hand baggage supplemented by an estimated additional 400lb of small Irish purchases, the Tudor's centre of gravity at the moment of impact must have been 109in aft of datum and in all possibility 2-3in further behind still. Regrettably, extrapolations from official Tudor trials showed that with full power applied while gear and flaps were down, no effective elevator control remained at about 94kt when the centre of gravity position was 106.5in aft or 112in aft at about 105kt.

Going back to the accident, as G-AKBY reached 100-150ft on the Llandow approach, the flying pilot finally realised he was too low and increased power. This proved insufficient so he applied full power to get to the runway. The aircraft's nose rose, but whether initiated by the pilot or the automatic result of full power application was irrelevant. At low approach speed with gear and flaps down and centre of gravity too far back, the Tudor would have been extremely unstable and the elevators incapable of arresting the nose-up pitching moment.

From then on, control was lost. Examination of the wreckage showed that one of the pilots had switched off the ignition, which accounted for all engine noise ceasing abruptly, but it was a futile gesture because there was no recovering from a Tudor stall turn that close to the ground.

Don Bennett, who had personally trained Capt Parsons on the Tudor and who knew his aircraft backwards, disagreed with the inquiry's findings. Harkening back to his own flight tests, he was satisfied that fully effective elevator control could be retained as far back as 112in. Inquiry members listened patiently while one of Britain's great aviators strove to justify his undiminished faith in the Tudor, but as Bennett had carried no recording instrumentation on his trials and flew a much lighter aircraft, they felt unable to accept that his arguments displaced their own.

They also expressed the opinion that Bennett possessed a level of piloting skill and sense of anticipation that was out of the ordinary. It was a valid point. Bennett was an exceptional pilot who managed to land a Tudor during the Berlin Airlift despite the elevator locks being left in. Perhaps G-AKBY would never have crashed in his hands, but the rules must be written for average operators. Fairflight did not appear to have issued any clear guidelines to comply with the compulsory conditions of the new Certificate of Airworthiness, nor did the aircraft commander seem overly concerned about the fact. There were no facilities for weighing passenger baggage at Llandow, and Capt Parsons did not avail himself of Aer Lingus' services for passenger handling or weighing in Dublin. Baggage, weighing, load sheets, centres of gravity — they all sound very mundane and yawn-inspiring — yet while some aircraft can be very forgiving of neglect, they will all bite if pushed too far.

At the time the Llandow accident was the biggest single disaster in British aviation history, and it went down as the final great black mark against the poor old Tudor. But was the aircraft really a repetitive failure, or was it let down on every occasion by human frailty? We will never know for sure, but there is more than a suspicion that the Avro Tudor was more sinned against than sinning.

PYRAMID OF CIRCUMSTANCES

When the British set up their Aeronautical Inspection Directorate at Farnborough in 1913, one of its responsibilities was the investigation of military aircraft accidents. This role then passed to the Accidents Investigation Branch (AIB), founded in 1915, when Capt C. B. Cockburn was appointed to the independent post of 'Inspector of Accidents' reporting to the Director General of Military Aeronautics in the War Office.

After World War 1, when two commercial companies started operating between London and the continent, it became clear that some organisation needed to take responsibility for the safety of fare-paying civilian passengers. A Department of Civil Aviation was therefore set up within the Air Ministry, and the AIB transferred to it in 1920 with a brief to investigate civil and military accidents. The new Inspector of Accidents was Maj J. P. Cooper MC, an engineer who worked directly to the Air Minister so that 'he would be able to speak without fear or favour'. His small team of four were all civilians, and AIB would always remain civilian-manned so that experience would not be lost on postings or promotion.

By 1937, coincident with the expansion of British military flying, the AIB was expanded to encompass seven inspectors of accidents working under the first Chief Inspector of Accidents, Wg Cdr Vernon Brown. Although he retired officially from the RAF on taking up his appointment, Vernon Brown was to oversee a branch that investigated almost nothing but military accidents during World War 2. Moreover, the AIB's workload increased to such an extent — from 91 to 333 investigations a year between 1938 and 1943 — that a year later, although still Chief Inspector, Brown had been elevated to Air Cdre status.

With the coming of peace, a separate Ministry of Civil Aviation was created to co-ordinate the subsequent growth in commercial air travel. The AIB was transferred to it in 1946, marking a formal separation from the Air Ministry, though Sir Vernon Brown continued as Chief Inspector of Accidents.

The Ministry of Civil Aviation soon learned that airliner crashes made front page news. An early example concerned Lockheed Constellation PH-TEN belonging to the Royal Dutch Airlines (KLM). Although the beautifully curved Constellation at last provided the world's airlines with a commercially viable trans-Atlantic land-plane, they would still have to wait until the mid-1950s, and the appearance of the Bristol Britannia or DC-7C genre, before being in a position to mount regular non-stop schedules in both directions. Meanwhile, in the face of prevailing westerly winds, airlines would stage through the European gateway airports of either Shannon or Prestwick.

Christened *Nijmegen* after the old Dutch town close to the West German border, PH-TEN left Schiphol airport, Amsterdam, at 21.11hrs (GMT) on 20 October 1948

Above:
The Flying Dutchman — KLM Constellation PH-TEN Nijmegen. The Constellation's Speedpak detachable under-fuselage freight container, devised by Lockheed to augment the somewhat limited capacity of the two underfloor freight holds, is about to be fitted.

Below:
Plan view of Nijmegen *hitting electric high tension cables three miles east of Prestwick Airport in level flight. As the aircraft's speed was 170mph, it would have travelled from A to B in one second.*

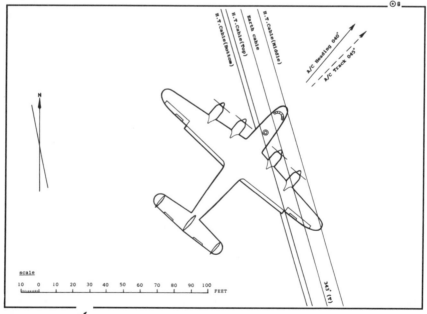

bound for New York with 30 passengers and a freight cargo of watches, textiles and mail. Apart from three cabin attendants, the crew consisted of two flight engineers, two wireless operators and three pilots. Second Officer Parks and First Officer O'Brien were both ex-RAF, but perhaps most reassuring to the fare-payers was the presence on board of KLM's Chief Pilot, Capt K. D. Parmentier.

Dirk Parmentier had learned to fly with the Dutch Air Force before transferring to KLM in 1929. He became one of the handful of pilots who pioneered the 10,000-mile air route from Amsterdam to Batavia (now Jakarta) in the Dutch East Indies, before making up the piloting half of the KLM team which won the handicap section of the London-Melbourne air race in 1934. Having been established as a Dutch celebrity, Parmentier was eventually given responsibility for test-flying all new KLM aircraft.

When his homeland was overrun in 1940, Parmentier ferried a load of important Dutch passengers to Britain. For the rest of the war he served as chief pilot of the KLM crews who operated a regular DC-3 schedule between Lisbon and the UK. It was pretty dangerous work, and the way in which Parmentier used cloud cover to escape from the attentions of six attacking Ju88s over the Bay of Biscay in 1943 only enhanced his reputation for superb airmanship. Some less eminent pilots regarded the short and powerfully built Parmentier, with his abrupt and determined movements, as a bit of a cold fish, but there was no denying his energy and inquiring mind. Blessed with administrative as well as flying skill, the trip to New York on 20 October should have been just another flying day for Capt Parmentier.

First stop was Prestwick, sited on the west coast of Scotland for its good weather record. The flight over the North Sea and England having passed uneventfully, radio contact was established with Prestwick Approach Control when *Nijmegen* was at 9,000ft about 70 miles southeast of the airport. A GCA letdown procedure was carried out through cloud, initially for a landing on Prestwick's main 2,200yd-long Runway 32. But while on the approach, Parmentier found the crosswind to be outside KLM limits for a landing on the northwest runway, so as soon as he broke cloud he overshot into a visual left-hand circuit to the south and east of the airport for an arrival on the shorter (1,500yd) Runway 26.

All seemed to be going to plan until around 23.32hrs when, three and a half miles to the east of the airport, the Constellation collided in dense fog with high tension cables forming part of the British Electricity Authority's national grid system. *Nijmegen* was set on fire and subsequently crashed in flames at Auchinweet Farm, about five miles east-northeast of the airport. Everybody on board lost their lives.

Technical records told the AIB inspectors that Constellation PH-TEN had amassed only 3,552 flying hours since leaving Lockheed's Burbank factory in May 1947. It had been regularly maintained and inspected thereafter, as had its four Wright Cyclone engines. On examining the wreckage, the airliner's five altimeters were found to be correctly calibrated with no signs of pre-impact malfunction, and there was no evidence to suggest that navigation aids on board had failed to function properly. 'Up to the conclusion of its first approach to Prestwick airport,' stated the experts, 'the aircraft was airworthy in every known mechanical sense'.

The ground to the east of Prestwick airport gradually rose to a height of over 400ft. Making allowances for the sagging of electricity cables between their pylons, the Constellation must have struck them a mere 40ft above the ground. Given the experience of the flight crew and the international dimension of the whole business, the Minister of Civil Aviation appointed Mr T. P. McDonald KC, together with an experienced Constellation pilot, Capt Bernard Frost, to ascertain through the medium of a public Court of Inquiry why the aircraft flew where it did at such a dangerously low altitude. All possible assistance was given by the various Dutch agencies involved, and an official representative of the Netherlands government was present throughout the proceedings.

When Capt Parmentier went to the Schiphol office of the Royal Dutch Meteorological Institute for his pre-flight briefing, he was given the aerodrome forecast issued by the Prestwick met office for the period up to 03.00hrs: 'Surface wind, 240° at 18kt. Intermittent slight rain, occasionally becoming moderate. Visibility two to six miles. Cloud base 1,000ft, occasionally 5/10 base 800ft.' The Prestwick weather outlook worsened as the evening progressed, and had PH-TEN taken off on schedule at 20.30hrs, Parmentier and his crew would have picked up the 21.06hrs Prestwick Sub-Area W/T broadcast which predicted a lowering cloud base of '9/10, base 600 to 1,000ft'. But there had been a last minute change in *Nijmegen's* routeing to include a freight off-load in Iceland. Consequently, PH-TEN did not get airborne until five minutes after the broadcast, and there is no evidence that the flight crew ever received the Prestwick weather update by other means. Not that it should have mattered overmuch — the Constellation carried enough fuel to fly to Prestwick, divert to Shannon if necessary, and still return to Amsterdam.

Nijmegen's crew made radio contact with Prestwick at 22.55hrs, and although several airfield weather updates were passed by ATC thereafter, none of them put the cloud base lower than 700ft even though visibility and cloud-base continued to deteriorate. 'The absence of this information,' stated the inquiry report tersely, 'was due to the failure of the meteorological observer to include this item in either of the reports which he sent to the Flying Control Officer (Tower Control) at or just after 23.00hrs'. By the time of the accident, Prestwick weather was '6/10 at 300ft, 10/10 at 700ft, 3,900yd visibility in drizzle' with worse to come, yet at no stage was this conveyed to PH-TEN's crew. In fact the Flying Control Officer told the inquiry that 'it was not the normal procedure (to) pass on deterioration messages to aircraft'.

The Court accepted the view expressed by Capt Snitslaar, KLM's new Chief Pilot, that if Dirk Parmentier had been briefed on the 300ft ceiling, he would not even have tried to land at Prestwick but would have diverted. KLM's North Atlantic Route Manual certainly laid down clear instructions: 'The decision as to whether or not a landing can be made at a certain airport will be considered according to the following factors: in the first place the captain will be directed by his own idea of safety, in the second place by the orders of the local ATC, and in the third place by the KLM landing limits. He will not make any landing when this involves disregarding . . . KLM regulations when another airport with better landing conditions could be reached safely . . .

'Unless otherwise stated in the route book, no landing can be made if either the cloud base or visibility is below the minima quoted . . . The following limits apply to instrument low approach procedures at Prestwick:
— GCA Assist, Runway 32, Night, 5/10 at 300ft, 0.5 mile visibility
— Runway 26, Night, 5/10 at 700ft, two miles visibility.'

Finally, the Manual was emphatic that the landing advice and limits contained within it 'are effective for all pilots, irrespective of rank'. That was pretty unequivocal and Dirk Parmentier would not have disregarded KLM operating instructions especially in front of subordinates. As Chief Pilot, he was responsible not only for the compilation of the Route Manuals in the first place, but also for being seen to maintain the company's impeccable flight safety record of which he was justifiably proud.

Above:
Capt Dirk Parmentier, regarded by many as among the top six civil pilots of his generation. KLM

Below:
Prestwick Airport of yesteryear with the main 32 instrument runway running from left to right. On the night of 20 October 1948, Capt Parmentier overshot from an approach on 32 and turned left into a visual circuit to position for a landing on the shorter Runway 26. The 26 threshold is in the bottom left hand corner. Prestwick Airport

Unaware that the weather was already outside limits, *Nijmegen*'s crew pressed on with Parmentier flying and O'Brien working the radios. At 22.55hrs the first officer had asked Prestwick Approach Control, 'Is the GCA serviceable and what runway are they using?' Back came the answer, 'GCA is set up on Runway 32. Runway in use 26. GCA can give you overshoot on 32.' Although O'Brien acknowledged — 'We will do GCA and overshoot on Runway 32, and will land on Runway 26' — at 23.16hrs the Prestwick GCA Director advised that, 'the wind is southwest 12 to 15mph. You may land on Runway 32 and if you find the wind too strong, you may land on Runway 26.' Came the reply: 'Roger. We will attempt to land on 32.' No sooner were the words out of O'Brien's mouth than the CCA Director seemed to regret his earlier optimism by transmitting, 'There is strong drift (cross-wind) on Runway 32'.

At this stage *Nijmegen* was some 20 miles northeast of Prestwick descending through 4,000ft. On levelling out at 2,500ft, Parmentier was told to reduce to circuit speed 'and perform your cockpit check for overshoot'. Two minutes later, still about 12 miles inland, he was directed to turn south. On reaching Cumnock, 11 miles southeast of the airfield, clearance was given down to 2,000ft.

The Constellation was then turned west and after two minutes on the new heading, cleared down to 1,500ft. Completely surrounded by cloud and locked firmly onto instruments, Capt Parmentier intersected the glidepath around 23.27hrs. He maintained a nice approach all the way down. Finally the GCA Director said, 'Check undercarriage and flaps for landing . . . advising you of a strong cross-wind (from your left) on 32. Do not acknowledge further instructions . . . track good, look ahead for overshooting. How do you read me?'

'Receiving you very good and perfectly readable. Will make landing on Runway 26.'

'Roger. Call Prestwick Approach Control on this frequency.'

'Your message received. Will you turn lights on on Runway 26?' (Only one Prestwick runway could be illuminated at a time, so the 32 lights had to be switched off before the 26 lights could be switched on.)

'Your message received. Standby.'

After checking in with Approach Control, the pilots were told: 'Surface wind southwest 15mph. Give me a check call when downwind for Runway 26'.

'Your message received.'

Although KLM issued no specific instructions to pilots on the safest method of overshooting from Runway 32 and landing on 26, its Route Manual did say: 'In using circling limits as applied to landings on the long runway at Prestwick (14 or 32), pilots will be aware that manoeuvring must be confined to the west side of the airport and that flight should not extend beyond the east side of the airport.' The reason for this was that 'the terrain to the east gradually slopes upward to a point where the ground contour is nearly 400ft above mean sea level . . . Therefore the circling limit (for) landing on 26 must be used with extreme caution . . . the night limits for use of runway 26 require a ceiling of 700ft and visibility of at least two miles.'

Given that some radio masts to the east of the airfield rose to 585ft above sea level, the Court was of the opinion that KLM's circling limits for Runway 26 were too low. Be that as it may, without any precision guidance from the ground or even a stopwatch on board to time a downwind leg accurately, Capt Parmentier would have known that the transition from Runway 32 to 26 could only be executed safely so long as he retained visual contact with the ground. The GCA controller confirmed

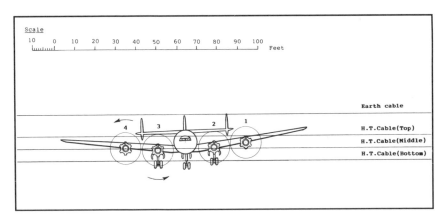

Above:
Head-on view of Nijmegen *about to hit the cables. The earth cable cut off the top of its port fin. The top HT cable would have been lifted clear of 2, 3 and 4 airscrews by the fuselage roof, but the other cables were cut and partly wound in by the propellers.* Nijmegen *must have absorbed 132,000V which caused the fire.*

Below:
The last remains of Nijmegen *scattered over Auchinweet Farm near the village of Tarbolton, Ayrshire. Of the 40 people on board, six were found to be alive when medical aid reached the scene. Despite being moved to hospital, all were so severely burned that none survived.* Outram Press

to the inquiry that, 'he (presumably O'Brien) told me he was visual and that he was landing on 26.'

Sweeping round in a fairly tight turn, Parmentier climbed the Constellation to 450ft to start the downwind leg with wheels and flaps down. Almost at once he ran into cloud, and the next thing known for certain was that around 23.32hrs the Constellation collided with four high tension cables some three and a half miles to the east of the intersection of the Prestwick runways. These cables were suspended from two pylons 1,013ft apart; the topmost was the 'earth' and the others were phase conductors carrying 132,000V from a power station at Kilmarnock to South Scotland. About midway between the two pylons — the top of one being 455ft and the other 477ft above mean sea level — the 'earth' cable was damaged in two places but not broken. The other three cables were severed by the propeller blades, and many broken pieces were found on the ground.

In among the debris were the top of the port fin and rudder which had been cut off by the topmost cable. If that was not bad enough, the Constellation also took the full force of a voltage sufficiently high to cause fusing of any thin gauge metal acting as a conductor and to ignite any exposed flammable substances such as fuel in the wing tanks. Apart from flickering airfield lights, the first Prestwick knew anything was wrong was when a fading, 'We have hit something . . . Fire Control . . . We are climbing' was heard from First Officer O'Brien. The GCA controller noticed a 'blip' five miles east-northeast near the village of Tarbolton, and he called 'What is your position?' O'Brien and Capt Parmentier were probably too busy working like one-armed paperhangers to even try answering this question, especially after what started as a left turn in the vague direction of the airport developed into an uncontrollable complete orbit to port with the Constellation neither climbing nor descending. By the time ground witnesses saw or heard PH-TEN pass over Tarbolton for a second time, it was torching flame. 'Have you any idea where we are?' came the last plaintive cry from *Nijmegen* around 23.34hrs, but there was nowhere left to go. Heading northeast, the airliner finally crashed some 90sec later at Auchinweet Farm where the ground altitude was about the same as that of the high tension cables. The inquiry came to the opinion that 'the aircraft was doomed to destruction from the time fire broke out, and that notwithstanding the best efforts of the pilot and crew, nothing could have been done thereafter to prevent the disaster'.

There was no doubt in the inquiry's mind 'that the cause of the ultimate destruction of the aircraft was its collision with the high tension cables'. Up to completion of the overshoot from Runway 32, PH-TEN seemed to be fully serviceable and under the control of an experienced and competent crew. 'The problem is to discover why the aircraft was flying at an altitude between 400 and 450ft over ground which was largely above the 400ft contour.'

Much was made in the inquiry report of the failure to warn *Nijmegen*'s crew of the deteriorating weather situation at Prestwick, and the conclusion was reached that, 'there was a grave lack of supervision in the Meteorological Office at Prestwick'. The Court was little more impressed with the sense of effective responsibility shown by the Flying Control Officer in the Tower. 'May I ask you,' recorded the President, 'to answer a plain question. As a pilot, would you not want to know if the ceiling was getting lower and the visibility getting worse?'

'Approaching an airfield, yes.'

'And did you pass that information?'

'I did not.'

Add to this the statement that, 'at least 40min of the delay (in sending assistance to the crash site) . . . could have been avoided if the organisation for emergencies at Prestwick Airport had provided for proper liaison with the police and medical and fire services', and the Prestwick organisation came across as a bit of a shambles. Nevertheless, although the accident demonstrated the critical importance both of pilots receiving accurate and adequate information on current weather conditions and of flying supervisors supervising effectively, none of the airport's failings could honestly be said to have been a primary cause of the Constellation disaster. Capt Parmentier may well have behaved differently had any of his conversations with the airfield mentioned the word 'deterioration', and certainly neither of the other two large airliners scheduled to arrive between 22.00 and 23.00hrs even tried to get in when they were given the true weather situation, but by the time *Nijmegen's* flight crew discovered the extent of the low cloud base and visibility for themselves – at the latest when turning downwind for a visual approach on 26 – they still had plenty of opportunity to climb away and divert.

Why then did Capt Parmentier, vastly experienced as a pilot yet still with all his wits about him at the age of only 44, and First Officer O'Brien, with over 3,000 flying hours under his belt and old enough at 29 not to keep quiet in the face of a serious flying risk, appear to behave like greenhorns by stumbling on in solid cloud vainly seeking the 26 runway lights? Given that all altimeters were conveying the true height above ground, both pilots must have failed to appreciate the rising ground ahead.

On the face of it, the reason lay on the Approach chart held by Kevin O'Brien. Printed and issued by KLM, the chart for Prestwick was erroneous and misleading in two respects. First, the section illustrating approaches to Runway 26 in side elevation showed that the ground out to 14 miles in a northeasterly direction never rose above 200ft. In fact the ground rose to 400ft between three and four miles in this direction, and reached nearly 1,000ft by 14 miles out. Second, at a place one-third of a mile from the electricity cables it marked a '45ft' spot height which should have read '450ft'. Poignantly, on recovering the burnt remains of the chart from the wreck of PH-TEN, it was found that the charring had stopped within one-eighth of an inch of the false '45' marking. This was sufficient though to show that no correction had been made to the chart.

The offending charts were based on US Army Air Force maps, which were just as incorrect. The KLM derivatives were never checked by any KLM representative visiting Prestwick, nor was the KLM Flight Operations Officer at the airport ever asked to confirm their accuracy. The final insult was that perfectly accurate British European Airways' approach charts were available in the Prestwick briefing room. 'It appears quite extraordinary,' recorded the inquiry, 'that instrument letdown charts for airports in Great Britain should be based on those of a foreign authority, when detailed and accurate (locally produced) maps are available for such a purpose'.

If incorrect height information was not bad enough, there was also no mention of the line of high tension cables on any chart carried in *Nijmegen*. Another lesson from the accident is clear – flight crews should always use the best data available, because precision approach information that is incorrect or out of date is precisely useless!

That said, it must be remembered that the KLM Manual prohibited all their pilots 'irrespective of rank' from using Runway 26 by night if the ceiling was lower than 700ft or visibility less than two miles. Notwithstanding the chart's accuracy, there is no getting away from the fact that in the pertaining weather conditions, Capt Parmentier should not have carried on flying downwind for 26.

In spite of both pilots' considerable experience of staging through Prestwick, it seems that they ignored the weather, the high ground to the east and the flight limitations that flowed from them. Such a lack of situational awareness could only have resulted from one thing – a major in-flight distraction. The inquiry considered several hypotheses, including the sudden onset of massive turbulence or a collision with a large bird, but there was no evidence to support any of them.

In the end the Court found it 'impossible . . . to reach any conclusion of the precise cause of the accident'. It was left with the feeling that the loss of *Nijmegen* and all on board resulted not from any single factor but rather from what the inquirers termed 'a pyramid of circumstances'. The lack of any mention of cloud and visibility deterioration during the GCA, the absence from the pilot's instructions of any detailed directions on timed visual runway approaches in bad visibility, and the misleading character of the approach charts carried in the aircraft, would have stretched any flight crew no matter how well qualified. It might only have taken one more distraction to push them over the edge.

The most likely answer to the final link in the chain lay in the wreckage of PH-TEN. Damage to the propellers (one blade of each had broken off near the hub) suggested that the 2,200hp engines were rotating at high speed on impact, except possibly No 2. It was possible to say from inspection of the damaged electricity cables that the Constellation hit slightly right wing down. The top 'earth' cable was therefore severed by No 1 airscrew, and the middle and bottom cables by Nos 3 and 4 on the starboard side. This was confirmed by the presence of one very deep cable cut on the leading edge of one blade of each of these airscrews, but there was no corresponding deep cut on any No 2 engine blade.

In addition, the remaining blades of the port inner engine were twisted in the opposite direction to the remaining blades of the other airscrews. A strip inspection showed that the pitch setting of No 2 was abnormally coarse, rendering it incapable of delivering the same power output as the other three engines. Such an abnormality could have resulted from impact with the ground, but as all four engines crashed in much the same attitude, there was no reason why No 2 should have sustained any peculiar damage. A much more likely explanation was that the pitch change was pilot-induced, most probably during an attempt to feather No 2 engine. Certainly the wrecked cockpit interior revealed that the engine fire extinguisher selector cock at the Flight Engineer's station had been moved from its normal neutral position to select No 2 engine. This indicated that either the engineer thought a fire existed there and intended to extinguish it, or that No 2 propeller was being closed down because such a selection was part of the feathering drill.

Unfortunately, by the time the inquiry decided it needed to look deeper into this possibility, the engines had already been sold for scrap. Nevertheless, if No 2 engine had been feathered before PH-TEN struck the high tension cables, it would have explained why Parmentier appeared to have difficulty in climbing once the collision occurred especially as the gear and flaps were still down. If one port engine plus a damaged rudder proved incapable of balancing two live starboard engines, it might also have accounted for the continuous port turn.

Let us return to the point where the Constellation became established downwind for 26 in cloud. From the weather information he had been given, Capt Parmentier could have assumed that this was an isolated patch and that he would soon be through it. Just as the true weather situation became apparent, No 2 engine suffered a serious malfunction. By the time subsequent emergency and feathering drills had been completed, *Nijmegen* would have been well downwind, but then came another brain teaser to preoccupy the flight crew. It was clear from KLM instructions that the commander should have initiated a diversion in view of the prevailing weather, but that would involve at best flying over the Irish Sea to Shannon and at worst returning over the North Sea to Amsterdam. The loss of No 2 engine was bad enough, but who knew what it could develop into on a long diversion? Overriding all other considerations in the KLM Manual was the first priority statement that 'the captain will be directed by his own idea of safety'. Might it not have seemed more prudent to the crew to continue with the circuit in order to get the aircraft down safely at Prestwick as quickly as possible?

Although the theory is not watertight, it offers the best explanation of why Capt Parmentier continued to fly as he did when everything else cried out for him to discontinue the visual approach to 26. Tired brains suddenly finding themselves in bad weather shortly before midnight, and then faced almost immediately afterwards by a serious emergency and consequent airmanship considerations, are not best placed to recognise cartographical errors or remember circling weather minima. It may just be that a problem No 2 engine acted as the final brain-toppling layer in the pyramid of circumstances, ensuring that the flight crew finally ran out of spare capacity to appreciate the onset of the biggest threat of all.

The final lesson therefore comes in two halves. First, a chain of seemingly minor omissions and errors can build up to become far more life-threatening than the sum of its parts. Second, such a chain of misfortune can afflict all pilots irrespective of their experience or credentials. Dirk Parmentier, widely acknowledged as one of the great airline pilots of his generation, not only knew the book backwards but also had drafted a large proportion of the warnings contained within it. Yet despite being fully conversant with Prestwick, oozing with the experience that came from nearly 16,000 flying hours including 413hrs that year, and being at the top of his form, even the great Dirk Parmentier eventually ran out of airspace and ideas. Lesser pilots should never fly so close to their personal limits that a poor weather brief or an incorrect chart can mean the difference between life and death.

SMOKE GETS IN YOUR EYES

British civil air accidents are now the responsibility of the Department of Transport's Air Accidents Investigation Branch (AAIB). Those of a semantic bent might dispute whether accidents ever befall the 'air' ('aircraft' was felt to be too narrow a definition in the space age), but the Branch's objectives are as clear as they ever were: 'to determine the circumstances and causes of an accident with a view to the preservation of life and the avoidance of accidents in the future.' In the interests of impartiality, the AAIB does not apportion blame or liability; such post-inquiry matters are left to the Civil Aviation Authority (CAA) and airline operator concerned.

Although the Minister can still order a Public Inquiry whenever an accident stimulates particular public interest or has serious implications, he has not seen the need since 1972. This, it is argued, is a measure of the AAIB's investigative expertise and widely respected judgement. The AAIB Chief Inspector currently heads a staff of around 40 of whom nearly two-thirds are inspectors: about half are operations inspectors, the others engineers. They all work out of the Royal Aircraft Establishment at Farnborough, where they are adjacent to the fount of British aeronautical expertise and the RAF's Institute of Aviation Medicine. A senior duty co-ordinator is on hand night and day, and he can call on one of three teams, each comprising an operations and an engineering inspector, on constant stand-by to attend the 25-30 reportable accidents that occur annually over the UK. If an accident happens to a UK-registered aircraft over international waters, it is also AAIB's responsibility. The tricky bit comes when a crash happens on some foreign turf — in that case, representatives of the state of registry are usually invited to attend, but some sovereign states need a little more persuasion to invite AAIB than others.

Other major nations work along similar lines. When a US registered aircraft is involved in an accident, the National Transportation Safety Board (NTSB), a division of the Department of Transportation, sends an investigating team to ferret out the cause or causes of the accident. The NTSB then makes recommendations to the aircraft operators for action, or to the Federal Aviation Authority (FAA) for permanent regulations, to lessen the probability of repetition.

As in Britain, US air accident investigation came of age in the late 1940s and 1950s as both airlines and airliners developed and expanded. In the immediate years after 1945, airlines were forced to rely on modified military aircraft types such as the Douglas DC-4. Though undeniably economical to operate, this four-engined transport was soon found to lack the pressurised comfort of the Boeing Stratoliner or Lockheed Constellation. Nothing daunted, Douglas simply enlarged the DC-4's fuselage to fit pressurised accommodation for 68 passengers plus a crew of three, improved aircraft performance and christened the result the DC-6. Once teething bugs were ironed out, the DC-6 came to be regarded as the ultimate in piston-engined airliners.

On 10 August 1956, Northeast Airlines inaugurated a new franchise between New York and Miami to cater for the growing traffic to the sun. Pending build-up of its own fleet of DC-6s, Northeast sustained a regular timetable by leasing a DC-6A, N34954, from Flying Tigers. On 1 February 1957, N34954 was scheduled to fly a full passenger load non-stop to Miami. Take-off time from La Guardia was supposed to be 14.45hrs, but wintery weather caused numerous delays. After trying ineffectually to keep N34954 clear of snow at the loading gate, Northeast's lead foreman had the DC-6 taxied into the partial protection of a hangar. His men could now brush off the snow, and spray de-icing fluid on the wings and control surfaces, without feeling that they were wasting their time.

Capt Alva Marsh had flown N34954 up from Florida and after the frustrating wait, he finally received clearance for the return leg. At 17.50hrs, Northeast Airlines Flt 823 was at the holding point for La Guardia's Runway 4. Falling darkness together with thickly drifting snowflakes made the densely built-up Bronx across the East

One of the shortest flights on record — Northeast Flt 823 on 1 February 1957.

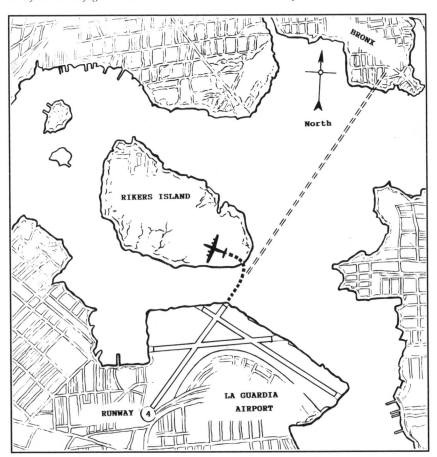

61

Flying Tigers DC-6A, N34953. Utilising the same basic wing as the DC-4, the DC-6 was 6ft 8in longer and had a pressurised fuselage. The DC-6A was in turn 5ft longer than the DC-6 with a strengthened cabin floor for freight carriage. N34953 was to survive a forced landing in Jamaica Bay, NY in 1957 but its sister aircraft, N34954, was not to be so lucky after it crashed on Riker's Island on 1 February 1957.

River barely visible. After an inbound aircraft turned off Runway 4 at 18.02hrs, Flt 823 was cleared for take-off. Capt Marsh noted some snow on the runway but very little on the wings, and what bit was there blew off as he opened all four throttles. Roaring down the runway, N34954 carved through the slush and lifted off at the right place and normal airspeed of 111kt before disappearing into the grey overcast.

Michael McNamara, La Guardia's radar departure controller, picked up Flt 823 as it climbed past 75ft. The radar head swept the screen every 2sec and on the third sweep after identifying Flt 823, McNamara saw its 'blip' suddenly veer to the left. Despite watching radar scopes for over a decade, he had never seen anything like it. Turning to alert the tower flight control officer, McNamara saw a diffused, pinkish flash through the murk to the north. Although he did not know it at the time, Flt 823 had remained airborne for only 52sec. It came back to earth on Rikers Island, a feature that squatted like a giant turtle in the middle of the East River and which was known only for the penitentiary complex on its western side.

Within 15min a Coast Guard rescue helicopter was airborne from Floyd Bennett Field. Visibility was so bad that the crew only navigated across Long Island by following car lights, but the rescuers were pleasantly surprised to find that the DC-6A's crew of six were all alive although two stewardesses had suffered burns. Because the prison island was so isolated, it was spared the ground casualties that would have resulted had the DC-6A come down anywhere else that close to La Guardia. It was equally gratifying that a large majority of the 89 adult passengers plus six children in arms managed to scramble from the burning wreckage to safety. Yet of the 101 souls on board Flt 823, the emergency services found that 20 had died from smoke suffocation.

Probe as they might, the expert investigators were unable to determine the accident cause with any degree of certainty. The DC-6A was 1,000lb underloaded and clear of snow and ice on take-off. Although the weather forecast predicted possible carburettor icing up to 5,000ft, other aircraft had been into and out of La Guardia all afternoon without problems. Most surprising of all, neither Capt Marsh nor his co-pilot, Capt Dixwell, noticed anything untoward after take-off. Marsh was climbing straight ahead at an indicated 800ft/min as he called for gear up, and airspeed had increased to 140kt as he asked for flap retraction. Both pilots did not recall any of the flight instruments, including turn and slip indicator, registering anything but normal. Full power appeared to be being delivered, there were no signs of fire, loss of airspeed, or sensation of turning and sinking until Dixwell saw the ground rising up. The DC-6A just seemed to veer imperceptibly of its own accord and fly gently into the ground. After nine days of public hearings which proved irrefutably inconclusive, a frustrated news reporter declared, 'For all we've heard here, that plane should have landed in Miami'.

The DC-6A crash is interesting not just for its uncertain cause. Despite flight deck unawareness of the turn and descent until co-pilot Dixwell yelled, 'Al, the ground!', Capt Marsh managed to control the crash on to Rikers Island in such a way that everyone survived the impact. In most air accidents this would have been the difficult bit, and Capt Marsh should have been pleased with himself as he unlocked his seat belt and went back to check on his passengers. Only then did he see that 'smoke was thick in the cabin and there was confusion in the dark till flames appeared'.

When N34954 struck the ground, investigators found that its left wing including engines and fuel tanks had been driven back, blocking the main cabin exit. As the wing tanks ruptured, fuel sprayed over the fuselage and into the cabin through cracked walls. Survivors were generally agreed that there were no signs of fire until the wing hit the ground, and the evidence bore this out. A passenger with a private pilot's licence said that as soon as the left wing tip hit, 'there was a ball of flame going past my window, the ship shuddered to a stop and the cabin immediately filled with smoke. Choking, I got up and started toward an emergency exit . . . I covered my mouth and nose with a handkerchief to keep out the smoke'.

The fire spread slowly and there was so little damage to the fuselage that even though the main cabin door was blocked, all passengers should have been able to get out without difficulty through the emergency exits or holes ripped in the fuselage. Yet 20 passengers died from asphyxia and burns, the former probably leading to the latter. All were at the rear where a perfectly removable window clearly marked as an emergency exit was never opened: alongside it people died, several of whom stayed strapped in their seats. One theory is that they froze in panic, but why did 20 passengers freeze while the other 75 rushed out because their lives depended on it? Most probably by the time those at the back got over their initial shock, they were surrounded by choking and blinding fumes spreading forwards. Gasping for breath and rapidly becoming disorientated, some found even the relatively simple task of unfastening a seat strap beyond them. Panic would have set in, drawing even more foul air into lungs, followed in seconds by collapse leading to death.

Rikers Island showed that people could survive an aircraft crash and yet still die in appreciable numbers because smoke and fumes prevented them reaching safety just a few paces away. Subsequent tragedies highlighted similar respiratory risks. The FAA report on a United Airlines DC-8 accident at Stapleton Field, Denver, on 11 July 1961 stated: 'During evacuation, the principal environmental hazard was smoke. When the aft galley door was opened, a 'chimney effect' developed, drawing outside smoke into the overwing exits, down through the aft section of the cabin and out of the open door. For this reason, the concentration of smoke was heaviest in the aft cabin . . . Just prior to opening of the galley door, the passengers had promptly left their seats and began to queue-up in the aisle. From all accounts, this was done in an orderly and relatively calm manner . . . As this line was forming, dense black smoke began filtering into the cabin, making breathing difficult and obscuring vision. Many passengers became frightened for the first time'.

The same effect was noted after a United Airlines Boeing 727 landed short of Salt Lake City Airport on 11 November 1965. A localised fuel-fed fire began as the aircraft slid along the ground, generating 'dense, acrid smoke that rapidly filled the cabin. Many passengers stated that after a breath or two they could no longer breathe or utter any sound . . . Other passengers recalled that after a few initial shouts and cries, the cabin suddenly became quiet with the only sounds coming from the flames and the muffled efforts of passengers struggling towards the exits'.

There were therefore good grounds for the American Airline Pilots' Association suggestion in March 1966 that passengers be equipped with smoke masks to give them that extra bit of time to find their way to safety. All aircraft belonging to the FAA were equipped with passenger smokehoods in 1967, and two years later the FAA proposed that such hoods be mandatory on all passenger transport aircraft. But the instruction was withdrawn on 11 August 1970 because the donning of hoods might cause delays in evacuation. There the matter rested.

Dawn was breaking on Thursday 22 August 1985 as two pilots and four cabin crew of British Airtours reported to Manchester Airport for a charter flight to Corfu. Their Boeing 737, registration G-BGJL, was scheduled to take-off at 06.00hrs. While the purser briefed his three stewardesses, the pilots discussed an entry in the previous day's technical log relating to slow acceleration of No 1 (the left) engine. Co-pilot Brian Love, a senior first officer, had been a member of G-BGJL's crew on that occasion, but no problems had been reported on the two flights since remedial action was undertaken.

With 131 holiday makers including two infants boarded, the co-pilot started the engines and made ready to fly the leg to Corfu. At 06.08hrs the commander, Capt Peter Terrington, a 39yr old 737 training captain, obtained clearance for Flt KT28M to taxy for Runway 24. The weather was typical for a Lancashire early morning in summer — surface wind westerly at 6kt, temperature 13°C, no low cloud to speak of and 1,000m visibility in smoke. The runway was dry as G-BGJL was cleared to line up and then take-off at 06.12hrs. The purser and No 4 attendant working the forward cabin strapped into their rearwards-facing seats while Nos 2 and 3 stewardesses sat facing forwards on the left side in the rear galley.

After lining up, the co-pilot requested take-off power. Capt Terrington opened the throttles and declared No 1 engine acceleration to be acceptable — First Officer Love agreed that it was better than on the previous day. During the take-off run the captain made an 'eighty knot' routine check call. Twelve seconds later, a 'thud' was heard. Thinking that the 737 had suffered a burst tyre or bird strike, the commander ordered 'Stop', closed the throttles and selected reverse thrust on both engines.

After peaking at 126kt, indicated air speed decelerated through 85kt some nine seconds after the 'thud'. As the commander started to tell ATC of the abort, the fire bell on the flight deck started ringing; cancelling reverse thrust, he declared, 'it looks as though we've got a fire on number 1'. Three seconds later the air traffic controller, Brendan Kelly, confirmed, 'there's a lot of fire, they're on their way now'. As groundspeed reduced through 50kt, the commander sought ATC advice on whether he needed to evacuate the passengers. Kelly replied, 'I would do it via the starboard side'.

Turning off the runway into link Delta, the commander warned his crew that an evacuation would be necessary from the starboard side of the aircraft. As speed reduced through 17kt, the purser sought confirmation of the evacuation order. Back came the order, 'Evacuate on the starboard side'. Eight seconds later, G-BGJL came to a halt. Terrington ordered the co-pilot to carry out the fire drill on the left engine, while he shut down the right engine in preparation for the evacuation.

Passenger evacuation was a non-memory drill read out from the handbook by the co-pilot, but before it was complete the commander saw fuel and fire spreading

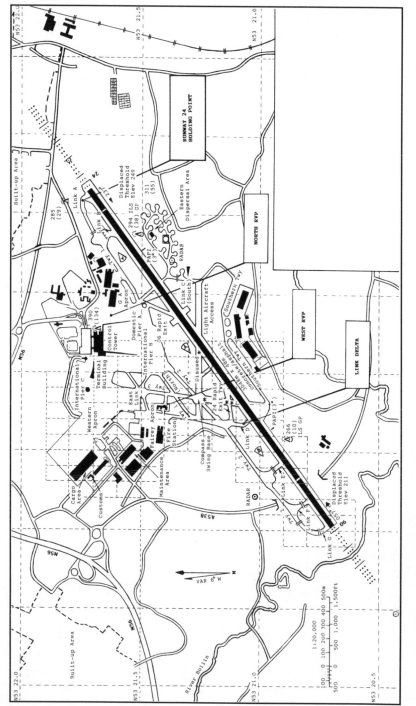

Geography of the accident to British Airtours Flt KT28M at Manchester Airport on 22 August 1985.

Above:
The cause of the accident to Boeing 737, G-BGJL, at Manchester Airport — the ruptured left engine's No 9 combustor can and adjacent holed fuel access panel.

Below:
G-BGJL aborting take-off. As long as the airliner rolled down the runway, its turbulent wake kept the blazing fuel fire plume below the tailplane and away from the main structure.

forward along the left side. In fact the fire was so intense that the tail section and fuselage aft of the wings were to collapse on to the ground through thermal weakening of the structure within minutes. All the commander knew at this stage was that the fire was getting too close for safety, and after opening the co-pilot's sliding flight deck window, both pilots lowered themselves down a fabric escape strap to the ground.

Most passengers aft of row 5, particularly those on the left side, must have been immediately aware of the fire as smoke came up from the back and flames started to crack windows even before the aircraft stopped. However, people right at the front of the 737 cabin appear to have been initially oblivious to the danger. Certainly there was no fire or smoke apparent to purser Arthur Bradbury who, on seeing passengers standing up and moving into the aisle, made a public address announcement to 'sit down and remain strapped in'. As the aircraft was about to stop, he went to open the right front door and release the inflatable escape slide. The door unlocked normally but as it was moving out, the slide container lid jammed in the doorframe. Unable to clear the restriction, Bradbury crossed to the left front door. He cracked that open, checked that the forward spread of the fire was slow enough to allow evacuation from there, and then opened the door fully. The slide was inflated manually 25sec after the aircraft stopped, about the same time as the first fire vehicle to arrive began discharging foam. No 4 stewardess, Joanna Toff, then supervised passenger evacuation down that slide, though to start the flow she first had to free some passengers who had become jammed together between the forward galley bulkheads.

Having got people moving, the purser returned to the right side where he eventually managed to clear the obstruction and open the right front door. Seventy seconds after the aircraft stopped, evacuation began from that side as well though smoke started to enter the galley area at the same time. A total of 51 passengers managed to get out through the front left and right doors before the smoke became so dense and acrid that the forward cabin crew had to slide out too.

As the 737 came to a halt, a young woman sitting in row 10 beside the right overwing exit tried to open it at the instigation of other passengers. After watching her pull to no avail on the right arm-rest mounted on the exit hatch, her companion stood up and reached across to the handle at the top of the hatch marked 'Emergency Pull'. The hatch, weighing 48lb, then fell into the aircraft, trapping the woman in her seat. With the assistance of a man in row 11, the hatch was removed and placed on seat 11D which was fortunately vacant. Forty five seconds after the aircraft stopped, passengers started to leave through the overwing exit on to the wing; 27 got out that way including one infant and a child in arms.

During the latter stages of the abandoned take-off and just as the aircraft cleared the runway, external witnesses saw the right rear door open and its slide deploy. A stewardess was initially visible in the doorway, but both slide and door were then obscured by thick black smoke as the 737 stopped. The aft cabin suddenly filled with thick black smoke which induced panic and a consequent rapid passenger movement down the aisle. Someone from the front row of seats, looking back as he waited to exit the aircraft, saw a mass of people tangled together and struggling in the centre section. The mass appeared incapable of moving forward and 'people were howling and screaming'. Two passengers remembered seeing one of the rear stewardesses struggling to direct passengers in the rear aisle, but no-one managed to escape through the right rear door.

Two airport fire vehicles arrived at the aircraft just as the first passengers were about to evacuate down the left slide. A pair of major foam tenders arrived about half

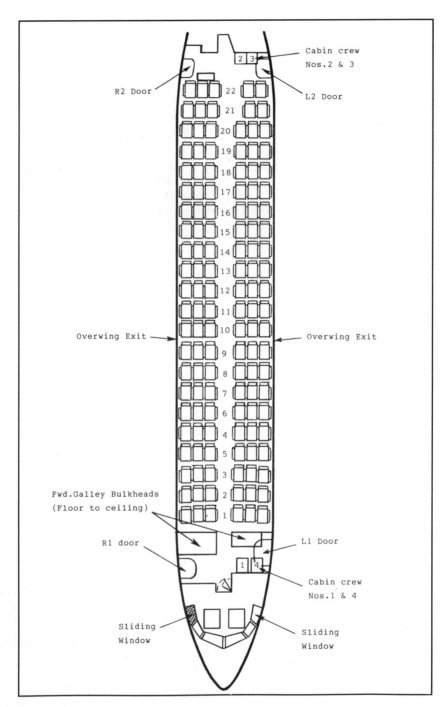

Interior of G-BGJL showing doors, overwing exists, passenger and cabin crew seat locations.

All that remained of British Airtours' G-BGJL. After the tragedy, the CAA ordered UK airlines to improve access to overwing emergency exits and install floor level emergency escape path lighting. These relatively simple measures were to cost £2.5 million.

a minute later, and they were positioned to try and keep escape routes clear while attacking the fire source.

A British Airways crew coach arrived at the scene after about four minutes, carrying a TriStar cabin crew who rendered first aid and comfort. A third foam tender arrived shortly afterwards, having been retrieved from the paint shop. Its driver saw a hand move above a man trapped in the right overwing exit, so he left his cab and climbed on to the wing. Some five and a half minutes after the aircraft stopped, the driver pulled a young boy clear over the trapped body: he was to be the last evacuee to survive the accident.

Approximately seven minutes after the aircraft stopped, it became clear that no more passengers were likely to get out unaided so firemen equipped with breathing apparatus entered the right front door. (It was policy that firemen delayed entry in such circumstances to avoid conflict with evacuating passengers.) An explosion then blew one of the firemen out of the door and the officer in charge, worried about the limited amount of water remaining in his fire fighting vehicles, ordered that no further attempts be made to enter the cabin until a reliable water supply was established. All nearby hydrants were found to be dry.

The Greater Manchester Fire Service was left waiting for an escort on to the airfield for some minutes, so their vehicles did not arrive at the burning 737 until 13min into the incident. Shortly afterwards, two men with breathing apparatus entered through the front right aircraft door and reported finding a number of bodies. About 33min after G-BGJL stopped, a male passenger was found still alive but unconscious in the aisle near the front of the aircraft. Despite valiant medical efforts, he died six days later in hospital, bringing the total number of fatalities on Flt KT28M to two stewardesses and 53 passengers.

The AAIB team, which began work straight away, soon found that the left engine combustion casing had split open, causing substantial damage to the Pratt and Whitney JT8D engine and nacelle. Debris strewn around the runway where the engines would have been coming up to full power showed that the left engine's No 9 combustor can exploded, the forward section of which was ejected through the damaged engine casing. This punctured a large hole in an adjacent fuel tank access panel, releasing fuel directly into combustion gases from the ruptured chamber. Thereafter, a fire was inevitable.

Yet those circumstances in themselves should not have been catastrophic. The aircraft remained mobile and controllable, and no-one was injured during the abandoned take-off. The volume of fuel initially involved in the fire was relatively small, the fire cover available at this major airport was well in excess of that required to deal with a 737, and fire vehicles were in attendance within 30sec of the aircraft stopping. Why then did an engine incident turn into a tragic accident costing 55 lives?

It was just bad luck that the wing tank access panel had an impact strength only one quarter that of the lower wing skin; had the ejected piece of combustor can hit elsewhere, it is probable that the fuel tank would have remained secure. Yet while the aircraft continued to roll down the runway, the blazing fuel remained entrained within the strong turbulent wake generated by the extended thrust reverser buckets. In other words, the fire remained an external one unregistered by a detection system designed only to detect internal temperature rises.

The pilots' response on hearing the 'thud' on take-off was quite reasonable given the limited cues available to them. Having decided to abort and decelerate in a measured manner suited to a burst tyre or birdstrike, a full nine seconds passed before the flight deck crew received any indication that they might be facing the more serious problem of fire. With hindsight, the decision to turn right off the runway was critical. In the pilots' defence, they were in maximum workload mode and the quoted take-off wind of 250°/7kt would have seemed of little relevance. As the AAIB report stated, 'There is no doubt that this crew, and indeed the aviation community at large, were quite unaware of the critical influence of light winds on a fire'.

Photographs taken by witnesses showed that aircraft movement was sufficient to keep the fire from the aircraft cabin, but when the 737 slowed to a halt, fire and smoke swung progressively forward. As the aircraft came to rest, smoke completely enveloped the rear fuselage including the right rear door. At this stage, the wind's influence became paramount. It drove the now-static fire plume against and beneath

As the 737 swung to a stop on Taxiway Link D, the wind from the left was such that fire and smoke from the burning No 1 engine swung progressively forward to envelope the entire rear fuselage. There was nothing that the fire vehicles, shown here in their initial positions, could do about it.

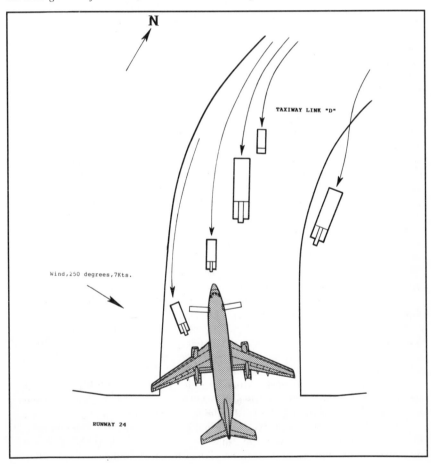

the hull such that initial fire penetration of the aluminium alloy fuselage occurred within 20sec, and it was estimated that the fire had direct access to the cabin interior within one minute of the aircraft stopping. In addition to channelling the fire to such an extent that both rear fuselage and tail soon collapsed to the ground, the wind also created an aerodynamic pressure field around the fuselage which, once exits were opened on the side opposite the fire, sucked flames and smoke into and along the length of the cabin interior.

The internal fire spread forwards from the aft cabin section as roof panels and overhead lockers ignited and collapsed down on to seat furnishings which added to the blaze. Yet there was no great conflagration inside the cabin. The evidence pointed to a series of localised fires, some becoming very severe, possibly resulting from burning duty-free spirits, the discharge of portable therapeutic oxygen cylinders or exploding aerosol sprays in hand baggage, all of which were in the overhead lockers. Those areas of the cabin interior which escaped direct fire damage were nevertheless covered with a thick coating of viscous soot.

It was interesting to note that the last evacuee, the 14-yr old boy pulled clear over five minutes after the aircraft stopped, had only superficial burns on his hands. Although some victims were so badly burned that they could only be identified by their designer shoes or spectacles, approximately 50% of the passenger seats, none of which were finished in fireblocking materials, survived the cabin fire as did many plastic safety cards and magazines stowed in seat 'net' pockets. This showed that temperatures within the cabin were not universally unsurvivable, as did the discovery of a man still alive in the forward aisle some 33min after G-BGJL stopped. His eventual death was primarily due to lung damage and associated pneumonia rather than external burns, and over 80% of the 55 Manchester fatalities died from carbon monoxide and hydrogen cyanide poisoning rather than exposure to excessive heat.

It would only have taken a few breaths in that atmosphere to rapidly incapacitate. When they burned, G-BGJL's furnishings not only consumed oxygen but also emitted a cocktail of poisonous gases plus floating solid debris which blocked mouths, noses and, just as crucially, eyes. Many Manchester survivors told of their inability to see because of the extreme density of smoke and the chemical effect of high concentrations of acid gases. After Manchester, it became mandatory for civil airliners to have emergency lighting showing the path along the cabin floor from each passenger seat to the nearest exit. However, the AAIB inquiry concluded that 'escape-path' cabin lighting would have been of very limited value unless passengers' eyes had been protected.

The 25sec delay in opening the front door was bad enough, but a survivor recalled that the heavy smoky atmosphere 'blanketed' sound within the cabin, even assuming that anyone could have shouted out directions. The physical and physiological effects of dense smoke combined with a tightly packed cabin interior made worse by the bottleneck between front-cabin bulkheads must have increased fear and panic. Moreover, the right overwing exit was the first available evacuation point for 100 passengers at the back, so any delay in getting them out because of debilitation and incapacitation was potentially very serious.

There were many lessons to be learned from the tragic fate of Flt KT28M. First, there was the obvious one that components can fail with dire effect even on systems as well designed and proven as the JT8D engine. After the accident, both the CAA and FAA issued mandatory directives requiring operators to inspect their engines often enough to detect any combustor can weakness at an early stage. All aircraft exit doors were modified to prevent repetition of the jamming problem.

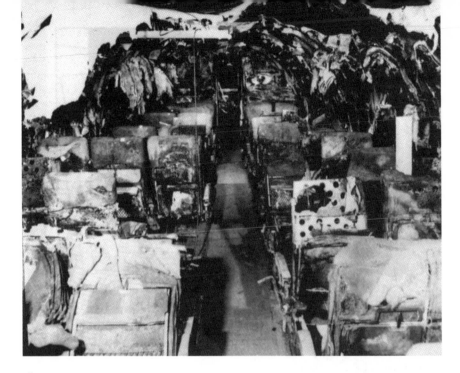

Above:
Cabin interior looking forward.

Below:
Cabin interior looking aft.

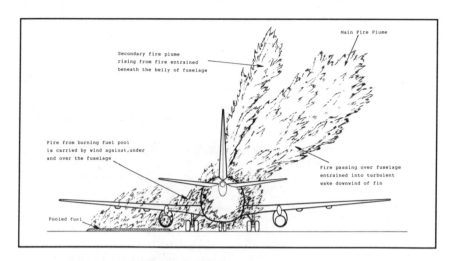

In the diagram:
- Main Fire Plume
- Secondary fire plume rising from fire entrained beneath the belly of fuselage
- Fire from burning fuel pool is carried by wind against,under and over the fuselage
- Fire passing over fuselage entrained into turbulent wake downwind of fin
- Pooled fuel

Above:
Representation of the static fire plumes as viewed from the rear of G-BGJL.

Left:
One means of providing individual passenger protection in a toxic environment — the Survivaid smokehood. It is easy to don, can be worn either way round and will not impair vision, speech or hearing. However, reliance on such simple smokehoods could have drawbacks. For instance, unless flight attendants hand them out and take them back on an individual basis, these valuable and attractive items will soon 'walk'. Fighting over the limited ones that remain should an emergency occur, or delays while the elderly or hamfisted took them out of their plastic wrappers, could delay evacuation when speedy egress was of the essence. Dowty

Next came the human factors. Despite the professional and prompt response by both Airport and Greater Manchester fire services, the effectiveness of the first was curtailed by the need to replenish its water supply and of the other by being kept waiting for an escort onto the airfield.

At the time of the accident, the airfield water hydrant system was being modified, a process that made it necessary to isolate sections of pipework periodically. Post-accident investigation revealed that the contractor's personnel had become used to turning valves off and on without telling the fire service. Shortly after the accident, water supplies were restored.

Turning to assistance from the local fire brigade, it had been standard practice for them to respond to the West Rendezvous Point (RVP) where they would be met by an airport police escort vehicle. However, less than a month earlier, the Head of Airport Services, the Airport Fire Officer and a Senior Fire Officer from Greater Manchester had met to agree that for all future incidents the external emergency services would congregate at the North RVP. By some oversight, the police were not informed of the meeting or of the change. Suffice to say that when G-BGJL caught fire, the external emergency agencies went to the new RVP while the police dispatched their escort vehicle to the old. The delay attributed directly to this confusion was put around three minutes.

Although the inquiry considered it unlikely, the possibility that the combined reduced fire fighting capability 'at that critical time led to loss of life cannot be discounted'. It certainly proved that even the best laid plans and procedures are very dependent on human awareness.

Yet to show the other side of the human coin, G-BGJL's cabin crew reacted to the accident commendably and with courage. Despite being urged by firemen to get out, the purser and No 4 stewardess remained on board until they were on the point of being overcome themselves. A number of survivors owed their lives to the direct actions of Arthur Bradbury and Joanna Toff.

At the rear, Nos 2 and 3 stewardesses must have been in a very difficult situation. Though least experienced of the cabin staff, they would have appreciated the extent and effects of the fire at an early stage while being aware of the general rule that aircraft doors should not be opened until an aircraft stops. Faced with an atmosphere getting ever hotter and a melee of disturbed passengers, such evidence as there is indicates that the two ladies, both of whom were only employed on seasonal contracts, stuck to their duties to the best of their abilities. A number of witnesses saw a stewardess, probably No 3, standing in the right rear doorway; she certainly appeared to have had a fleeting chance of saving her own life but she stayed on board.

Out of the 22 rows of seats in the cabin, there were only five survivors aft of row 16. The rearmost, and sole survivor from row 20, remembered a stewardess in the aisle next to him, apparently trapped in a scrum of passengers. This was probably No 2 stewardess, like her colleague trying to restore order from chaos until both of them collapsed under the rapidly deteriorating conditions. The inquiry felt it might be prudent in future for the most experienced crew members to be positioned at either end of the cabin in an aircraft the size of a Boeing 737, but no-one could have asked any more of the cabin staff than that given by those on Flt KT28M to Corfu.

Turning to the fire itself, we must learn from the loss of G-BGJL how best to minimise its effects. As even light winds can escalate the destructive power of fire, operators and air traffic services should try to ensure that all abandoned take-offs and emergency landings come to a halt on the runway. Aircraft should never be stopped with a fire upwind of the fuselage if at all possible. When in doubt, turn the aircraft towards the engine fire.

That is the relatively easy and cheap part. When it comes to aircraft interiors, cabin designers have always had to balance profitability against safety. But the process must have swung too far one way when cabin interiors are flammable, their furnishings emit too many lethal fumes when lit, yet they are far from easy to evacuate.

Cabins must have sufficient emergency exits, and access to them all should not be impeded by structural bottlenecks or too many seats. Having ensured this, the greatest lesson from Manchester is that passengers must be kept conscious and mobile until such time as they can be got out successfully.

The spread of fire can be greatly reduced by finishing cabins in fire-hardened materials, and since December 1987 all replacement seats on British airliners have had to be covered in fireblocking fabrics. Furthermore, the Manchester inquiry recommended that urgent consideration be given to providing passengers with individual smokehoods to provide protection in a toxic environment. But in 1991, after six years effort, the CAA announced that smokehood research was being abandoned.

There is a wide variety of smokehoods on the market and they differ widely. Some are easier to put on than others, but in the past some of the simplest to don gave least protection. There are other drawbacks. Not everyone would be happy to put on a 'plastic bag' over their heads, especially as hoods can impair speech and hearing. Furthermore the thought of old grannies scrabbling around seats trying to find hoods, let alone put them on properly and expeditiously, fill some experts with horror. Delays as even younger passengers tried to pull hoods over heads, or from fighting if a passenger could not find a hood and tried to appropriate one from a neighbour, could actually negate the effects of other safety measures introduced after Manchester. Overall, hoods were found to be unsafe because they delayed the evacuation process. A study of 14 aircraft fires since 1985 went so far as to conclude that, for every life they saved, hoods would contribute to the deaths of eight others.

Even a user-friendly smokehood can only preserve life for a finite time. A better long term option may be something that remains completely independent of passenger error — the onboard water spray extinguisher. Experience shows that survivable airliner crashes usually occur on or near airfields with local fire services arriving within three minutes. During this critical interval, water from the aircraft's domestic tanks could be used to suppress the cabin fire. A spray of fine mist would make the widest use of onboard water to rapidly and dramatically improve the whole passenger cabin environment by reducing temperatures and 'scrubbing' particulate and soluble gases from the atmosphere. Internal spray pipework can be triplicated with special check valves to maintain effectiveness even if the fuselage breaks up. Once the fire engines arrive, their hoses could be plugged into external connection points to continue spraying until all passengers are evacuated. Therefore, unlike smokehoods, water spraying can provide an infinite amount of protection time for as long as a water supply is available. However, spray systems will be very expensive to retrofit and are only likely to appear on new aircraft.

But the final links in any safety chain must be the passengers. When Mr Bernard Brown, the CAA's chief fire officer, examined 325 fires reported on British airliners during the late 1980s, he found that one had been caused by a passenger singeing her hair with lighted matches, another involved petrol leaking from a chainsaw in a passenger's hand baggage, and at least 13 others came from passengers dropping lighted cigarettes down seat backs after falling asleep.

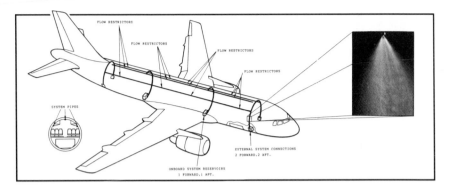

A typical SAVE water spray fire suppression system. In the UK it is felt that the future lies with fitment of such 'passenger-independent' protection in preference to 'passenger-sensitive' smokehoods. However, water suppression systems are expensive to retrofit and the travelling public may have to wait on the next generation of airliners arriving with water suppression built in from birth. Darchem Engineering

Moving on from near-negligence, how many travellers pay attention to mandatory briefings given before take-off, read the safety cards provided in seat pockets or pre-plan how they would get to their nearest escape exit if the need ever arose? Far too many burrow into books or newspapers in almost ostrich-like fashion during briefings, as if unwilling to face even the very thought that something might go wrong. And if an accident happens, will those wasting valuable time collecting personal belongings come into conflict with those trying to get to the head of the queue, thereby creating chaos that no amount of cabin crew intervention will resolve? In this litigious age, it has become the fashion to seek a scapegoat when an accident occurs, but it is arguable that if a safety route is provided and passengers neglect to bother to find out how to use it, they have no-one to blame but themselves.

Tied in with this is the presumption that the public will only tolerate low air fares. In the overhead lockers on Flt KT28M were bottles of duty free spirits, which together with those for sale on board added to the conflagration. It has been calculated that the amount of booze carried on an average airline trip approximates to the volume of water needed to feed an effective fire suppression spray system. Airlines and airport authorities argue that revenue from duty free sales is essential to keep ticket prices down. The same argument applies to seating: the wider the gangways and clearer the access to emergency exits, the fewer the seats that can be carried and therefore each ticket will cost appreciably more. In the final analysis, this debate is too important to be left to the experts and vested interests. The promotion of flight safety awareness stands or falls by the effectiveness of its publicity, and perhaps all travellers should be briefed on the Manchester accident before determining the right level of personal responsibility for their own safety. And when faced by those unwilling to make hard choices, the CAA's Director General Airworthiness would quote St Paul's advice to the Romans: 'You wish to have no fear of the authorities? Then continue to do right and you will have their approval, for they are God's agents working for your good'.

CREW OVERBOARD

Every so often a really seminal aircraft emerges, which then stays around in one form or another for ages. The Boeing 707 family of airliners is a prime example. Created and funded on the back of the military KC-135A tanker/transportation programme, the long-range 707 had such appeal that its makers soon developed a short/medium range version known as the 727. The 727 filled a gap in the market, but then Boeing took the bold step of designing the 737 for the short-haul, twin jet market where two rivals, the BAC 111 and Douglas DC-9, were already well established. Nothing daunted, Boeing based their approach on commonality of structure and systems where possible between the 707, 727 and 737. When customers realised that they could standardise on such features as seats and galley equipment, the 737 made up in sales appeal for its late entry into the field. By June 1987, the Boeing 737 became the world's best selling commercial airliner when it surpassed the previous record of 1,831 sales for the 727.

The first 737 version had 100 seats, but it was not long before airlines started demanding more. This led to the standard model — the 737-200 — which had a longer fuselage accommodating two extra rows of seats. The first 200-series started earning its airline money on 29 April 1968, and on 10 May 1969, No 152 on the 737 production line, N73711, was delivered to Aloha Airlines of Hawaii.

Aloha eventually procured 11 of the type. For 20 years they flew mainly short haul hops between the Hawaiian islands such that by 27 April 1988, N73711 had amassed 35,496 flying hours and carried out 89,680 landings. Only one other 737 in the world — N73712 — had flown a higher number of landings, and that too belonged to Aloha.

On 28 April 1988, N73711 was programmed for yet another round of inter-island flights. Capt Robert Schornstheimer, a 44-yr old who had joined Aloha back in 1977, was assigned to command that day. He was to be assisted by one first officer for the first six flights, whereupon another would take over to complete the remainder of the schedule.

The initial first officer checked in around 05.00hrs (Hawaiian Standard Time) with the dispatch office at Aloha Operations, Honolulu International Airport. After bringing himself up to speed on the flight operations paperwork, he went out to the parking apron to carry out the inspection required by company procedures before the first flight of the day. Finding nothing unusual with either the aircraft or its maintenance log, the first officer was satisfied that the 737 was ready for flight.

Capt Schornstheimer reported for duty about 05.10hrs, completed his pre-departure duties in the dispatch office, and then joined the first officer and flight attendants on the aircraft. The crew then flew round-trips from Honolulu to Hilo, Maui and Kauai. All six legs were uneventful and the aircraft performed normally.

At 11.00hrs First Officer Madeline Tompkins, a 37-yr old who had been with Aloha for 10 years, took over in the right hand seat as planned. The crew then flew from Honolulu to Maui, and from Maui to Hilo, again noting nothing untoward.

Neither pilot left the aircraft while N73711 stood on the ground at Hilo, nor was there any requirement for the crew to carry out a visual exterior inspection.

At 13.25hrs, Aloha Flt 243 departed Hilo Airport en route for Honolulu. The two pilots had been joined in the cockpit by a FAA air traffic controller seated on the observation seat, while down the back the three cabin attendants looked after 89 passengers. Planned routeing was direct to Honolulu at FL 240 with Maui listed as the alternate. First Officer Tompkins flew the take-off and en route climb from Hilo; she did not recall using the autopilot, and the departure and climb out were conducted in visual meteorological conditions with neither pilot noting anything unusual.

As Tompkins levelled the aircraft at 24,000ft, both pilots heard a sudden loud 'clap' or 'whooshing' sound followed by a wind noise behind them. The first officer's head was jerked backwards and she noticed debris, including pieces of grey insulation material, floating about the cockpit. The commander observed the cockpit entry door to be missing and 'blue sky where the first-class ceiling had been'. He immediately took control and found the aircraft to be rolling slightly left and right with the flight controls feeling 'loose'.

Flt 243 had suffered an explosive decompression, so both pilots and the air traffic observer donned oxygen masks. The captain began an emergency descent at 280-290kt with speed brakes extended, the first officer observing a 4,100ft/min rate of descent at some point. Deafened by wind noise, the pilots initially had to use hand signals to communicate.

Capt Schornstheimer actuated the passenger oxygen switch. When decompression occurred, all passengers were seated and the seat belt sign was illuminated. The No 1 flight attendant, Clarabelle Lansing, was reportedly standing at seat row 5. According to witnesses, she was immediately swept out of the cabin through a hole in the left side of the fuselage. No 2 flight attendant, standing by row 15/16, was thrown to the floor and sustained minor bruises. She was subsequently able to crawl up and down the aisle to render assistance and calm the passengers, which showed remarkable fortitude and presence of mind given that she must have been as shocked as anyone. No 3 attendant, standing at row 2, was struck on the head by debris and thrown to the floor. She suffered serious injuries, including concussion and severe head lacerations.

The first officer tuned the transponder to emergency code 7700 and tried to tell Honolulu Air Route Control Center (ARTCC) that Flt 243 was diverting to Maui. Because of the cockpit noise level, she could not hear if there was any reply. Although Honolulu ARTCC did not receive the first officer's initial transmission, the controller working Flt 243 observed the emergency 'squawk' painting about 23nm south-southeast of Kahului airport, Maui. The controller tried to raise Flt 243 several times but without success.

As the 737 descended through 14,000ft, the first officer switched the radio to Maui Tower frequency. At 13.48hrs she informed the tower of the rapid decompression and declared an emergency. A minute later, Honolulu Center advised Maui Approach Control that they had received an emergency code 7700 transponder return that could be an Aloha 737 and stated, 'You might be prepared in case he heads your way'. Approach then advised Honolulu Center that Flt 243 was indeed diverting to Maui.

As the descending airliner was still outside the local controller's area of radar authority, Maui local instructed Flt 243 at 13.51hrs to change to approach frequency. Although the request was acknowledged, Flt 243 continued to transmit on the local frequency. Two minutes later the first officer informed the local controller that, 'We're going to need assistance. We cannot communicate with the flight attendants. We'll need assistance for the passengers when we land'.

The commander began slowing down as he approached 10,000ft. He retracted speed brakes, removed his oxygen mask and began a gradual turn towards Maui's Runway 02. At 210kt the flight crew could communicate verbally again, and Capt Schornstheimer gave the order to lower flaps. Flaps 1 were selected initially and then flaps 5, but on attempting a further extension, the aircraft became less controllable and the commander decided to return to flaps 5 for landing. He also elected to use 170kt for the approach and landing because he found N73711 to be less controllable below that speed.

The first officer was still unable to establish contact with the flight attendants either via the PA system or the onboard telephone. She then selected landing gear down on the captain's command at the normal point in the approach pattern, but although the main gear indicated down and locked, the nose gear position indicator did not illuminate. Manual nose gear extension was then selected but there was still no green light. However, the good news was that no red landing gear unsafe indicator light illuminated either. After another manual attempt, the handle was pulled down to complete manual gear extension procedure. The captain did not order a visual inspection using the nose gear downlock viewer because the centre jumpseat was occupied: he also believed that the priority was to land the aircraft immediately.

At 13.55hrs the first officer advised the tower, 'We won't have a nose gear.' This warning was followed a minute later by, 'We'll need all the equipment you've got'. Then, while altering the throttles, the commander sensed a yawing motion and determined that No 1 engine had failed. He tried to relight but there was no response.

Normal descent profile was established four miles out on the final approach, though the captain noticed that the aircraft was 'shaking a little, rocking slightly and felt springy'. Nevertheless, Flt 243 landed at Kahului airport just before 13.59hrs. Capt Schornstheimer felt able to make a normal touchdown and landing, using No 2 engine thrust reverser and brakes to stop the aircraft. Towards the end of the rollout, flaps were extended to 40° as required for emergency evacuation which was then accomplished on the runway. Only afterwards did a passenger state that, as she was boarding N73711 through the jet bridge at Hilo, she observed a longitudinal crack in the upper row of fuselage rivets about halfway between the cabin door and edge of the jet bridge hood. She made no previous mention of this sighting to either the airline ground personnel or flight crew.

Although many passengers were able to disembark unaided, it took Maui emergency services 25min to clear all the injured on board. Two passengers in row 2 of the first class cabin had received multiple lacerations and electrical shock burns when struck by debris and wiring. Passengers seated in the window seats two rows behind sustained serious injuries including cerebral concussions and multiple lacerations to their heads and faces. An 84-yr old lady seated in 5A was the most seriously injured, with skull as well as skeletal fractures plus lacerations. In addition to the missing stewardess, one crew member and seven passengers were classed as seriously injured while another 57 passengers received minor injuries.

To understand what had happened, we must go back to first principles. All activity in the body depends on oxygen being conveyed through the blood stream. Air pressure at ground level effectively forces oxygen into the blood, but as we climb a

Above:
An Aloha Airlines Boeing 737 at Honolulu. Military Aircraft Photographs

Below:
The picture that shocked industry and public alike — paramedics help evacuate passengers from N73711
at Kahului airport on Maui after a large part of the upper fuselage had been ripped away at 24,000ft.
Not surprisingly, the $5 million aircraft was assessed as beyond repair. Associated Press

mountain or fly upwards in an aircraft, air pressure reduces and the body will soon show the effects of lack of oxygen unless remedial action is taken.

As fare-paying passengers would not take kindly to wearing oxygen masks on long trips, the whole cabin is pressurised. No matter how high the aircraft flies, passengers stay under the same air pressure as if they were at 8,000ft and feel no major discomfort. But when flying around in what amounts to a giant aerosol, puncturing the skin is not recommended. Individual emergency oxygen masks can keep everyone alive until the pilot descends to more hospitable levels, but in the words of an old technical manual, 'It should be remembered that perhaps the greatest danger from failure of a pressure cabin wall is the forceful expulsion of the cabin contents, including unsecured crew members, in the immediate neighbourhood of the defect'. So it came to pass when Flt 243 was rent asunder; passengers by the unfortunate flight stewardess stated that they saw her pulled upward and ejected through the cabin side. The only good part was that explosive decompression occurred at 24,000ft; many more people would have been lost had it happened 20,000ft higher where the pressure differential between outside and inside would have been much greater. For three days a full search effort by ships, helicopters and fixed wing aircraft was made to try and find Ms Lansing, but without success.

If explosive decompression was the effect of the accident, what was the cause? Basically, one-third of N73711's forward upper section of the fuselage behind the cockpit came off in flight as if ripped away by a giant hand. The damaged area extended back about 18ft from slightly aft of the main entrance door (around the beginning of the first class cabin) to just forward of the wings, and from the left side of the cabin at floor level round to the windows on the right. The left engine failed because its control cables separated under increased tension caused by cabin floor deformation. However, examination of the nose gear position-indicator light revealed nothing more dramatic than a burnt out bulb.

On Flt 243 the 737's skin had peeled away exposing the frames, stringers and window forgings. As the crucially-failed pieces of N73711 were now at the bottom of the Pacific, NTSB investigators had to determine the root cause of the disaster by examining the airliner's remaining structure and airworthiness history.

Skin panels of 737s were joined longitudinally at lap joints where the sheet metal of the upper skin panel overlapped the sheet metal of the lower skin panel by about three inches. This overlap was cold-bonded with adhesive on early 737s before the whole structure was riveted to the frame. Boeing expected each airliner to have an 'economic service life' of 20 years involving 51,000 flight hours and 75,000 cycles (landings).

Everyone had taken comfort from the fact that the 737 was built to 'fail-safe'. Not only was the fuselage designed to withstand a 40in crack without catastrophic effect, but also should a progressing crack occur, it was calculated that the fuselage skin would only 'flap' open, releasing cabin pressure in a controlled manner without adversely affecting residual structural strength. What Boeing never considered in its initial fatigue evaluation was the possibility of disbondment or corrosion affecting fuselage lap joint strength.

After all their studies, including examination of other Aloha aircraft and the remains of N73711, safety board experts concluded that it was probable that numerous small fatigue cracks eventually joined to form a large crack (or cracks) similar to that seen by the passenger as she boarded at Hilo. But why did this not lead to fail-safe 'flapping' of the skin as advertised? Basically because unforeseen factors had entered the equation. First, the experts found that corrosion on N73711 had had the double effect of thinning the metal and contributing to fatigue. Then there had been lap joint disbondment. In other words, the 737 literally came unglued in flight, a failure that had its origins back in manufacturing difficulties encountered with surface preparation and/or the bonding process. Deterioration of the bonding accelerated multiple-site fatigue cracking of the skin adjacent to the lap joint upper rivet row, thereby negating the fail-safe characteristics and resulting in catastrophic failure of a large section of the fuselage skin.

If that was not bad enough, the safety board went on to imply that Aloha Airlines could have done more to prevent the occurrence. The one previous accident involving in-flight structural failure of a 737 fuselage — to a Taiwanese aircraft in 1981 — was caused by extensive corrosion damage. Boeing had been issuing service bulletins since 1970 on the protection of bonded structures from corrosion, followed later by minimum requirements for maintaining lap joint structural integrity. If ever an airline operated in a salty, harshly corrosive environment it was Aloha. All things considered, the Board felt that the airline should have followed a maintenance programme designed to detect and repair cracking before it reached a critical condition.

There was also a well-known correlation between flight cycles and aircraft fatigue. Taking off, raising the undercarriage, pressurising, descending, lowering the gear and landing, all imposed strains on aircraft structures, but the problem was much worse for operators such as Aloha. The Hawaiian airline clocked-up many flight cycles each and every day on short-duration, island-hopping flights. When Aloha's three other high-cycle 737s were checked following the accident, two had to be scrapped on the spot and the third was out of service for a year.

It is easy to criticise Aloha's apparent lack of management awareness and deficient maintenance procedures, but that would mask the fact that Aloha's 737s accumulated cycles at a faster rate than any other airline, and certainly at twice the rate around which Boeing's structural integrity guidelines were formulated. Moreover, Aloha was far from alone in not appreciating how much their aircraft were suffering from wear and tear. Reports of fleet-wide cracks received by the FAA after N73711's accident indicate that insufficient critical attention to lap joint inspection and fatigue crack detection was an industry-wide deficiency.

Thus although the board concluded that, 'the probable cause of this accident was the failure of Aloha Airlines' maintenance programme to detect the presence of significant disbonding and fatigue damage, which ultimately led to failure of the lap joint,' one member disagreed sufficiently to file a dissenting statement. In Mr Joseph Nall's opinion, 'Industry's best engineers reviewed the carrier's record, knew of its high-cycle operations and even inspected some of Aloha's 737 fleet. No one — not Boeing nor the FAA principal maintenance inspectors — recognised or predicted the critical nature of the multiple cracking or that the aircraft hull was about to rupture.' Consequently, he preferred to cite the probable accident cause as 'the presence of undetected disbonding and fatigue cracking,' with Aloha management deficiencies downgraded to contributing factors.

It is hard not to disagree with Mr Nall's conclusion that, if anybody failed, it was a collective failure. Boeing admitted it was not until after the Aloha accident that, 'we became aware that we did not have a single corrosion document'. The FAA also failed to evaluate properly Aloha's maintenance programme or assess its inspection and quality control. It was not until the day after the accident that the Authority issued structural inspection guidance applicable to Boeing 737s with more than 55,000 landings, which only went to show that others besides the airline needed to wise up.

Flt 243's flight crew used a target speed of 280-290kt plus speedbrakes in the descent, which the safety board did not think was wise. If structural integrity is in doubt, airspeed should be limited as much as possible and high manoeuvring loads avoided. That said, the board felt that the magnitude of the accident was well beyond anything the flight crew had ever had thrown at them in the simulator, and their success in managing the multiple failures and recovering to a safe landing spoke well of their training and airmanship. Although Robert Schornstheimer and 'Mimi' Tompkins received awards from the Air Line Pilots' Association, the bravery of the two surviving cabin attendants — Michelle Honda and Jane Sato-Tomita — was also exemplary.

Yet in spite of apparent failings in construction and maintenance of the aircraft, matters must be kept in perspective. By 1 April 1989, the worldwide fleet of Boeing 737s had carried an estimated 2,175 billion passengers, recorded 32.75 million revenue hours and covered a combined distance of nearly 12.8 billion miles. It was a remarkable record for a family of remarkable aircraft, and it was so unusual for a 737 to have an accident that the whole world sat up and took notice when one did occur.

Nonetheless, the dramatic photographs of Aloha passengers strapped to the seats of what became known as the '737 convertible' pushed the question of aircraft ageing to the forefront. Airlines suddenly realised that they were in danger of suffering from their own success. It was not that new 737s were too expensive at around $30 million a go; it was more a case of too many airlines chasing too little manufacturing capacity. With hundreds of airliners reaching their design lifetimes during the 1990s, and promised delivery dates stretching out towards the end of the century, many airlines retained old stagers, such as N73711, and bore consequent higher maintenance costs, because 19-yr old aircraft seemed to be essential to meet traffic demands.

Before the Aloha accident this did not seem to matter overmuch. Comfort had been taken from the belief that elderly aircraft would give sufficient warning before any drastic failure occurred. Unfortunately, that faith proved to have been misplaced and the fact that the top could come off an airliner concentrated minds wonderfully. A whole raft of improvements, such as better maintenance and inspection schedules, and better trained personnel working to more authoritative data, were introduced. The FAA recommended that all 13,000 rivets on cold-bonded aircraft be replaced, and it also gave birth to an Ageing Aircraft Forum to take a detailed look at maintenance and monitor what was going on. Individual airlines realised that excessively elderly airframes were going to be a real turn-off with the public; the average age of Aloha aircraft for instance soon dropped from 15 to 10 years, and their average cycles fell from around 55,000 in 1988 to about 33,000 a year later.

In fact Aloha Airlines appeared to weather its problems well. Being a close, family orientated company, its employees leant on each other through the bad times, and management even provided psychiatric help for those who felt in need of it. 'We came out of it stronger than we went in', declared Aloha's President Maurice Myers; unfortunately, while all airlines try to ensure that the same can be said for their aircraft, every so often something happens to show that they still need to keep on their toes.

On Friday 8 June 1990, a British Airways BAC One-Eleven underwent routine servicing during which all six panels which made up the aircraft's windscreen were replaced. Two days later, the airliner took-off at 08.18hrs from Birmingham Airport with 81 passengers on board bound for Malaga in Spain. The One-Eleven had just reached 23,000ft in the climb over Oxfordshire when one of the two largest front windscreen panels together with its frame fell away. As pressurised cockpit air rushed towards the thinner air outside, it pulled Capt Timothy Lancaster from under his seatbelt. Despite grabbing on to his steering column, Capt Lancaster was sucked out of the cabin into a 500mph slipstream. Fortunately, at that moment steward Nigel Ogden, who had been serving hot drinks to the pilots, grabbed hold of the captain's legs. He managed to hold on to them, despite gashing his hand in the process, until another steward, Simon Rogers, arrived on the flightdeck, strapped himself into the vacant seat, and took over from Mr Ogden.

With his emergency oxygen mask in place, co-pilot Alistair Atcheson initiated an emergency descent. It was fortunate that he was wearing full restraint harness, but he was also prevented from being swept out because his commander was filling much of the gap. Capt Lancaster remained halfway out of the aircraft for 15min. Because there was nothing to cling to on a nose structure designed to cut smoothly through the air, his salvation relied almost entirely on the two stewards hanging on to his legs until Flt BA5309 made an emergency landing at Southampton-Eastleigh at 08.58hrs. The errant windscreen, measuring 3ft by 2ft 6in, made a solo touchdown at a farm near Wallingford.

Capt Lancaster, aged 41 at the start of the flight but who could be excused for feeling much older at the end of it, was so far out of the aircraft when the BAC 111 landed that firemen were able to remove him through it. His first thought on being sucked out had been that he should keep breathing. 'I tried to shout back to the crew who were holding on to my legs but I am sure they could not hear me. The temperature must have been at least minus 25C. I was not in pain while it was happening but I remember the buffeting of the winds.' The captain's jacket, which was ripped off when he was plucked out, was found in a field near a public house at Beenham, Berks. On landing, the aircraft's side was stained with blood and the remains of a white shirt. Amazingly, Capt Lancaster suffered only frostbite and a fractured elbow, wrist and thumb, and he soon recovered. The two stewards were treated for cuts and six passengers for shock.

Although the BAC 111 was 19 years old, longevity played no part in this accident. The disappearing windscreen should have been held in place by 90 bolts, each of which passed through layers of glass and transparent vinyl butyl before fitting securely into nuts anchored to the cockpit frame. When AAIB investigators examined the evidence, they found that when the windscreen had been replaced two days earlier, no fewer than 84 of the bolts were 'of smaller diameter' than that called for in the specification. Although the bolts were only a little smaller, otherwise they could not have been tightened to what would have appeared to be normal tautness, they were insufficient to withstand pressurisation and so the windscreen blew out.

The cause of this accident was put down to human error. Investigations were set in train to find out if the installers were at fault — normally working in teams of two, mechanics can change a 111 window in 90min — or whether the problem lay with packaging or quality control of replacement parts. But that was shutting the stable door. It must never be forgotten that behind the smooth face of airline PR, and underneath the photogenic skin of the shiny airliner, lies a greasy mechanical network of pipes that can burst, metals that can fracture, electrics that can go on the blink and nuts that can wriggle free. The trusty pilots up front can only do so much to prevent problems. If they spend too much time poking here and double-checking there during pre-flight inspections, they risk unsettling the boarding public. That is why leading carriers such as British Airways employ 7,000 engineers to maintain and sustain 200 aircraft; crucial work, such as anything to do with flying controls, is not only checked by one licensed engineer but also double-checked by another. But sufficient numbers of people are only part of the equation. Are they rostered properly, is their knowledge kept up to date, are they encouraged to use their initiative or do they see themselves treated as mere 'spanner bashers'? Aircraft do not fly by themselves — people keep them up there, and if the human dimension is allowed to fail, aircraft may come down a lot faster than they went up.

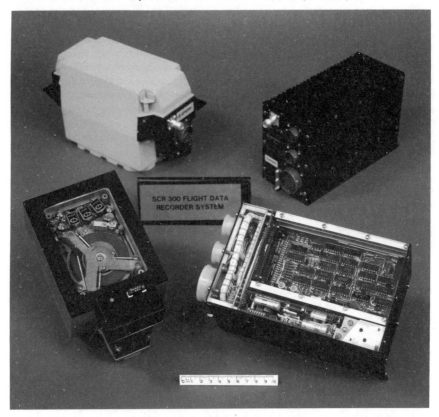

The SCR 300, a typical Flight Data Recorder (FDR). It has two airborne units; a fire and crash-proof accident data recorder (ADR) on which digital data and audio information is recorded on an endless loop of magnetic tape, and a data acquisition unit (DAU) containing the electronics to process the data to be recorded on the ADR. Speedy recovery of the ADR is of prime importance after an accident, so the crucial 'black box' is in fact painted bright orange so that it stands out in any wreckage. Mine detectors should not be used in the search for an ADR because they can erase everything on record. BAe

FLY THE AEROPLANE

In late 1964 the US Air Force funded preliminary studies by Boeing, Douglas and Lockheed into a heavy-lift military cargo aircraft. The winner would eventually be the Lockheed C-5, but whereas Douglas made only desultory concurrent efforts to examine alternatives, Boeing hedged its bets by initiating work on a number of commercial derivatives immediately after submitting its C-5 proposals in April 1965. Such astute forward planning was to give Boeing a head start with what came to be designated its Model 747. Moreover, apart from its great size and the use of big new turbofans, the 747 made such good use of existing technology that by the time the 747 first flew in early 1969, it had already been ordered by 27 airlines.

Up to 490 passengers could be carried in what was to be the world's first 'jumbo' jet, though 350 in a mixed-class configuration was more typical. Other 'wide body' offshoots from the C-5 programme were to follow in the shape of the Lockheed TriStar and Douglas DC-10. Having some two-thirds of the passenger-carrying capacity of the 747, the TriStar and DC-10 were better suited to long-range routes with only moderate traffic, but whichever way you looked at it, the relative difference counted for little in accident terms. Whenever a 'wide body' went down, the loss of hundreds of passengers as distinct from dozens invariably made bigger headlines and generated more public concern.

Yet although aircraft accident investigators are usually portrayed probing smouldering wreckage or examining minutiae in laboratories, not every case involves crashes and deaths. If something happens that could so easily have resulted in a major accident, the specialists can still be called in to proffer impartial advice on preventing a similar occurrence in future. If the aircraft and its systems (in particular the flight data recorder [FDR] and cockpit voice recorder [CVR]) survive, not to mention the crew, it can make the investigators' task so much easier.

On 19 February 1985, a China Airlines Boeing 747-SP, tail number N4522V, was carrying 251 passengers and 23 crew across the Pacific from Taipei, Taiwan to Los Angeles, California. Five flight crew were up front to share the strain of the long haul, and for some 10hr they had little to bother them. Then, while flying at FL410 and approaching reporting point Redoo about 300 miles northwest of San Francisco, Flt 006 encountered light clear air turbulence caused by a polar jet stream. The time was around 10.10hrs (Pacific Standard Time) and the primary flightcrew, consisting of Capt Ho Min-Yuan, First Officer Chang Ju-Yu and Flight Engineer Wei Kuo-Pin, was on duty. Capt Ho switched on the 'fasten seat belts' sign, but he left the autopilot engaged to control the 747's height, speed and heading.

The autopilot was operating in Performance Management System (PMS) mode, which meant that the PMS provided pitch guidance and maintained a selected 41,000ft; roll guidance was provided by the Inertial Navigation System (INS). The autopilot used only the aircraft's ailerons and spoilers for lateral control, ignoring the rudder and rudder trim. The PMS was also expected to maintain a datum speed of Mach 0.85 (254kt indicated), but this fluctuated between Mach 0.84 (251kt) and Mach 0.88 (264kt) in the turbulent conditions.

As speed increased to about Mach 0.88, PMS automatics retarded the throttles. When the aircraft decelerated to 0.84, the PMS moved the throttles forward to halt the speed decay, except the flight engineer noticed that No 4 engine did not respond. He moved No 4 throttle forward and aft manually, but still nothing happened; No 4 engine appeared to have flamed out. The airliner continued to decelerate, marking the start of a very interesting few minutes.

The captain directed the first officer to request a lower altitude from ATC so that they could descend to restart No 4 engine. After telling the relief flight engineer to come forward and help his 'on duty' colleague, First Officer Chang asked for descent clearance from Oakland Air Route Traffic Control Center (ARTCC) at 10.14:11hrs. He did not tell Oakland about the engine failure or declare an emergency. The ATC transcript shows that Oakland cleared a descent to FL240 at 10.15:01hrs. ARTCC subsequently made another six transmissions, but received no acknowledgement from Flt 006.

Although maximum engine restart altitude was 30,000ft, Capt Ho directed Flight Engineer Wei to try and relight No 4 while at 41,000ft. As speed continued to reduce through Mach 0.80 (240kt), the captain turned the autopilot's speed mode selector from PMS to 'Off'. This released the autopilot from the altitude hold command, enabling the captain to use the autopilot pitch control wheel to lower the nose attitude in an effort to arrest any further speed decay. Unfortunately the inertial navigator continued to feed inputs into the autopilot roll mode irrespective of what the pilot was doing. As the 747's rudder was out of the autopilot loop, the airliner yawed to the right and rolled to the left while the INS tried to maintain heading. Eventually the limit of the autopilot's roll authority was reached and, despite the application of full left aileron, the aircraft started to roll gently to the right.

About this time the first officer 'looked up' after completing his radio call and saw that the aircraft had banked 'slightly' to the right. Just afterwards the captain finally disengaged the autopilot. Airspeed was still decreasing and Capt Ho wanted to push the 747's nose down manually at a faster rate to arrest speed loss. When the autopilot was disengaged, the 747 immediately yawed and rolled further right, but the captain did not apply any counteracting rudder.

As Capt Ho concentrated on his attitude director indicator (ADI) to make a left-wing-down correction, the descending 747 entered cloud around 37,000ft. The captain then became disorientated. Being uncertain of the roll attitude, he alternated between moving the control wheel to the left and right; not surprisingly, he was unable to recover to normal flight. In fact, while descending to 30,000ft, the 747 completed a 360° aileron roll. As all the flightdeck ADIs rotated, the flight engineer felt the aircraft enter an abnormal attitude and then he saw that Nos 1, 2 and 3 engines had lost thrust. After telling his captain, who must have needed this information like a hole in the head as he strove to recover the situation, Second Officer Wei found the 'g' forces becoming so great that he could no longer lift his arms and his head was forced down against the centre pedestal.

It was subsequently found that the 747's speed fell as low as 54kt indicated (101kt below basic stalling speed) and twice exceeded the aircraft's maximum limiting speed of 394kt. The second time indicated airspeed went over the top, the captain and first officer combined to pull the control column back. As speed came back under some semblance of control, the 747 emerged from the clouds at around 11,000ft. Now that he had visual references, Capt Ho was finally able to regain straight and level flight at about 9,500ft. The flight engineer said that Nos 1, 2 and 3 engines 'came in' while descending through 10,000ft, and he then managed to restart No 4.

After the aircraft was stabilised, Oakland ARTCC was contacted and, at 10.17:03hrs, Flt 006 reported that it had experienced a 'flameout, ah, we emergency . . . we are niner thousand feet...'. A further minute passed while breathing rates in N4522V's cockpit returned towards normal, and then Flt 006 requested clearance to climb. Radar vectors were given to regain course and at 10.19:17hrs, Flt 006 told Oakland that 'we can control the aircraft'. However, on checking his instruments, the flight engineer found that the body landing gear indicated down and locked and that No 1 hydraulic system fluid level gauge showed empty. Having the gear down reduced N4522V's cruising level and range, which combined with having distressed and possibly seriously hurt people on board made Capt Ho decide to divert to San Francisco. There followed a descent into a long final approach for runway 28L at San Francisco International Airport. After landing there safely, it seems amazing that only two people out of the 274 passengers and crew on board were found to have been seriously injured — a cabin crew member received an acute back strain and a passenger suffered lacerations and bone fractures on his right foot.

N4522V did not get off so lightly. After rolling through the sky, its nose pulled up with such force that the flight data recorder indicated +4.8g. The instrument was so taken aback by this unusual loading that it ceased functioning correctly for the remainder of the flight, but it was subsequently found that the aircraft pulled +5.1g at 19,000ft. N4522V's wings were bent upwards by 2-3in at the tips, and the left outboard aileron upper panel was broken. The trailing edge wedge was cracked in several places, while some 10-11ft of left tailplane, including the left elevator, had separated. The right tailplane tip ended up five feet shorter than it should have been, and a further section in the box beam area was no longer in place. Finally, left and right undercarriage uplock assemblies had come away from their fuselage attachment points and the auxiliary power unit had separated from its mounts such that it was found resting on the two lower tail cone access doors.

Yet in spite of an NTSB assessment that the 747 was 'damaged substantially . . . (as) a result of the acceleration forces and high airspeeds that occurred during the upset and recovery manoeuvres', the engines carried on working normally and the aircraft remained airworthy. It is to Boeing's great credit, as well as reassuring to all prospective travellers, that the 747 stood up so well to such un-airliner-like manoeuvres.

Although no crash or loss of life resulted from this incident, it could so easily have proved otherwise. Since N4522V was a US registered aircraft leased by China Airlines, a NTSB investigation was initiated into what was termed the 'in-flight upset'. The board found that the first officer had performed satisfactorily throughout the emergency, as had the flight engineer except that during the attempted engine relight, he did not close the bleed air valve before advancing the throttle.

However, the NTSB was critical of the captain's actions. Although the training manual recommended that the autopilot be disengaged following engine failure, the captain left it in rather than assume the more difficult and time-consuming task of flying the aircraft manually. He then became preoccupied with the decreasing airspeed and his overall instrument scan broke down to such an extent that he failed to spot the signs of impending departure from normal flight. Thereafter, he became spatially disorientated and remained so until he regained visual clues below cloud.

In Capt Ho's defence, it has to be said that the 747 had been airborne for about 10hr, had crossed several time zones and the incident occurred at about 02.14hrs Taiwan local time, some four to five hours after the captain's normal bedtime. Consequently, the captain's ability to obtain, assimilate and analyse all the data

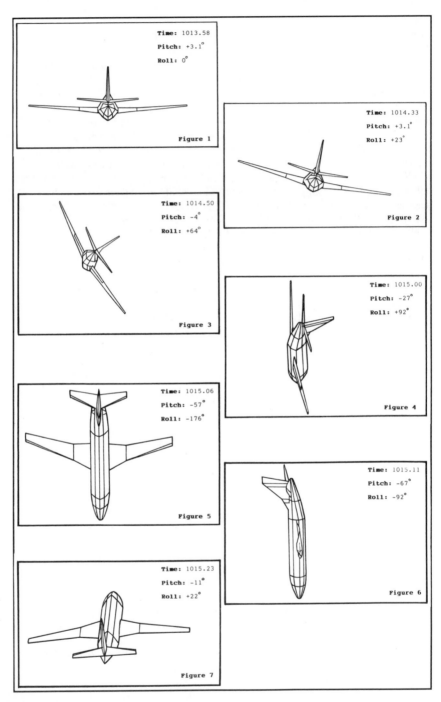

Excerpts from the NTSB computer animation illustrating China Flt 006's Pacific roll.

presented to him could have been impaired by the effects of monotony, boredom and fatigue. Nevertheless, the board did not accept these factors as justifications. Capt Ho had been relieved by the augmentee captain for about five hours, resuming commander duties about two hours before the incident, and he was alert to the situation as it developed. Being an experienced commander with over 15,000 flying hours in all and 3,748hr on 747s, Capt Ho should have known how loss of the thrust of an outboard engine would affect his ability to control the aircraft. He should also have been aware that the autopilot control did not include rudder authority, so that the net effect of flying on autopilot in this configuration would be to roll to the left thereby inducing sideslip, increasing drag and decreasing speed.

The board therefore concluded that the near-disaster had little to do with No 4 engine, which as it turned out had not flamed out but merely stagnated at an idle power setting. Indeed, a single engine failure while cruising along in a Boeing 747 places the aircraft in so little jeopardy that China Airlines' operating manual did not even classify such a happening as an emergency. Nevertheless, the engine malfunction did trigger the chain of events. It caused the captain to become distracted from his normal instrument scan, propelled him towards evaluating the engine problem with the flight engineer, and tunnelled his vision towards rectifying the decaying airspeed. He did not disengage the autopilot as he had been taught in training, and the autopilot effectively masked the impending loss of aircraft control.

Controls on this mark of Boeing 747 were such that they could be programmed for automatic flight along the whole route. As more and more aircraft become similarly endowed, pilots will find themselves increasingly responsible for computer supervision at the expense of physical workload. There is a drawback. Monitoring modern autopilots (and other flight systems), which so rarely go wrong and which can often operate more effectively than humans *when all is going well*, can be mind-numbingly tedious particularly at 2 o'clock in the morning after 10 hours flying. Herein lies the contradiction inherent in technology taking over from humans: the emphasis in the modern airline pilot's role is switching from performing to monitoring, but there is ample evidence, from both research and accident statistics, that humans are poor monitors.

The speed with which this frightening incident developed should serve as a salutary reminder of the need to remain alert for the unexpected. If pilots are aware of the perils of being in system-monitoring mode, they might be more ready to make a positive change to system-controlling mode in response to a malfunction. Given that someone else might not be so fortuitous in finding a cloud base sufficiently high to enable visual recovery, there are three other major lessons to be learned from Capt Ho's misfortune. For a start, do not get preoccupied with a distraction. In so many accidents, the first event is a malfunction, often of a relatively minor nature. Even if it is something major like a fire, the wing will not burn off in a nanosecond. Completing all the emergency drills to a standard that would gladden the heart of a simulator instructor will be of little avail if the airliner is allowed to depart from controlled flight. Whatever the emergency, the first and foremost rule is: FLY THE AIRCRAFT.

Second, in a multi-crew aircraft there are other experts about so use them. In this case the commander got too closely involved with everything from trouble-shooting the engine snag to flying the beast. There was a fully trained first officer with 4,553hr on type in the next seat; the flying controls should have been handed over to him, leaving Capt Ho free to concentrate on the wider airmanship and command issues. A flight deck is no place for a one-man band, and a good captain uses his crew to the full.

Finally, although the NTSB indicated that the co-pilot performed satisfactorily, all flight deck crew members have a duty to check each other's performance. Everyone in receipt of flying pay should monitor the pilot-in-control's flying and be ready to shout out if he looks like going awry. Whatever your aircrew specialisation on the flight deck, you are never a passenger.

First of the 'wide body' jet airliners, Boeing 747s initially weighed 710,000lb and carried up to 490 passengers in 10-abreast seating. Among later developments was the 747-SP (Special Performance) which was designed for routes of lower traffic density by sacrificing passenger capacity for very long range. The Aer Lingus BAC-111 passing by a China Airlines 747-SP gives some idea of the size of the 747-SP which was involved in the 'in-flight upset' over the Pacific on 19 February 1985. Alan J. Wright

WEATHER LORE

Many features of modern life seem to originate in the USA. Perhaps North Americans have more disposable cash, time or unfettered imagination than most to undertake new ventures, but certainly the US of the late-1930s had a distinct geographical advantage in that its peaceful skies, far removed from any battlefield, enabled embryo airlines to develop around a burgeoning network of scheduled passenger routes. Nevertheless, as every silver lining masks a cloud, the downside to this trailblazing was that the US pioneered new categories of commercial aircraft accidents as well.

On 31 August 1940, a Pennsylvania Central Airlines DC-3 was flying through a severe electrical storm when a flash of lightning erupted directly ahead. Ground witnesses saw the DC-3 immediately nose over and plummet into the ground near Lovettsville, Va, killing 24 people. The FBI seized on a battered alarm clock from the wreckage as a possible bomb trigger, but it proved to be a red herring. In the end, after months of painstaking research, a small hole was noticed on a line of the salvaged passenger manifest. It was most probably caused by a bolt of lightning, and a severe storm brought down the aircraft.

Forty four fatalities resulted from two more thunderstorm accidents before the end of the war. Thereafter eight air disasters, generating a total death toll of 270, were attributed to storms up to 1959. They all occurred over the USA, demonstrating not simply that airline travel was more a way of North American life but also that one should never underestimate continental weather. Yet, as the scheduled airline system fanned out, the rest of the world soon learned that the weather threat to airliners was not just a US preserve.

After finally losing faith in the Avro Tudor, BOAC ordered 22 Canadair DC-4Ms for its Empire routes. A DC-4 variant which made maximum use of British equipment, including Rolls-Royce engines, the DC-4M (known in BOAC service as the 'Argonaut' class) also had a pressurised fuselage to take full advantage of the better performance at higher altitudes conferred by four supercharged Merlins.

Over the space of seven years, BOAC's Argonaut G-ALHE amassed 18,000 in-service hours carrying up to 40 first class passengers at a time in its roomy interior. By June 1966 when its Airworthiness Certificate was renewed, 'Hotel Echo' was to be found on the busy London-Lagos route. After yet another unremarkable outbound trip from UK, the Argonaut flew the first leg back on 24 June. It was a 550-mile hop from the Nigerian capital to Kano, a bustling city on the high interior plateau, and 'Hotel Echo' completed it successfully at 16.40hrs.

The relief flight crew of five plus three flight attendants, who would take the Argonaut on to London via Tripoli, had arrived at Kano airport 40min earlier. Capt H. V. Tomlinson and First Officer John Slatford checked in with BOAC ops before moving on to study the weather forecast for the 1,400-mile leg to Tripoli. They found the weather over the entire northern Nigerian region to be typical for the time of year: a moist southwesterly air current surmounted by a dry easterly one, resulting in a combined unstable air mass.

Capt Tomlinson was a 36-yr old ex-RAF pilot who had great experience of flying in all weathers. He noticed the overhang of a storm seemingly near the edge of the airport, but there was no sign of the roll-type cloud associated with line squalls which could generate dangerously violent turbulence. In fact the meteorological forecaster put the nearest line squall about 400 miles to the east; despite gathering momentum as it moved westward, this squall was not expected to reach Kano until the next day.

Once the incoming Argonaut commander cautioned that a storm, now some 8-10 miles out, was moving around the airport from the northeast, Capt Tomlinson proposed to his navigation officer that they extend slightly towards the west just after taking-off on Runway 25 to avoid the worst of the weather. After ensuring that he had surplus fuel on board to cope with this detour, Tomlinson concluded by saying that he wanted to get off as quickly as possible.

British Ministry of Civil Aviation advice to pilots at that time on the effects of thunderstorms included the following statement: 'Before take-off, make a thorough analysis of the weather situation to determine the probable location of thunderstorms. Plan the flight to avoid them. Special attention should be given to thunderstorms in the vicinity of the airfield.' Capt Tomlinson had done all this, and as stewardess Kay Buckley checked off the names of the 38 boarding passengers, the commander paused during his usual visual pre-flight inspection for a further scan of the dark cloudy skies. Just then another Argonaut landed on Runway 25. Noticing that it made a normal landing despite passing much closer to the rumbles of thunder and lightning flashes than he intended to do, Tomlinson saw no cause to heed the Ministry's concluding words of advice: 'If there is any risk of the aircraft flying into the influence of an active thunderstorm cell during its initial climb, it will be advisable to delay the take-off.'

At 17.16hrs the crew received clearance to taxy. As Capt Tomlinson arrived at the holding point for Runway 25, the Tower passed a surface wind of 300° at 15kt and a pressure setting of 1,012millibars. The Argonaut was now being drenched by a typical tropical downpour but the commander could see the end of the runway clearly through the windscreen wipers. Rattling through the pre take-off checks, Tomlinson obtained clearance to go. He shoved the throttle levers forward, four Merlin engines roared into life and after some 2,000yd, 'Hotel Echo' lifted off.

Wheels were retracted by the time the aircraft crossed the upwind end of Runway 25 at 100ft. Shortly afterwards Tomlinson called for a power reduction. Once established in a 300ft/min climb at 125-130kt, he asked for 'Flaps up' as the Argonaut disappeared into the murk. The commander remembered the altimeter reading 260-270ft as the flaps retracted, but then both pilots saw the indicated air speed drop steadily and quickly. 'Full power,' shouted Tomlinson as he eased the nose forward. Notwithstanding Slatford's efforts, the Argonaut was slow to respond. The speed stayed steady at 103kt, a mere 6kt above stalling speed, and so there was nowhere to go but down. By the time the pilots had sufficient spare capacity to look out, they found their aircraft to be only 15-20ft above the ground with a tree directly ahead. The commander tried to take avoiding action without digging a wing tip in, but the underside of the airliner's nose section and left wing still struck the tree 17ft above its base. Fire broke out as the left wing tanks ruptured, and a rapidly disintegrating Argonaut came to rest in a ball of flame. The final impact was so shattering that 21 passenger seats were hurled so far away that they were left untouched by the exploding fires. Although the captain and first officer survived, the navigator died along with the second steward and the stewardess. Despite brave rescue forays into the flames, 29 of the 38 passengers also perished.

At the instigation of the Nigerian Minister of Communications and Aviation, an inquiry was convened under the chairmanship of Mr E. H. Coleman, an ex-RAF Wg Cdr filling the impressively-sounding appointment of Director of Civil Aviation, West Africa. The first thing the board did was confirm 'Hotel Echo's' airworthiness. The airliner was over half a ton lighter than permissible maximum weight at take-off, and close examination failed to reveal any kind of significant defect. The engines had been at full power, the altimeters correctly set and the landing gear locked up.

As anticipated, the inquiry homed in on the weather. West African Meteorological Services reported that the main thunderstorm centre *did* pass a little to the north of the airport at the time of the accident. However, a new cell appeared to have developed in the overhang, giving heavy rain and squalls to the west of the airport at about 17.20hrs. When Capt Tomlinson was horrified to find his airspeed dropping quickly just after take-off, it was the hitherto unknown cell that suddenly changed a moderate headwind to a strong tailwind with a corresponding decrease in airspeed. On top of it all there may also have been a downdraught.

When it came to considering possible error, the board found that the commander had done all he could to assess the risk. Neither he nor the forecaster could have been aware that the offending thunderstorm cell was forming along the take-off path from Runway 25. The inquiry concluded: 'The board, therefore, is of the opinion that the Pilot-in-Command was justified in taking off in the prevailing conditions.' They also found that Capt Tomlinson and his crew had done everything possible to save 'Hotel Echo': the rapid descent was in no way caused by the attitude of the aircraft which remained level throughout.

In recommending further research and warnings into the potential dangers of operating aircraft near thunderstorms, the Kano board reinforced the point that bad weather remained a perennial cause of aircraft accidents. Yet as airliners of the Argonaut generation gave way to jet-powered successors, some people may have thought that here at last was a means of flying around and above trouble. Sadly, despite technological advances, natural phenomena can still add spice and interest to airline life, often at the most unlikely and unexpected moments.

A prime example occurred on 24 June 1982 when British Airways Flt 009, a Boeing 747 on the Kuala Lumpur-Perth sector of its London to Auckland run, suddenly lost all four engines in quick succession over West Java. Despite flying way up high at FL370, Capt Eric Moody, his crew of 15 and 247 passengers, had flown straight into a cloud of volcanic dust thrown up by an erupting Mount Galunggung.

It was about 20.45hrs local time and the night was dark. Relying on standby power — all four engine-driven generators were of little use — the crew initiated relight drills while descending at 250-270kt. The 747 manual advised that relighting was most likely to be successful in less rarified air below 28,000ft but no signs of engine life were forthcoming even well below that. The airliner was now over the Indian Ocean turning back towards the nearest diversion airfield at Jakarta, but on passing 15,000ft with a mountainous region (11,500ft safety height) up ahead, Moody feared that ditching might be the only option. Fortunately, at 13,000ft and some 13min after initial flameout, No 4 engine re-started. It was followed soon after by the other trio. After climbing back to 15,000ft to assist radar identification by Jakarta Control, descent clearance was given for an approach to Halim Airport's Runway 24 only for No 2 engine to surge repeatedly as the commander throttled back. Volcanic dust sucked inside was taking its toll.

Nursing the three remaining engines, and using speedbrakes against power rather than throttle movement whenever possible, the crew managed to get G-BDXH

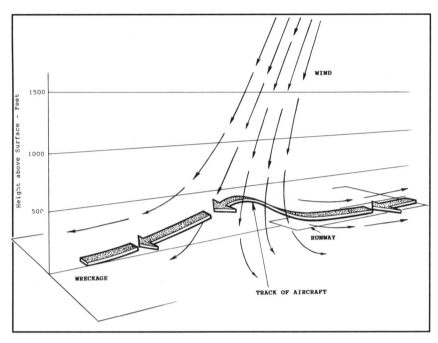

Above:
The effect of windshear and downdraught on G-ALHE as it lifted off from Kano's Runway 25 on 24 June 1956.

Below:
Flight plan route of BA 009 which was rudely interrupted by an erupting Mount Galunggung on 24 June 1982.

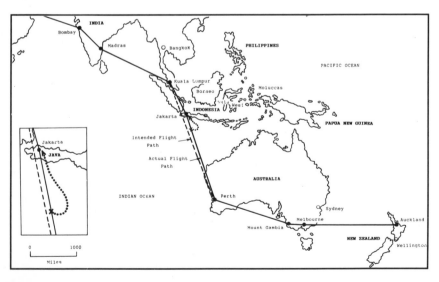

down safely. Sandblasted forward windscreens diffused the runway lights, making runway aspect unreadable, but Capt Moody was pleased with his landing. 'It was a good one,' he said afterwards. The subsequent awards for outstanding airmanship to Capt Moody and his crew were richly deserved.

The flight engineer remarked much later that the score was 'Jumbos — One, Volcanoes — Nil,' but if all the Rolls-Royce RB211 engines had taken in enough ash to prevent recovery, the final result could so easily have been different. Nor can it be said that running into volcanic ash seven miles up is a one-off experience.

On 15 December 1989, a KLM 747-400 Combi letting down through 26,000ft into Anchorage International Airport flew into an ash plume erupting from Mount Redoubt. All four engines failed, and after eight attempts, Capt Karel van der Elst and his crew managed to relight two at 13,000ft: the other pair restarted after three more tries. All 14 crew members and 234 passengers landed safely, but the aircraft's structure was so badly sandblasted, and its systems so severely contaminated, that the cost of the damage was put at around $80 million. All this from a volcano that only began to erupt 90min earlier, and whose ash cloud was no different from an ordinary cloud on radar.

But if jet flight has simply enabled airline operators to superimpose a new set of environmental risks on top of the old ones, traumas at height do at least give a crew time to take remedial action. It is those tried and tested weather risks down near the ground that really bite, and whatever the advances made by science and technology, the same sort of low blows that felled Capt Tomlinson and his Argonaut at Kano continue to creep under pilots' defences more than somewhat.

On 2 August 1985, Delta Air Lines assigned one of their Lockheed TriStars, N726DA, to Flt 191 — a regular passenger schedule between Florida and Los Angeles with a stop en route at Dallas/Fort Worth (DFW), Texas. Flt 191 departed Fort Lauderdale at 15.10hrs (Eastern Daylight Time) on an IFR flight plan with 152 passengers and a crew of 11 on board. The DFW terminal weather forecast given to the flight crew stated, among other things, that there was a possibility of widely scattered rain showers and thunderstorms, becoming isolated after 20.00hrs (Central Daylight Time). The crew's dispatch document package also contained a warning that 'an area of isolated thunderstorms is expected over Oklahoma and northern and northeastern Texas . . . a few isolated tops to above FL450'.

Delta Flt 191 was uneventful until passing New Orleans. As a line of weather was intensifying to the south along the Texas-Louisiana Gulf coast, the flight crew elected to change to the more northerly Blue Ridge arrival route into DFW. This late flight plan change resulted in a 10 to 15min hold at the Texarkana VORTAC, Arkansas, until the TriStar could be slotted into the arrival pattern for the world's third busiest airport.

At 17.35:26hrs, N726DA's CVR showed that the flight crew received an Automatic Terminal Information Service broadcast stating that DFW weather was 'six thousand scattered, two one thousand scattered, visibility one zero . . . wind calm . . . visual approaches in progress . . .' A few seconds later Flt 191 was cleared to begin descent for a Blue Ridge join.

On the way down to the initially cleared height of 10,000ft, Fort Worth Air Route Traffic Control Center (ARTCC) suggested a heading of 250°. The captain replied that he was looking at a 'pretty good size' weather cell 'at a heading of two five five... and I'd rather not go through it, I'd rather go around it one way or the other'. In response ARTCC passed another heading.

First Officer Rudolph Price, aged 42 with 1,200 hours on type and a Delta employee since 1970, was flying the TriStar while Capt Ted Connors, at 57 a very senior and experienced pilot and commander, worked the radios. At 17.48:22hrs Capt Connors told his first officer that he was flying well and that 'I'm glad we didn't have to go through that mess. I thought sure he was going to send us through it'. Soon afterwards flight engineer Nick Nassick said, 'Looks like it's raining over Fort Worth'. At 17.51:42hrs Flt 191 was instructed to contact DFW Airport Approach Control, and this was done while passing through 11,000ft.

At 17.56:28hrs, Approach Control transmitted a message which said in part, 'Attention all aircraft listening . . . there's a little shower just north of the airport and they're starting to make ILS approaches . . . tune up one oh nine one for one seven left'. Having dialled up the ILS frequency of 109.1, the flight crew made ready to pass over Blue Ridge, head 244° and intercept the centreline for an ILS approach to Runway 17L.

At 17.59:47hrs the first officer said, 'We're gonna get our airplane washed,' just before the captain switched to Arrival Radar and told the controller that they were at 5,000ft. Two aircraft were ahead of Flt 191 in the landing sequence for 17L, the first of which was American Air Lines Flt 351. Flt 351 was some 11 miles from touchdown as approach control asked if it was able to see the airport . Back came the reply, 'As soon as we break out of this rain shower we will'.

Just before 18.01hrs, the controller asked Flt 191 to reduce speed to 170kt and turn left onto 270° for feed-in behind a Learjet for landing on runway 17. At 18.02:35hrs, Flt 191 was told that it was 6 miles from the outer marker; the controller asked the flight crew to turn 180° to join the localiser at or above 2,300ft and stated that the TriStar was 'cleared for ILS one seven left approach'. A little later the controller requested 191 'to reduce your speed to one six zero please,' and Capt Connors replied, 'Be glad to'. The controller broadcast at 18.03:30hrs, 'We're getting some variable winds out there due to a shower...out there north end of DFW'. Flt 191 acknowledged and a flight crew member was heard on the CVR to remark, 'Stuff is moving in'.

At 18.03:46hrs, 191 was asked to reduce to 150kt and contact DFW tower. On checking in on the new frequency, Capt Connors stated, 'Tower, Delta one ninety one, out here in the rain, feels good'. Tower cleared the TriStar to land and briefed, 'wind zero nine zero at five, gusts to one five'. At 18.04:07hrs, the first officer called for the before-landing checks — gear was confirmed down and flaps extended to the landing setting of 33°.

A little later the first officer remarked, 'lightning coming out of that one'. The captain asked 'Where?' and received the reply, 'Right ahead of us'. Flt 191 continued in the descent passing 1,000ft at 18.05:05hrs. Just afterwards the captain warned the first officer to watch his airspeed and a sound identified as rain began to be heard on the CVR. At 18.05:21hrs Capt Connors warned, 'You're gonna lose it all of a sudden, there it is'. Five seconds later he stated, 'Push it up, push it way up'. The sound of three Rolls-Royce RB211 engines at high rpm was then heard on the CVR and the captain said, 'That's it'.

At 18.05:44hrs, the aircraft's Ground Proximity Warning System (GPWS) 'Whoop whoop, pull-up!' alert sounded. The captain cried 'TOGA', which was a call for flight engineer Nassick to select the Take-off/Go Around switch: when the aircraft was being flown manually, this switch provided flight director command bar guidance for an optimum climbout manoeuvre. Two more GPWS alerts were repeated six and seven seconds later, followed by the local controller telling 191 to 'go around'. The CVR recording ended at 18.05:58hrs.

As the local controller saw Flt 191 emerge from the rain at the north end of the airport, 'It just didn't look right to me (so I told the crew) "Delta go round"'. Sadly,

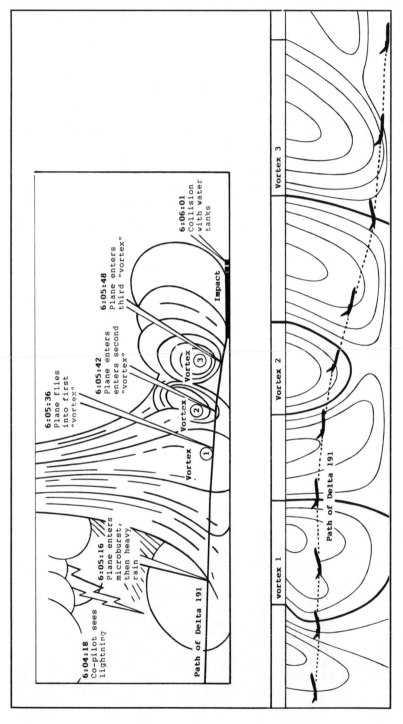

The final minutes of Delta 191's approach into Dallas/Fort Worth on 2 August 1985. The diagrams and flight path were plotted by Prof T. T. Fujita of the University of Chicago's meteorological department, assisted by Delta Air Lines.

6:04:18
Co-pilot sees
lightning

6:05:16
Plane enters
microburst,
then heavy
rain

6:05:36
Plane flies
into first
"vortex"

6:05:42
Plane enters
second
"vortex"

6:05:48
Plane enters
third "vortex"

6:06:01
Collision
with water
tanks

Impact

Path of Delta 191

Vortex
① ② ③

vortex 1

Vortex 2

Vortex 3

Path of Delta 191

Above:
Medical personnel recover bodies from the wreck of Flt 191 at Dallas/Fort Worth on Friday 2 August 1985. The TriStar's tail section was the only significant piece of structure left, and from it emerged 29 survivors. Associated Press

Below:
Delta Air Lines Boeing 727 N473DA lying all forlorn after coming to grief at DFW on Wednesday 31 August 1988. Lest anyone fear that DFW is an airport to avoid, when publishers Conde Naste examined scheduled airline flights worldwide between 1969 and 1988, the airline that emerged with the world's best safety record (zero fatal accidents from 1,876,448 flights) was Southwest Airlines, based in Dallas. (See page 109.) Associated Press

the advice came too late. At 18.05:52, the great airliner's main wheels made a glancing touch-down 6,336ft short of the 17L threshold. Flt 191 bounced back into the sky, only to come down again very rapidly towards State Highway 114, a ring road passing the northern end of DFW Airport. People standing by or driving along the highway at the tail-end of rush hour saw Flt 191 appear out of the gloom and strike a Toyota car on the westbound lane. As the port engine ingested bits of the Toyota, inside the TriStar a passenger actually said to his wife, 'Ya know, I've heard of rough landings but this is ridiculous'. He did not realise that the impact with the car slewed the TriStar some 10° left. As the 164ft-long aircraft cleared the eastbound lane, it snapped off a lamp-post whereupon witnesses noticed a fire near the left wing root. 'Oh, ****!' was the last human sound heard from the cockpit.

N726DA struck the ground in a left-wing-low attitude. The disintegrating left wing grazed the northernmost of two water tanks near the airport's east freight area, pivoting the fuselage counter-clockwise into the southernmost tank. N726DA then broke apart, a large explosion and fireball obscured the scene, and out of it all emerged the tail section skidding backwards. This finally came to rest on its left side before being blown back upright by the wind; it was the only significant piece of structure left. From here emerged the 26 passengers and three cabin attendants to survive. Although the DFW emergency services swung into action in a timely and effective manner, out of 163 people on board the TriStar 134 (plus the driver of the stricken Toyota) perished.

Once again the weather was the culprit left holding the smoking gun. North Texas was a very hot place to be on 2 August, with the surface temperature eventually rising over 100°. Through conduction and convection, a mass of air above warmed and rose to create a thunderstorm of enormous power. Given the imprecise nature of the airport and area weather forecasts available to the flight crew, a more timely and accurate update should have been available from the weather radar at Stephenville, Texas. This was located some 72nm from the approach end of runway 17L, and at 17.48hrs, 17min before the accident, it picked a Level 2 weather cell which the NTSB christened 'Cell C'. (There is a correlation between associated thunderstorm features such as turbulence and the intensity of a radar weather echo, and Level 2 equated to 'moderate' intensity.) Four minutes later Cell C had grown to Level 3 ('strong'), and a new pinpoint radar echo, Cell D, had developed to the south of it.

As luck would have it, the upper air radar specialist on duty at Stephenville left his radar position at about 17.35hrs to go for dinner. After eating and tending to some other duties, he returned to the radar around 18.00hrs where he noticed Cell D. At about 18.04hrs he called Fort Worth Forecast Office to advise them of the Cell's presence. He was required to do no more. The radar specialist was not a meteorologist, he was not qualified to issue either a forecast or a prediction about what Cell D would do, nor was he required to notify anyone when a thunderstorm was located near DFW Airport or brief anyone at that airport. After notifying Fort Worth Forecast Office, the radar specialist turned to analysing other echoes. He did not turn his attentions back to Cell D until about 18.21, by which time the top of the Cell had reached 50,000ft, its intensity had increased to Level 5 and Flt 191 had disintegrated.

The Fort Worth Forecast Office served both the general public and the aviation community. It had a television monitor which was set to the Stephenville weather radar on the day in question. The forecaster-in-charge heard the Stephenville radar specialist's 18.04hrs brief on Cell D and he saw the cell for himself on the television monitor, but he did not believe it was a storm of sufficient intensity to warrant issuing an Aviation Weather Warning.

Going back a few minutes, this very strong weather echo complete with thunderstorm was sitting off the north end of DFW Airport and Flt 191 was flying straight into it. As if that was not bad enough, this particular thunderstorm was about to spill out a strong downdraughting outburst of highly divergent damaging winds known as a microburst.

Microbursts may only be a few thousand feet across — the diameter of this particular one was 3.4km — but insofar as the jet of air downdraughting from them slams into the ground, causing violent wind eddies, they make take-offs and landings particularly hairy. An aircraft traversing a microburst initially encounters the outflow on the front side. This increases the headwind component, causing the aircraft to rise and indicated airspeed to increase. Several seconds later, the headwind component starts decreasing and the aircraft encounters the central core downdraught. Finally, the aircraft enters the back side of the microburst with its strong increase in tailwind component, which causes the aircraft to sink and indicated airspeed to decrease. The whole business can be over in anything from 20-40sec — Delta 191 entered the microburst at 18.05:14hrs and crashed at 18.05:52hrs — but there may well be not much recognisable aircraft left at the end of it.

The centre of the DFW microburst was just under 2 miles north of the approach end of 17L, and about 1,000ft west of the extended runway centreline and ground track of Flt 191. The airliner underwent an intense initiation into the theory of microbursts by first encountering a maximum headwind component of about 26kt at 754ft in the descent. By this time, despite setting power and attitude to maintain 150kt as instructed by ATC, Rudy Price found his indicated airspeed climbing of its own accord to 173kt. 'Watch your speed,' counselled Connors just as the deluge began; 'you're gonna lose it all of a sudden.' No sooner were the words out of his mouth than the airspeed indicator needle fell away.

Although indicated airspeed was to fall as low as 129kt, the first officer successfully transitted this phase by rotating the aircraft above a 15° nose-up pitch attitude and by increasing thrust to almost take-off power. The TriStar then entered the central core where the headwind component decreased in consequence. The aircraft stabilised momentarily around 500ft, and the pilots probably assumed they were through the worst. But 17sec before initial impact, the aircraft encountered rapid reversal in the lateral, horizontal and vertical winds. As if an increasing tailwind component was not bad enough — 20kt fell off the clock in the space of one second, activating the stickshaker — the TriStar then fell foul of three successive vortices which caused very severe up- and downdraughts. 'You really had a three-pronged attack here, in all the axes,' summarised a NTSB engineer. N726DA rolled wildly to port, the left wing dropping by a full 20°. 'Hang on to the ****' shouted Connors, but there was nothing left to hang on to. Rapidly decaying indicated airspeed, alternating updraughts and downdraughts, and severe gusts which required almost full lateral flight control authority to counter, combined to bring N726DA down.

The NTSB inquiry concluded that the probable cause of the accident to Delta 191 was the 'flight crew's decision to initiate and continue the approach into cumulonimbus cloud which they observed to contain visible lightning . . . This resulted in the aircraft's encounter at low altitude with a microburst-induced, severe windshear from a rapidly developing thunderstorm located on the final approach course'. Yet in fairness to the flight crew a stream of other aircraft flew into DFW that afternoon and none of them, including the two just ahead of Flt 191, reported landing difficulties or unusual conditions on the approach. This may have led Capt Connors to believe that, despite appearances to the contrary, the storm did not contain any overly dangerous features. In other words if Ted Connors, with his 29,300 flying hours and type ratings on a whole host of airliners from Douglas DC-3 to Lockheed TriStar, and Rudy Price, assessed by Delta as 'above average' and good enough to help rewrite Delta's TriStar operating manual, could misread the signs, few could honestly say that they would never have fallen into the same trap.

The natural inclination is to blame that hardy perennial, the weather forecasts, but it is extremely doubtful whether any radar specialist, forecaster or other modern shaker of bones or prober of entrails could have made a significant difference to the outcome of this accident in the time available. One transmission from a DFW controller at 17.59:44hrs (not received by Flt 191) stated that, 'there's a little bitty thunderstorm sitting right on the final; it looks like a little rain shower'. The fact that man still cannot tell, with sufficient accuracy on a significant proportion of occasions, whether or not a 'little bitty' thunderstorm will rapidly develop into one which will kill hundreds, illustrates how much predictive progress we still have to make.

Consequently, despite all the good recommendations that come out of investigations into weather accidents, such as pleas for expensive studies into 'gee-whizz' equipment or more refined procedures, warnings and guidelines, man deludes himself if he thinks he can counter the effects of severe weather at an electronic stroke or wave of the pen. There are certainly some good low level windshear warning systems around, but it is going to take many years before any device emerges which can guarantee to detect shears of every intensity, in all circumstances and in time to be of use.

Meanwhile, fliers must remain ready to deal on their own with unexpected phenomena such as microbursts. The first step to that end is to understand what the weather can do, and the extent of human limitations in the face of it. Twenty seven aircraft fell foul of low level windshear in the US between 1964 and 1986, and not all were really big microbursts such as that at DFW. Flt 191 encountered a horizontal windshear of at least 73kt — a Boeing 727 was brought down with the loss of 153 people at Kenner, La, on 9 July 1982 by an 'average' shear of 47kt.

In an ideal world, microburst shear would be countered by avoiding flying under or close to the sort of towering cumulus clouds associated with thunderstorms. As a simple rule of thumb, if a pilot saw a thunderstorm lurking with intent he would either route round it or stand off until it cleared. Unfortunately, in a far from ideal world, that is easier said than done. At some times of the year in many parts of the world, afternoon thunderstorms are as regular as clockwork. Many of these are very intense, but the vast majority of aircraft get in and out of affected airports without experiencing anything more dramatic than a bumpy ride and a drenching.

If the paying traveller would not look kindly at any carrier that 'cried Wolf' too often, the best advice to pilots must be to rely on actions that stand the best chance of getting out of trouble safely should the need suddenly arise. Delta, like most other airlines, had thought about what might happen if a pilot inadvertently encountered windshear. Their simulator curriculum taught pilots to ram the throttles forward to maximum thrust while pulling the nose up, allowing airspeed to decrease to near stickshaker activation if necessary to avoid contact with the ground. Although trading speed for precious altitude went against everything ingrained into pilots from basic training, the technique had been proved to work and there was substantial evidence that First Officer Price attempted to fly a proper windshear recovery technique on 2 August. Right at the very end of the approach, he was exerting as much pull force on the control column as he could muster to avoid hitting the ground. Given that this would have brought the TriStar even more quickly towards the stall, it was not surprising that the stickshaker worked momentarily for the last time. Almost by force of habit and training, it seems that the first officer instinctively relaxed the pull force on the control column. From that moment on, contact with the ground became inevitable.

Yet like most accidents, it was not until relatively late in the approach that Flt 191 passed the point of no salvation. Notwithstanding all that had gone before during the first part of the microburst, N726DA had become restabilised momentarily on the glide slope at around 500ft. This was the last time the pilots would have felt reasonably in control of the aircraft rather than the other way around, and with hindsight they should have grasped the opportunity to climb away and out of the hostile environment while they still had time and height to spare. But Flt 191 carried on going dovn, and in believing that their aircraft had flown through the worst of the windshear, the pilots cut off their last line of retreat.

Moving towards the wider flight safety picture, even with today's sophisticated aircraft backed by the best information technology, pilots can still pay the ultimate price if they push, or are pushed by the agency holding the purse strings, beyond the limits to get their aircraft down on the ground. There are always *good* reasons why captains press on, not least because they fear being shown up as less capable fliers if someone just ahead has managed to sneak in and land. Perhaps it may dent the image to divert in the cause of safety, and generate a few snide comments from down the back, but nobody ever said that aircraft captaincy was easy. While dedication and perseverance are all very commendable, a pilot should never be too proud to overshoot and go round for another approach. The weather is one of the oldest causes of aircraft accidents, and it is likely to be one of the last to be defeated. Until that happens, always treat the elements with respect.

WHAT'S IN A WORD

It is a disturbing fact that more than two-thirds of aircraft crashes take place either in the first two minutes of take-off, when pressure is on the machine, or during the four minutes immediately prior to landing when pressure is on the pilot. And if that was not worrying enough, during 1989 at least six perfectly serviceable aircraft flew too low while on the approach, causing around 600 fatalities. Particularly noteworthy was Flying Tigers Flt 66, a Boeing 747, which took off from Singapore at 06.04hrs (local time) on 18 February 1989 for a scheduled cargo run to Kuala Lumpur. The planned flight time was only 33min, but even that was to prove too much; half an hour after take-off, the 747 flew into the ground.

It was established that the commander handled the radios while the first officer flew the aircraft. The flight proceeded routinely with the 747 being transferred from Singapore to Kuala Lumpur Control at FL200. While at height, the crew briefed that they would make an ILS approach to Kuala Lumpur International's Runway 33. Tiger 66 was cleared to route direct to the Kayell (KL) Beacon and then handed over to Kuala Lumpur tower. Events thereafter are best left to the transcript of radio communications between ATC and the 747.

06.25.10hrs

Tower: Tiger Six Six. Cleared to Kilo Lima, seven thousand, runway three three, QNH one zero one one, expect no delay, be advised Tower visibility all around is about three thousand metres.

Tiger 66: Okay. Is the full runway open?

Tower: Affirmative, full length available.

Tiger 66: Okay, we read a bunch of NOTAMs about holes and ditches and stuff like that. We just wanted to make sure.

06.27.00hrs

Tower: Tiger Six Six, report your distance now.

Tiger 66: Fifty miles, fifty DME.

Tower: Tiger Six Six, descend five five zero zero.

Tiger 66: Five five zero zero, Tiger Six Six, we're out of seventy-eight hundred.

06.28.54hrs

Tower: Tiger Six Six, descend three five zero zero.

Tiger 66: Roger, cleared thirty-five hundred, we're out of six thousand.

06.30.40hrs

Tower: Tiger Six Six, descend two seven zero zero.

Tiger 66: Roger, cleared to two thousand seven hundred, we're out of forty-five. Is your ILS in operation this morning?

Tower: ILS for three three not available. If you wish, ILS one five is available.

Tiger 66: No, that's okay, we'll come on straight in on three three.

06.31.51hrs

Tower: Tiger Six Six descend two (to?) four zero zero, cleared for the NDB approach runway three three.

Tiger 66: Okay, four zero zero.

The 747 descended to 437 ft above sea level before striking a ridge line just over one mile southeast of the Kilo Lima beacon. As the aircraft hit the tree tops, it shed portions of leading and trailing edge devices plus parts of the horizontal stabiliser. The aircraft continued in controlled flight until the undercarriage struck a path half way up the ridge. The landing gear then sheared off and the 747 pancaked in on the top half of the ridge. As the fuel tanks ruptured, leaking fuel ignited and consumed the cockpit. Fire damage to the rest of the aircraft was minimal but it was still destroyed on impact with the ground. The wreckage came to rest heading 295° at Puchong, one mile southeast of the KL NDB and nine miles from the airfield.

The crew probably never saw what hit them because early morning mist, as well as darkness, would have shrouded the crash valley. There was no evidence of engine failure or flight control problems, and it was ascertained that the 747 was controllable until the moment of impact.

The extensive construction programme then underway at Kuala Lumpur airport was reflected in numerous NOTAMs. The fact that the ILS on Runway 33 was unserviceable on the day of accident had also been NOTAMed for some time: all other airfield navaids were available.

From the recorded transmissions between aircraft and ground, the inquiry found that the air traffic controller used non-standard phraseology in the descent clearances issued to Tiger 66. According to Malaysian ATC instructions, altitude clearances should involve the pronunciation of each digit in the number of hundreds or thousands followed by the word 'hundred' or 'thousand' as appropriate. If this ruling had been observed, Tower would have given altitude clearances of, 'Two thousand seven hundred' and 'Two thousand four hundred' instead of 'Two seven zero zero' and 'Two four zero zero'.

When Tiger 66 responded, 'Okay, four zero zero' the improper read back of the clearance given (two four zero zero) should have been corrected by the controller. The unfortunate controller in question stated that he had recently started issuing clearances in the way he did because aircrews seemed incapable of understanding instructions issued as per the official manual. Senior pilots of other airlines which routinely transitted through Kuala Lumpur airspace indicated that controllers seemed to have difficulty pronouncing the 'TH' sound, and that they found it much easier to pronounce each number separately.

The loss of Tiger 66 showed that a chain of minor errors and omissions could combine together to bring about the loss of over $100 million worth of aircraft and the four people on board. Not for the first time a run of the mill sortie turned out to be anything but, and perhaps the root cause of such disasters is complacency. The first lesson that should emerge from the 747 wreckage in the Malayan jungle is that every flight, including (especially?) straightforward transits, deserves to be planned and executed meticulously. The length and complexity of the NOTAM list relating to Kuala Lumpur airport that day made it even more important that each notice be reviewed and analysed fully beforehand rather than during a 33 min flight.

NOTAMs apart, had Tiger 66's crew asked about the serviceability of their selected approach aid – the ILS — before they let down, they would have gained themselves more time to study the charts, consider the implications and allocate individual responsibilities to ensure that the NDB approach was executed successfully and safely. As it was, the crew was *passing* 4,500 ft in the descent before they realised that reliance on the ILS was a non-starter. We know from the recordings that they did not rebrief the alternative approach procedure.

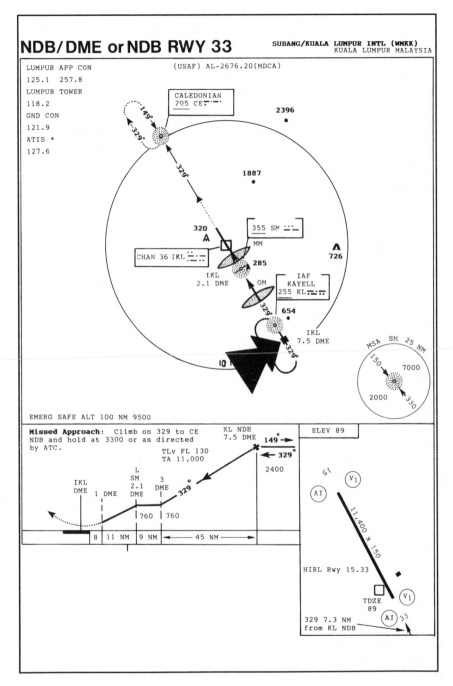

NDB/DME or NDB RWY 33

SUBANG/KUALA LUMPUR INTL (WMKK)
KUALA LUMPUR MALAYSIA

(USAF) AL-2676.20(MDCA)

LUMPUR APP CON
125.1   257.8
LUMPUR TOWER
118.2
GND CON
121.9
ATIS *
127.6

CALEDONIAN
205 CE

2396

1887

320
CHAN 36 IKL
IKL
2.1 DME

355 SM

MM

285

OM

IAF
KAYELL
255 KL

726

654

IKL
7.5 DME

MSA   SM   25 NM
150   7000
2000   330

EMERG SAFE ALT 100 NM 9500

Missed Approach: Climb on 329 to CE NDB and hold at 3300 or as directed by ATC.

KL NDB
7.5 DME   149→
            ←329°

ELEV 89

TLv FL 130
TA 11,000

2400

IKL
DME   1 DME
L
SM
2.1
DME
3
DME   329°

760   760

8   11 NM   9 NM   ←— 45 NM —→

HIRL Rwy 15.33

TDZE
89

329 7.3 NM
from KL NDB

V₁
AI

11,400 × 150

V₁
AI 33

Terminal Procedure Chart for an NDB approach to Runway 33, Kuala Lumpur International. The Chart clearly shows minimum descent height to be 2,400ft until within 7.5 miles DME.

107

It is hard not to conclude that from this moment on, the crew of Tiger 66 was behind rather than up with what was going on. Had they been *au fait* with the NDB Rwy 33 terminal approach chart, would they have accepted unquestioningly a clearance down to 400ft when the chart clearly showed the minimum height to be 2,400ft until past the KL Beacon? What is more, their aircraft was fitted with a ground proximity warning system (GPWS). This device worked as advertised, at 17sec before impact (for 1.7sec) and continuously from 8sec down to impact, but these warnings elicited no response from the flight crew. A properly executed escape manoeuvre would have averted the crash; a better appreciation of what they were about should have prevented the crew getting anywhere near disaster in the first place.

The need for unambiguous radio transmissions is obvious. English is the *lingua franca* of aviation, which in theory should be a boon to universal understanding. In practice the aviation world has standardised on 'American' English, which has the advantage of being universally recognisable by anybody with a TV set from Tierra del Fuego to Timbuktu. But there are drawbacks. Sloppy phraseology such as 'Okay' is one, together with slurred diction aimed at making everyone down there realise that there is a John Wayne manque up here rather than some wimp. There are also the gratuitous interjections such as 'Sir' which, though designed to engender friendliness, are as likely to confuse, mislead or just plain irritate.

In other words, use standard RT. Apart from a lack of situational awareness aboard Tiger 66, the major cause of the accident was the misheard altitude clearance and failure of ATC to respond to the incorrect readback. Insofar as one simple misunderstood word caused so much death and destruction, it reinforces the point that an aircraft cockpit is no place for a brain in neutral. But those ground authorities who come up with mandatory procedures also have an obligation to ensure that no ambiguities are left to trap unwary non-native English speakers. It is not all that long ago that a Gatwick air traffic controller directed an aircraft to hold over Eastwood, only for the pilot to hear this as an instruction to turn eastward.

Finally after many such accidents, pleas are made for great sums to be spent on some new impending-collision detector, ground avoider or similarly wondrous device. Yet the plethora of attention getters already on modern aircraft are no more than background noise and pretty lights if they are ignored. Never treat any warning as routine — act on it first, and investigate the cause afterwards.

COCKPIT
INDISCIPLINE

On 31 August 1988, Delta Air Lines Boeing 727, N473DA, was allotted to a regular scheduled passenger flight from Jackson, Mississippi, to Salt Lake City, Utah, stopping off en-route at Dallas/Fort Worth (DFW). It departed Jackson as Flt 1141 at 06.30hrs (Eastern Daylight Time) with only one logged fault — an inoperative No 1 main fuel tank quantity gauge. The first officer flew the leg to DFW, during which nothing out of the ordinary was noticed. Flt 1141 reached DFW's Gate 15 at 07.38hrs (Central Daylight Time).

Captain and first officer went to company operations on arrival, leaving the flight engineer/second officer to carry out a walkround inspection. The duty mechanic noted the unserviceable main fuel tank gauge in N473DA's logbook, but as Delta's minimum equipment list did not classify this as a 'no-go item', the mechanic had no other involvement with the flight.

The 727 was refuelled on the instructions of the Delta agent responsible for aircraft loading. The second officer having received weight and balance data plus the final weather briefing, and his flight deck seniors having returned, 'pushback' went ahead at 08.30hrs on schedule. In addition to the three men up front, there were 101 passengers and four cabin crew on board. At 08.37:20hrs, the DFW east ground controller instructed Delta Flt 1141 to '. . . join the inner for standard taxy to Runway 18L'. All three engines were started but the captain shut down No 3 as a fuel conservation measure once it became clear that there would be a lengthy delay before departure.

By 08.57hrs Flt 1141 had moved up to No 4 in the queue for take-off. The second officer alerted the flight attendants to prepare for departure, and the captain ordered No 3 engine restarted. At 08.58:38 the local controller instructed, 'Delta 1141, taxy into position Runway 18L and hold . . .' This clearance effectively directed Flt 1141 to pass the aircraft ahead of it on the taxiway and take the No 1 position. Just after 08.59hrs, Delta 1141 was cleared for take-off.

Being some 18,000lb below maximum permissible take-off weight, the crew of Flt 1141 was authorised to use a flap setting of 15° and reduced thrust. From the flight deck the take-off roll appeared to be normal in all respects; there were no warning lights, audible warnings or unusual engine instrument indications. The green 'Auto Pack Trip' arming light did not illuminate as the throttles were advanced, but as this system was not required in that particular configuration, the second officer forbore to inform the captain. Witnesses in the tower and on the ground agreed that Flt 1141 progressed normally until rotation. Thereafter the aircraft seemed to rotate to a higher than normal pitch angle with flames or sparks emanating from behind. It then appeared to continue down the runway, apparently out of control with the wings rocking from side to side.

Inside the cockpit, the crew found the right wing dropping just after lift off and the second officer heard the comment 'Engine failure' from either the captain or first officer. The captain felt that 'all was normal . . . everything was routine' until, as the main gear wheels left the ground, he heard 'two explosions'. It felt to him as though the aircraft had gone into reverse thrust before beginning to 'roll violently . . . it was all I could do to control the airplane'.

Approximately 22sec from lift off, the 727 struck an ILS localiser antenna array some 1,000ft beyond the end of Runway 18L. Although the aircraft remained airborne for another 400ft, pieces of right wing tip and right inboard and outboard aileron began to come adrift. N473DA then came down again on the main gear, traversed a 150ft-wide by 16ft-deep depression, and hit the ground on the far side. The wreckage trail showed it gradually swerved right for some 800ft, slid sideways for another 600ft, and came to rest near the airport boundary fence about 3,200ft from the departure end of runway 18L. What had not been ravaged by impact forces was then destroyed by post-crash fire. Two flight attendants and 12 passengers were fatally injured. Another 26 people, including the flight crew, sustained serious injuries, but fortune smiled on the 68 remaining passengers who received minor or no injuries. The value of the written-off Boeing 727 was estimated at $6-6.5 million.

A NTSB investigation was immediately set in train. Its members soon confirmed that the Delta crew was properly certified and qualified for the flight, and that the aircraft had been equipped and maintained to FAA standards. Neither weather, wind shear nor wake turbulence vortices from a previously departing 727 were found to be factors, and inspection of N473DA's three aft-mounted turbofan engines disclosed no pre-impact mechanical problems. Although No 1 fuel gauge was inoperative, there was no evidence of any fuel imbalance that would have caused flight control problems.

The inquirers turned to what remained and here the CVR came into its own. The tape started off with quite a bit of non-duty related chat among the flight crew, including casual conversations with a flight attendant who was in the cockpit on two occasions during taxying. The change was made from ground to local control frequency at 08.57:22hrs. Ten seconds later, the flight attendant left the cockpit and the door was closed in response to the second officer telling the cabin crew to prepare for departure. No 3 engine was restarted at 08.57:42hrs and the last part of the taxy checklist initiated. In response to the second officer's challenge of 'Flaps', the first officer replied 'Fifteen, fifteen, green light'. Around a minute later, the flight was cleared for take-off.

The sound of increasing engine noise could be heard at 08.59:35hrs. Take-off appeared normal for 40sec but then the aircraft's stall warning was heard. Shortly after, the CVR picked up engine compressor stall/surge sounds. A crew member called 'Engine failure', followed by the captain demanding 'Full power' 0.6sec before the sound of the first impact. Three more distinct impact sounds were on the final four seconds of the recording.

N473DA never lifted above 20ft before it began to descend. The first impact mark was made by the tail skid striking the runway centreline about 5,000ft before the upwind end of Runway 18L. The right wing hit the right side of the runway some 650ft further on, but the airliner staggered along for another 5,300ft before wiping out the ILS antenna.

All of which, combined with the engine compressor surges, pointed towards a stall on take-off. The 727's stall warning system is designed to stickshake when a wing sensor detects the approach of a stall angle of attack of 11° for flap settings from

0-2°, and 14° for flap settings of 5-15°. N473DA's warning system started stickshaking some 1.7sec after the estimated lift-off point, and continued for 20.2sec until the sound of first impact. Working from the dispatch papers, the aircraft's weight at brake release was put at 157,683lb for which the required take-off flap setting was 15°. The Flight Data Recorder showed the 727 getting airborne 807ft beyond normal lift-off point, and the tail skid hitting the runway at or immediately after the main gear lifted off. A tail strike on that mark of Boeing 727 required a body angle of around 10°, but in that configuration with 15° of flap there should have been 53,105lb of lift available over and above aircraft weight. That was more than enough to prevent the 727 settling back down again, but if flaps had been up at that point, the aircraft would have weighed 984lb more than the lift produced.

A Boeing test pilot stated that the 727's wing leading edge devices greatly improved lateral stability. He noted that with flaps up, the aircraft is less tolerant of sideslip and will tend to drop a wing as angles of attack increase. Every possible combination of extended and retracted aerofoil devices, both deliberate and inadvertent, were therefore considered. Nothing was overlooked by the NTSB, including the chance that lift spoilers might have deployed during the attempted take-off. But all bar one of the spoilers were found to be stowed and locked, and after careful examination of other mechanisms, many of which were found to be irreversible or not susceptible to movement as a result of impact loading, the board had to conclude that the wing was in a clean configuration — all flaps and slats fully retracted — before impact. Most apparently damning of all, examination of the flap control mechanism in the cockpit wreckage showed it to be in the flap up position.

According to Delta's procedures at the time, the first officer was to set wing flaps to the take-off position after departing the ramp area, but only after all three engines had been started. When it became clear that Flt 1141's departure was to be delayed, the flight crew shut down No 3 engine and put a hold on carrying out the remainder of the TAXY and the BEFORE TAKE-OFF checklist items. The crew began to restart No 3 when they believed they were No 4 for take-off, but within 15sec they received clearance to enter the runway and hold for take-off. At this point the CVR showed a marked change. Up to then the checklist had been actioned in an orderly and measured manner, but thereafter the tone became rushed as second and first officers appeared to hasten through the challenges and responses while the aircraft moved from Taxiway F to the runway. Upon the second officer's prompt of 'Flaps', the first officer responded 'Fifteen, fifteen, green light', only there were no background sounds on the CVR to suggest that controls or switches were being manipulated. Furthermore the time between challenge and response was less than one second, which was not really adequate to complete the drill properly.

All three members of the flight crew told the NTSB that, by habit, they would have verified the trailing edge flap indicators and leading edge flap and slat light indicators; unfortunately, none specifically recollected having done so on the day of the accident. It is likely that the captain's attention was diverted by the visual task of taxying the 727 on to the runway and that the second officer was striving to complete the checklist in preparation for flight. Consequently, neither of these two men looked specifically at the instrument panel to verify the first officer's response.

But the 727 is equipped with a system whereby a horn blows to warn the crew when the aircraft is improperly configured for take-off. This system is activated when No 3 thrust lever is advanced and, among other things, the outboard trailing flaps are less than 5° and/or No 4 or 5 leading edge slats are not extended. The lack of any sound of this warning horn on the CVR should have proved the crew to be blameless, but post-crash investigation identified an intermittent problem in N437DA's take-off warning system that had not been detected or corrected during last scheduled maintenance. If this problem had manifested itself during Flt 1141, there would have been no aural warning of a misconfigured aircraft.

When engine power was advanced during the fateful take-off, the second officer noticed that the green 'Auto Pack Trip' arming light did not illuminate. The 727's 'Auto Pack Trip' system is designed to shut down the air conditioning system automatically in the event of an engine failure during take-off, thereby ensuring that thrust produced by the remaining engines was not reduced by air being bled off for air conditioning. One of the requirements for normal arming of the system is that the inboard trailing edge flaps are out of the 0° position. Failure of the 'Auto Pack Trip' system to arm on Flt 1141 was corroborating evidence that the inboard flaps were retracted when the take-off roll was initiated.

Once they had satisfied themselves that the 727 had not been in a 'split flap' configuration, ie 15° of flap had been selected but only the outboard flaps had extended (the inboard remaining retracted), or that the flaps had not been suddenly selected in before impact, the NTSB finally had to conclude that trailing edge flaps and leading edge devices were fully retracted when Flt 1141 began its take-off roll.

Given that the checklist had called for 15° of flap to be selected prior to take-off, but that it did not appear to have been done so, the board determined the probable cause of this accident to be 'the captain's and first officer's inadequate cockpit discipline. This resulted in the flight crew's attempt to take-off without the wing flaps and slats properly configured...Thus the flap lever was not set to the 15° detent during pre take-off activities; the first officer, as well as other crew members, did not note the actual flap position when he responded to the checklist challenge, and the airplane's take-off warning systems did not provide a warning of improper take-off configuration'.

Anyone who has worked an aircraft challenge and response checklist system day after day knows that it is all too easy to fall into the habit of answering challenges by rote. When the pressure suddenly increases, as on Flt 1141, there is even more impetus to scamper along to complete the checks expeditiously. The safety board concluded that the first officer responded to the flap challenge without looking at the status of the light and indicators.

Unfortunately for the flight crew of Delta 1141, this was not the only evidence of cockpit indiscipline. The CVR held no record of the mandatory captain's briefing prior to take-off; he allowed events to happen rather than control what was going on. While the first officer acted as the social focus in the cockpit, it seemed to be left to the flight engineer to be businesslike and professional. For instance, in the absence of any requests for specific checklists, he seemed to keep track of events and initiate appropriate checklists on his own. He subtly prompted the flight attendant to leave the cockpit when the 727 became No 4 for departure by announcing over the cabin PA system that the flight attendants were to prepare for flight. This action by the second officer may also have been a not-so-subtle reminder to the captain that No 3 engine had still to be restarted.

The safety board believed that the second officer's actions were appropriate and played no part in the flap position anomaly that brought about this accident. However, they did hold the captain responsible for the logical and timely completion of cockpit duties by his crew members. The board believed that, had the captain exercised his responsibility and asked the flight attendant to leave the cockpit or, as a minimum, stopped all the non-pertinent chat, the 25min taxy period could have been utilised much more constructively and the flap position discrepancy might have been discovered in time. Furthermore the captain never perceived a need to check visually or tactually whether the first officer lowered the flaps.

And if all this was not bad enough, it should not be forgotten that a 727 can still cope on take-off with a clean wing provided that stickshaker angle of attack is not exceeded. The investigation found that the most appropriate reaction after activation of the 727 stickshaker was to apply maximum thrust and lower the aircraft nose. Had the captain of Flt 1141 done no more than apply full power within three seconds of the stick starting to shake, the aircraft would have gained 20kt and over 200ft of precious height before reaching the ILS antenna. If stickshaker angle of attack had not been exceeded, even more height would have been gained, and if either pilot had moved the flap control immediately, the extending leading edge devices would have provided sufficient stall margin to regain control. Yet far from doing any of these, the captain continued to increase angle of attack after the onset of stickshake and he never applied maximum power. Little wonder that the NTSB was not impressed.

To maintain a sense of balance, the safety board acknowledged that the accident to Flt 1141 was not unique. During the middle of 1987, Delta flight crews were involved in no less than six incidents resulting from pilot operational errors, and it was felt that the airline's management should have been more positive in its training and crew checking programmes. The NTSB went so far as to say that Delta's 'corporate philosophy of permitting maximum captain discretion contributed to the poor discipline and performance of Flt 1141's flight crew'. Furthermore, FAA inspectors had been aware of serious failings in Delta's flight operations and training programmes a full year before the accident. Because 'neither the FAA nor Delta took sufficient corrective action to eliminate known flight crew performance deficiencies', one member of the NTSB felt that both the FAA and Delta must share direct rather than contributory responsibility for the accident.

All of which shows that there are lessons for everyone from the Flt 1141 accident. Right at the top, national aviation agencies cannot confine themselves to making lofty pronouncements on standards; having identified irregularities, they owe it to all concerned to ensure that remedial action is taken. One step further down, other airlines will doubtless follow the same path as Delta did in the mid-80s involving a period of rapid growth including merger with another airline. Yet no amount of wheeling and dealing in the market economy should ever make an airline so big or so busy that it loosens its grip on training, checking and operating programmes.

But if evidence was ever needed that the buck stops with the aircrew, it was provided on 1 August 1989. After an 'exhaustive' internal inquiry, Delta Air Lines found that the flight crew on Flt 1141 'failed to set the aircraft's flaps and slats in the proper take-off configuration as required by established Delta practices and procedures'. In consequence Delta fired the 49-yr old captain, a 24-yr veteran of Delta with about 17,000 flight hours at the time of the crash, the 38-yr old first officer, a 10-yr Delta veteran with some 6,500hr, and the 32-yr old second officer who had about 1,500hr.

For those who felt such action to be hard, the CVR transcript indicated that the captain did not initiate even one checklist; the second officer called out only one checklist complete; required callouts were not made by the captain during engine start; the captain did not give a take-off briefing; the sterile cockpit policy was violated, and all crew members did not notice that the flaps were in the up position prior to take-off. It is a harsh truth that aircrew are paid large sums not simply to pose in designer uniforms but in preparation for that possibly once in a lifetime emergency when a human has to be on hand to take over from an errant machine. To put it bluntly, if you take the money and status while the flying is easy, you must be willing to carry the can if you screw up an emergency. Worse still, if you cause an emergency that kills people where none existed before, just be grateful to be alive.

If there is any sympathy around after Flt 1141, it ought to go to the poor flight engineer. He had been with Delta less than a year, and he alone on that 727 flight deck appeared to try his best to operate in a professional manner. But the whole crew hung together as Delta reacted to the NTSB observation that the difference in safety performance between air carriers 'appears to be the strong emphasis by top management on safety issues and management's acknowledgement of its accountability in that regard'. As an official said, 'We don't stand up when the news is good and duck it when it's bad'.

Delta made positive changes after the crash of Flt 1141, not least in the establishment of a programme which retaught each flight employee the paramount importance of cockpit discipline in the accomplishment of checklists. On Flt 1141, the first officer substituted expectation for reality in his rush to complete the checks in time for take-off. But over-hastiness should not be regarded as the only potential pitfall. The repetitive nature of the whole challenge and response business, carried out in the glowing darkness of a cockpit, can come to resemble the lulling intonation of a sacred mantra. Unless concentration is maintained, it becomes all too easy to chant the expected response from memory without actually observing the

The Fairchild Metro 3, a commuter airliner that will continue the safe and sterling work it has done around the globe over recent years provided it is handled properly. Fairchild

appropriate indicator, light or switch. Take care not to respond with the indication you have seen a thousand times before, rather than the one displayed there and then.

But in spite of all the psychologists' studies into man/machine interactions and evaluations of how interpersonal relationships among flight personnel affect performance of cockpit duties, nothing puts it better than Sod's Law — 'If something can go wrong, it will do'. On Flt 1141, the dreadful outcome of the human errors perpetrated on that flight deck should have been avoided by the take-off warning system highlighting that the 727 was misconfigured; after all, the device had only been installed by Boeing in the first place because too many aircrew in the past had done what the crew of Flt 1141 were just about to do. But on the very day that the flight crew left their collective minds in neutral, the kit that should have provided their aural salvation also chose to malfunction. Technology should never become a substitute for the human brain in any cockpit, or a crutch for human frailty.

Certainly no amount of technology will offset the truly negligent operator. At 18.20hrs (Mountain Standard Time) on 19 January 1988 a Fairchild Metro 3, belonging to Trans-Colorado Airlines and designated Flt 2286, departed Denver's Stapleton Airport. The twin Garrett-engined commuter airliner, registration number N68TC, had two pilots and 15 passengers on board. Once airborne, N68TC set off on a typical Metro commuter schedule around the state of Colorado.

First stop was Durango (DRO), situated some 240 miles southwest at the base of the San Juan Mountains. Founded by the Denver and Rio Grande Railroad back in 1880, Durango had served as gateway to Colorado's riches for Indians, fur traders, prospectors, ranchers, engineers and now tourists. But whomsoever came and went, the best description of this town of around 11,500 inhabitants remains that of Will Rogers: 'It's out of the way and glad of it'.

Trans-Colorado Flt 2286 climbed uneventfully out of Denver, reaching its assigned FL230 just after 18.53hrs. It was reasonable to assume that First Officer Ralph Harvey was flying because Capt Stephen Silver worked the radios throughout. He acknowledged the DRO 18.03hrs weather observation of, 'indefinite ceiling 800, sky obscured, visibility one mile light snow and fog, temperature 25, dew point 25, wind is calm'.

At 19.00:40hrs, Denver ARTCC asked the Metro crew if they would 'rather shoot the ILS or will the (VOR) DME approach to Runway 20 be sufficient?' The commander replied that they would take the DME approach, whereupon Trans-Colorado 2286 was cleared to proceed to the DRO 023° radial/11 miles Initial Approach Fix (IAF). At about 19.05hrs, the airline agent at Durango was advised on company radio frequency that the flight was 25min out and would not need to uplift fuel.

There is some pretty high ground around this part of the Rockies, and Durango airport is 6,685ft above sea level. At first therefore, Denver ARTCC cleared the Metro to descend at pilot's discretion to 16,000ft. At 19.10:19hrs this was extended to 15,000ft. Just over three minutes later, ARTCC told the pilots to cross the IAF at or above 14,000ft and cleared them for a VOR/DME Runway 20 approach to the airport. Capt Silver did not respond immediately and the clearance was repeated. He then came back with the statement that they were 'down at 14 (ie 14,000ft) and we're cleared for the approach'. At 19.16:15hrs, Denver informed Flt 2286 that radar coverage was terminated. Six seconds later, the captain responded, '2286 Wilco'. There were to be no more transmissions.

On commencing descent, a Metro crew member briefed passengers accordingly and asked them to fasten their seatbelts. One passenger noted flaps being extended

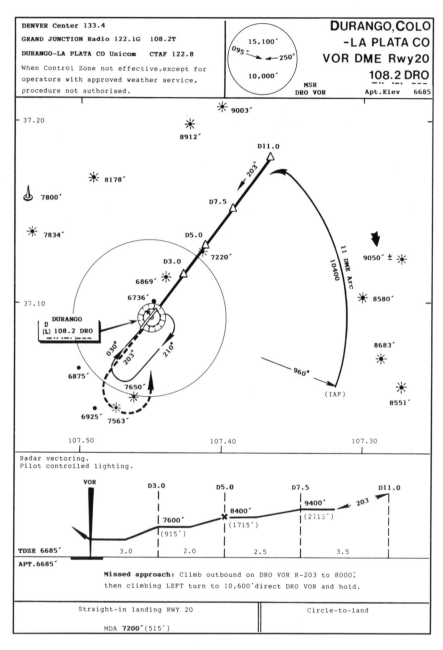

Published VOR/DME approach to Runway 20, Durango Airport. Instead of flying to the Initial Approach Fix (IAF), and then descending round the 11 DME arc to get down in a relatively sedate fashion, Trans-Colorado 2286 was brought straight in on a 203° heading to fly down a 023 radial. Given the Metro's routeing from Denver to the northeast, this direct approach saved the time involved in flying to the IAF and then backtracking, but at much greater eventual cost.

116

and saw houses and lights on the ground. There was nothing to alarm anybody until the last few moments when the Metro appeared to level off briefly, hit hard, followed by an abrupt pitch-up and increase in engine power. N68TC rolled several times laterally before striking some trees about 6-8ft below the top of a hill. Still maintaining a heading of about 198°, it then cleared the hill only to come down again near the bottom of the opposite slope. The Metro slid about 300ft along snow-covered terrain before coming to a stop some five miles from the airport.

At 20.04hrs DRO airport reported Flt 2286 overdue. Half an hour later a local resident rang in to say that a man had just reported surviving an aircraft crash. Five other passengers, including a 23-month old who had to be carried, walked together for 90min over the mile and a half to a highway. There they met a motorist who transported them until he met a responding rescue vehicle.

About 22.26hrs the crash site was located. Rescue units using snowmobiles, ambulances, ski patrol sleds and a bulldozer were directed to the remote location, where they found that the wreckage had stayed essentially upright though the wing had separated from its fuselage attachment fittings. The right engine and nacelle hung down from the wing, connected by little more than control cables, while the left engine had been torn completely from its mounting and was now buried in snow. The aircraft was crushed from the nose to first row of passenger seats, and both pilots died from multiple impact trauma. Four passengers were also killed, and rescue of the remainder was hampered by snow, darkness and extreme cold. Two more passengers died during evacuation, followed by another the next day. The last survivor was transported from the scene at 00.30hrs.

No defects were found in any of N68TC's systems, engines or airframe, and the NTSB found that all navigation aids were operating within acceptable parameters. The question to be answered was why the pilots let the Metro descend below minimum descent altitude (MDA) without keeping clear of the ground during the VOR/DME approach to Durango's Runway 20.

Although its value was put at $3 million, the destroyed Metro was not equipped, nor was it required to be equipped, with a FDR or a CVR. Notwithstanding, data provided by Denver ARTCC showed the safety board that at 19.15:48hrs, Trans-Colorado Flt 2286 was 11 miles on the 023° radial of the VOR/DME approach to DRO. However, it was still at 14,000ft flying at a ground speed of 195kt when at that stage of the approach it should have been down at 10,400ft. So instead of the crew only having to get rid of 3,715ft in order to arrive at DRO airport elevation in a leisurely and civilised fashion (a speed of 135kt and descent rate of about 900ft/min would have sufficed) ARTCC evidence showed the Metro's rate of descent increasing to over 3,000ft/min. N68TC crashed about 19.20hrs, and radar data revealed that its groundspeed rose to over 190kt in the last seconds of flight.

Had the flight crew followed the approach as published, they would have gone first to the Initial Approach Fix on the 096 radial. If they had then followed the 11 DME arc as advertised, they would have given themselves time to descend from 14,000 to 10,400ft with ease before turning on to the 203° final heading. Because they elected to fly straight in, the Metro had to descend at a rate more than three times that intended for this approach. Such a direct approach was not unusual, especially if the crew was behind time, but as one captain said, it was only safe 'as long as you're set up in advance and there's a minimum tail wind.' Met data showed that Flt 2286 was affected by a constant tailwind of at least 10-15kt throughout the approach.

The safety board believed that the short scheduled flight time between Denver and Durango discouraged Trans-Colorado pilots from flying the full approach pattern, and that such scheduling worked against prudent decision-making by flight crews. The captain of Flt 2286 also had a reputation for keeping to schedule. The board concluded that he chose the VOR/DME rather than the ILS approach to save time.

Yet irrespective of company schedules, the Metro's crew was still required to act in the best interests of flight safety: if that meant opting for a safer if longer alternative, so be it. Moreover, even though the 42-yr old first officer had accrued some 8,500hr of flight time, of which about 305 were on the Metro, his records revealed repeated weaknesses in his instrument flying. The safety board believed that by-passing the IAF and flying the VOR/DME approach to Runway 20 straight in from 14,000ft in instrument flying conditions required a high degree of skill and ability, and that on the basis of his past performance, 'the first officer did not possess these abilities.'

But this is being wise after the event. Back on the flight deck of Trans-Colorado Flt 2286, the crew was in possession of full weather information and in allowing his co-pilot to fly the approach into the restricted weather conditions around Durango, the captain behaved no differently from other company pilots. At that stage he was not supervising something that was doomed to fail. He just needed to ensure that crew co-ordination and judgement was of a particularly good standard given that the approach would be made more challenging by the high level at which it started and the tailwinds into which it ran lower down. An integral part of the captain's command role was to monitor his co-pilot closely to ensure that he maintained situational awareness and did not fly below the published descent profile.

In the event it is clear what happened. Locked on to instruments while flying a particularly demanding approach manoeuvre, the first officer must have lost a grip of the aircraft and its three-dimensional situation. His chances of seeing the airfield visually before MDA were lessened by the moonlight being blotted out on a particularly dark and overcast night. Eventually he allowed the aircraft to descend below permissible altitude and strike the ground.

But why did Capt Silver allow this to happen? Having been described by Trans-Colorado's Chief Pilot as a good operator, very intelligent and self-confident with a casual style, surely the captain would have talked his first officer through the approach or, *in extremis*, taken control himself to ensure that the Metro and all on board did not come to grief. The answer only came once the bodies had been examined by the Center of Human Toxicology at the University of Utah. Samples from the body of the first officer were found to be free of alcohol and all drugs, but the same could not be said of the captain. His body revealed the presence of the principal metabolite of cocaine in sufficient quantities to indicate that it had been ingested 12-18hr before the accident, which tied in with a reported statement by the captain's fiancee that, 'the night before we had done a bag of cocaine'. Moreover, there was evidence to show that the captain was not a novice cocaine user. The board concluded that ingestion of cocaine had impaired the captain's perceptual skills and piloting abilities at the time of the accident. In other words, the drug had made him so tired that he was unable either to monitor the first pilot's operation of Trans-Colorado Flt 2286 or fly the blessed thing properly himself. Therefore, although the NTSB found the probable cause of the accident to be 'the first officer's flying and the captain's ineffective monitoring of an unstabilised approach that resulted in a descent below the published descent profile', contributing to the accident 'was the degradation of the captain's performance resulting from his use of cocaine before the accident'.

Once the stone was turned over, all manner of other nasties crawled out. The 36-yr old captain had been involved in a Cessna 182 crash in 1983, but Trans-Colorado seemed unaware of this. There were further repeated instances of the captain violating rules and procedures, exemplifying what the board could only describe as 'a cavalier attitude to the need for rigorous adherence'. This indictment was reinforced by the captain's record of a relatively large number of road traffic convictions, plus falsification of both a state driver's licence application and a FAA medical certificate application. To crown it all, although the first officer's flying weaknesses had been noted by a previous employer, Trans-Colorado remained ignorant of these deficiencies when they hired him.

The safety board believed that more FAA guidance should be given to operators of scheduled revenue passenger services to help them obtain relevant information from previous employers about the skills and abilities of prospective pilots. But preventing other commanders behaving as Capt Silver had done was more difficult. None of his colleagues reported observing any actions that they considered unusual or indicative of drug use, although several witnessed behaviour variously described as 'angry', 'carrying on' or violating relatively routine company procedures. It was all so easy after the event to say, 'Someone should have noticed and done something before the accident happened', but real life is never that easy. Everybody has off-days, and it takes a very brave person to report another to higher authority especially if, as in the case of Capt Silver, he was regarded by many in the airline as a highly skilled pilot with whom it was generally enjoyable to fly. All the NTSB could say was that there was a need to pursue the detection of drug use among applicants for medical certificates more vigorously.

It may only have been a coincidence that within three months of the Durango accident, Trans-Colorado had filed for bankruptcy and by July 1988 had ceased operations altogether. 'Junkie in the Cockpit' does not make for good airline public relations, but it would be wrong to dismiss the Durango accident as a one-off affecting a now defunct minor airline. After a Boeing 737 crashed in New York in 1989 killing over 30 people, the aircrew vanished from the scene to cover up the fact that they had been drinking. The following year, a federal jury in Minneapolis returned guilty verdicts against three former Northwest Airlines pilots charged with flying a 727 after, in the case of the aircraft commander, imbibing 15-20 rum and Cokes the night before. Perhaps pilots are no more flying under the influence than they ever did, but it certainly seems that way.

Ever since the barnstorming age, professional aviators have been perceived as far from quiet and retiring individuals. Indeed many have thrived on, and encouraged the image of, being derring-doers who work hard and play hard, and not a few paying passengers have had cause to be grateful for having Capt Wonderful up front rather than Capt Meek. But with the adulation and the praise, especially from other pilots, can come the inflated ego and belief that regulations, especially those that cramp the life style, only apply to smaller fry. There is not much one can do about that in an open society other than beat the education drum and reinforce the point that use of drink or drugs before flight can easily render the greatest operator medically unqualified to act as a flight crew member. Apart from adding a whole new dimension to the term 'flying high', the Durango accident revealed both the danger of drug use in aviation and the difficulty faced by the aviation community in trying to control it.

POWER FAILURE

When the British aeronautical industry comprised a multiplicity of firms, each run by a distinguished name, one particularly noble Lord was asked why he made a habit of only flying in four-engined aircraft. Back came the answer in a flash: 'because there aren't any five-engined aeroplanes'. This was not strictly correct but the sentiment is understandable. Engines are pretty crucial to the whole business of heavier-than-air flight, and wise pilots soon come to appreciate the truth of the old adage that lift is a gift, but thrust is a must.

On 19 July 1989, United Airlines DC-10 N1819U took off from Denver with 285 passengers and 11 crew members bound for Chicago. Everything went to plan until United Flt 232 was cruising at FL370 across Iowa. Suddenly there was a 'severe explosion' of sufficient magnitude to throw the chief flight attendant to the floor. Capt Al Haynes, a United employee since 1956, reported at 15.16hrs that he had lost No 2 engine. Located as it was in the aircraft's tail along the centreline, this engine's loss should have posed little or no handling problems. But almost immediately after hearing the bang from the rear, flight engineer Dudley Dvorak saw his gauges indicate a total loss of hydraulic fluid. At 15.17hrs Capt Haynes reported that his hydraulic systems were not functioning properly, followed by the statement that he had 'almost no controllability, little elevator and almost no aileron'. By the time the chief flight attendant reached the flightdeck to report on her unnerving experience, she found the crew already struggling to control the DC-10. At 15.20hrs Flt 232 declared an emergency.

N1819U was turned back towards the nearest diversion airfield — Sioux City's Gateway Airport — where the primary 17/35 runway was 8,999ft long and 150ft wide. It is not often that a crew relishes having a checking officer on board, but they had cause to be grateful that Check Capt Dennis Fitch was sitting on the jump seat that day. As Al Haynes and First Officer William Records did 'double-time' with the yoke, Capt Fitch knelt between them manipulating the throttles at their direction. But in spite of this concerted effort, Capt Haynes finally reported that he was having difficulty controlling the aircraft. Gateway Tower pointed out smaller airports and four-lane highways in the vicinity, but ultimately it was decided to try and set the DC-10 down on Sioux City's Runway 22 which was only 6,888ft long and no longer actively in use. In fact 04/22 had been relegated to serve as a taxiway, and it was there that firefighting crews of the Iowa Air National Guard's 185th Tactical Fighter Group, which were based at the airport, assembled in preparation for the emergency landing. The 24 firefighters with their crash trucks and 2,000gal water tanker had to move off pretty sharpish once they realised where the DC-10 was attempting to land.

The time was now nearing 16.00hrs. USAF Maj Harry Greer, one of a quartet of A-7D fighter pilots who had just touched down, spotted the DC-10 when it was about two miles on finals for Runway 22. The airliner was wings-level and descending in an apparently normal landing profile when, at about 50ft above the ground, Greer noted a slight correction to the left followed by a right wing drop.

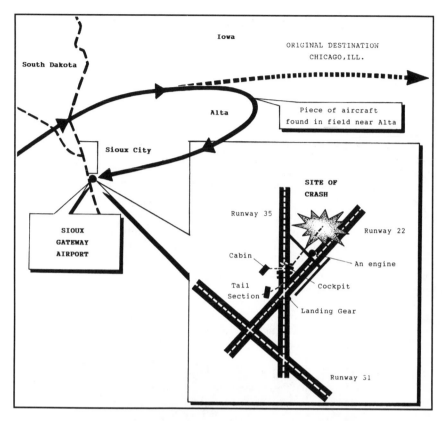

The path flown by United Flt 232 into Sioux City's Gateway Airport following engine and hydraulics failure on 18 July 1989. As the airliner turned back from the Chicago direction towards Sioux City, some pieces of engine and tail broke away, including an 8×12ft section which landed near Alta, Iowa.

The DC-10 still seemed to be in a position to land — fortunately, the landing gear could be lowered by gravity — but at about 20ft the right wing continued dipping to a 20-30° bank before finally hitting the ground. The aircraft then nosed in and rolled over, breaking up into three large parts while cutting a 4,000ft long by one foot deep gouge in the tarmac from the 22 threshold to a point across Runway 17/35 where the largest pieces came to rest. The aircraft was then engulfed in a fireball but to the amazement of those who fought the intense conflagration, many survivors walked away from the wreckage unassisted. It was the break-up of the DC-10 into sections which enabled just under 200 people, including all flightdeck personnel (once a forklift separated the tangled cockpit area wreckage), to get out before the blaze really intensified. Ten of these were to die later from serious burn injuries, but although this made a total of 111 fatalities (including 2 infants) from the United DC-10 crash, 185 of the 296 persons on board Flt 232 amazingly survived.

The DC-10's FDR confirmed that the crew had lost all hydraulic fluid and nearly all powered flying controls. As on all modern high speed jet aircraft, the DC-10 has no manual reversion, though with McDonnell Douglas providing so many back-ups

Above:
A United Airlines DC-10, a Series 10 version optimised for US domestic operations.

Below:
Part of the DC-10 fuselage, lying in a cornfield near the north end of Sioux City's Gateway Airport, after crashing on 19 July 1989. Associated Press

there should have been no need. DC-10 flight controls are powered exclusively by three hydraulic systems, unsurprisingly labelled Nos 1, 2 and 3, and driven by the left, centre and right engines respectively. Reversible motor-pumps can transfer power between Systems 1 and 3, as well as between 2 and 3. Aircraft can even fly with only one operative hydraulic system; a pilot who tried it found control authority to be limited and the controls sluggish and heavy, but the aircraft could be landed safely. Yet the DC-10 over Iowa should have been nowhere near as badly off as that. It had only lost No 2 engine; Nos 1 and 3 should have kept the controls functioning perfectly normally. Why then were two apparently serviceable engines incapable of providing a single hydraulic power source between them?

Although the once intact N1819U was fifteen years old, within a fortnight of the accident a FAA executive was able to say that, 'this is not an airplane problem, but an engine problem'. The DC-10 had been powered by General Electric CF6-6 engines which, in the airline's opinion, had established an 'admirable reliability record over the years'. When the No 2 engine was recovered from where it fell off during the crash, the entire fan section, including a 300lb disc, and part of the rotor were found to be missing. These key parts possibly separated at the time of the failure, and an intense search involving a whole host of people ranging from Iowa and Nebraska National Guards to the young men and women who worked the corn and bean fields at that time of year was mounted to try and find the remains.

Meanwhile the DC-10's tail was erected in a Sioux City airport hangar. No 2 engine was reinstalled in position with chicken wire filling the gaps and strings and ribbons tracing the paths of destruction. As part of the second-stage disc and much of the remaining engine were recovered, the first-stage fan disc of No 2 engine became the prime suspect. Investigators eventually found that when this fan disc disintegrated at 37,000ft, it flung out shrapnel in all directions. Fifty hits were found on the tail structure, including one measuring 10in x 12in, and among other effects the debris burst severed the three separate hydraulic lines. This led to the loss of all hydraulic fluid, leaving the crew with almost no aircraft control. 'The disintegration of the fan was of such magnitude that it tore all the lines . . . even in the side walls of the aircraft.' The experts were unsure whether any hydraulic system design could have survived the disintegration that befell United Flt 232.

The natural cry after such accidents is that 'something must be done' to prevent a recurrence. The key to the Sioux City accident was the failure of the first-stage fan

Rear fuselage detail of the McDonnell Douglas DC-10. The General Electric CF6-6 engine is well aft, above both the bulkhead-mounted hydraulic accumulator and associated hydraulic lines. Cross-section A shows where the hydraulic lines ran; all three systems served the flying controls in the tailplane and fin.

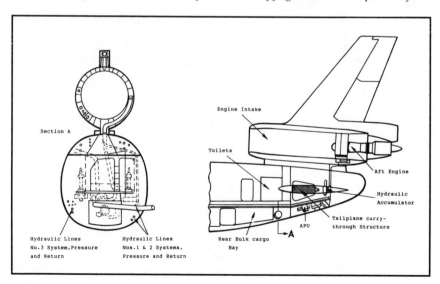

disc, and General Electric immediately recalled the discs from six engines in use with four world airlines that had been forged from the same block of titanium. Yet replacing discs was really only a palliative. Although CF6-6 fan sections had failed before, discs had always remained on the engine. 'We have never had anything like this one,' declared a NTSB investigator, and herein lay the rub. If a one-off accident occurs, how much time, effort and expense do you expend to guard against the effects of another chance in a million? Designers could quintuplicate hydraulic lines to give even greater redundancy, or shield potentially explosive rotating discs with armour plating, but there would be a considerable weight penalty. No cost-effective aircraft can be designed to withstand a freak event, and it invariably comes back to balancing risk against the maximum cost that the travelling public will pay for the convenience of flying from A to B.

So despite all the worthy checks that maintainers carry out on potentially vulnerable component parts of their aircraft, anything mechanical can fail and engines are no exception. Far more engine malfunctions occur in flight than the public hears about, but generally misbehaving engines are shut down and the remainder of the flight completed in a calm and organised manner by crews who spend many a flight simulator hour training for just such eventualities. One reassuring fact is that modern engines are much more reliable than their predecessors, and when something does go wrong, the average engine malfunction is no big deal even at great speed. On 1 January 1990, an Air France Concorde left Kennedy Airport for Paris. It had reached a speed of Mach 1.39 over the Atlantic when the root of a second-stage low-pressure compressor blade ruptured in one of the 38,400lb-thrust Rolls-Royce Olympus engines. The crew returned to New York where extensive damage was found to have been caused to both the engine and its adjacent plumbing. Apart from some delayed personal travel schedules though, this incident probably had no effect whatsoever on the passengers.

Yet that does not mean that crews can only wait stoically for the very rare occasion when things go really wrong. In the aftermath of his Sioux City experience, Capt Al Haynes paid credit to United's Cockpit Resource Management programme for enabling his crew to work as a team and maintain as much control as they did. This programme had its origins in a NASA study, initiated after a world-wide series of accidents affecting multi-crew aircraft, which revealed that in most cases these accidents were caused by a temporary loss of situational awareness brought about by a momentary but critical breakdown of crew co-operation on the flightdeck. The fact that many of the affected airlines already placed great emphasis on good crew co-operation and flightdeck discipline was irrelevant. It seemed to NASA that the airline operating environment had now become so complex that traditional methods of nurturing cockpit management skills could no longer adequately meet the demands being placed regularly on individual crew members in the normal course of their duties.

The NASA study led eventually to the development of a highly effective short training course pioneered by United Airlines but which later came to be adopted by many other operators around the world. Briefly, the programme balances human relationships with emphasised awareness of cockpit resources. Crew members learn how to contribute to the team effort through inquiry and advocacy, resolve conflicting viewpoints constructively, make effective use of criticism, and gain a better understanding of the decision-making process within a group. The end product is a crew member who is much more aware of the contribution he or she can make to the successful management of the flight, leading in turn to a more cohesive crew and thereby greater safety in the overall conduct of operations. In particular this form of training was found to engender a higher degree of situational awareness among the crew. From this came the increased possibility that some member would identify and speak out about those insidious situations where danger looms, but where the threat of catastrophe is not immediately apparent either to the flying pilot or to the aircraft commander who may be temporarily overloaded or preoccupied with more immediate concerns.

Proof of the pudding came when Capt Haynes said that his four-man DC-10 crew agreed among themselves 'before anything was done'. Some might argue that all this balancing concern for performance with concern for other people is so much mumbo-jumbo, and that is needed in an emergency is no more and no less than a bit of good old fashioned firm leadership. The only trouble is, as latest technology offers more airliners with less engines controlled by fewer aircrew, there can be times when circumstances drive two people to act with just as much haste and no less speed than one.

On 8 January 1989, G-OBME, a Boeing 737-400 operated by British Midland Airways, was scheduled to fly a double shuttle between London/Heathrow and Belfast/Aldergrove. G-OBME landed at Heathrow at 18.45hrs on completion of the first shuttle, and after a quick turn round and embarkation of 118 passengers (including one infant), took-off again for Belfast at 19.52hrs. Capt Kevin Hunt, aged 43 and a British Midland employee since 1966, commanded Flt BD092. He was to work the radios on this leg while First Officer David McClelland, aged 39, flew the aircraft. A flight service manager plus five cabin attendants brought the crew complement up to eight.

After a standard instrument departure from Heathrow, the 737's onboard computer was programmed to take it north into the Daventry control area. Having reached FL350, Midland 92 was to coast out over Wallasey and then fly Airway Upper Blue 3 across the Irish Sea. Estimated arrival time in Belfast was 20.50hrs, leaving only the return flight to Heathrow to complete the crew's working day.

At 20.05:05hrs, as G-OBME was passing through FL283 some 20nm south-southeast of East Midlands Airport routeing directly towards Trent VOR beacon, the crew suddenly experienced moderate to severe vibration and smelled fire. Although no fire warning or other visual or aural attention-getter made its presence felt, Capt Hunt took control of the aircraft and disengaged the autopilot. He did not glean any clear indication of the source of the problem from the instruments, but he thought that the smoke and fumes were coming forward from the passenger cabin. From his knowledge of the air conditioning system, this led him to suspect No 2 (the right) engine.

The first officer was also monitoring the engine instruments and, when asked by Capt Hunt which engine was causing the trouble, he replied, 'It's the le....it's the right one'. 'Okay', responded Capt Hunt, 'throttle it back', whereupon autothrottle was disengaged and No 2 throttled back. During the 11sec that had elapsed since Capt Hunt took control manually, the aircraft had rolled through 16° to the left but the commander applied no corrective aileron or rudder.

Within a couple of seconds of No 2 being throttled back, the 737 rolled level again, the shuddering ceased and both smell and visual signs of smoke appeared to have lessened. Meanwhile, the first officer was advising London Air Traffic Control (LATCC) that Midland 92 had an emergency situation which looked like an engine fire. The commander then ordered, 'Shut it down.' Some 43sec had now elapsed since the onset of vibration but then the commander said, 'Seems to be running alright now. Let's just see if it comes in'. Shutdown was further postponed as David McClelland responded to a LATCC query about which alternative airfield they wished to go to. The first officer said that it looked as if they would opt for East Midlands Airport (Castle Donington) but LATCC was to standby. He then told the commander that he was about to start the 'Engine Failure and Shutdown' checklist, adding 'Seems we have stabilised. We've still got the smoke'. Checklist action was further delayed while the commander called British Midland Airways (BMA) Operations to brief them on the situation. Two minutes and seven seconds after the start of the vibration, while waiting for a response from BMA Operations, No 2 engine fuel cock was finally closed and the auxiliary power unit (APU) started. The commander was convinced that he was taking the right action because as soon as No 2 engine was shut down, all evidence of smell and smoke seemed to clear from the flight deck. BMA Operations then transmitted, 'Divert to East Midlands please'.

Power was reduced on No 1 engine shortly afterwards at the start of the diversion. This engine continued to operate at reduced power with no signs of unserviceability other than higher than normal vibration and increased fuel flow indications. The high vibration reading continued for a further three minutes before falling progressively until it reached a little higher than normal on the cockpit indicator. For the remainder of the flight, the commander saw nothing on his instruments or from any other source to contradict his opinion that the emergency had been successfully concluded and that No 1 engine was operating normally.

The picture differed further back. As the 737 approached FL280 in the climb-out, the six stewards and stewardesses had already served complimentary drinks and were just beginning to distribute dinner — a pork salad — when both they and their passengers heard an unusual noise accompanied by moderate to severe vibration. Some were aware of smoke, variously resembling 'rubber', 'oil' or 'hot metal', while many saw 'fire', 'torching' or 'sparks' emanating from the left engine. Several flight attendants described the vibration as low, repetitive thudding, 'like a car backfiring', while the trio working the rear of the cabin saw evidence of fire from No 1 engine. Soon after No 2 engine was shut down, the commander asked flight service manager Ali Osman, 'Did you get smoke in the cabin back there?' Came the reply, 'Yes we did'. The commander then instructed that the cabin be cleared and everything packed away.

About a minute later Ali Osman returned to report, 'Sorry to trouble you...the passengers are very very panicky'. No 2 engine having been shut down only some five miles south of Castle Donington, Capt Hunt broadcast reassuringly over the public address system that trouble with the right engine had produced some smoke in the cabin, the engine was now shut down and they could expect to land at East Midlands Airport in about 10min. The flight attendants who saw signs of fire from the left engine later stated that they failed to hear their commander's reference to the right engine. Many passengers seated on the left side who had witnessed the same signs were puzzled by the apparent discrepancy, but despite continuing vibration no-one felt confident enough to say anything to the cabin crew.

Being so close to East Midlands Airport (EMA), there was no way in which the airliner could fly straight in from that height. Midland 92 was therefore cleared to turn right and descend initially to FL100, during which time it was handed over to Manchester ATC. Manchester then passed headings to enable the 737 to carry on descending to the north of the airport before being finally brought in for an ILS approach to Runway 27. During the descent, Capt Hunt continued to fly G-OBME manually while First Officer McClelland worked the radios, obtained EMA weather and wrestled unsuccessfully for two minutes to programme the flight management system to display the East Midlands landing pattern. At 20.12:28hrs the commander attempted to take stock of the situation by asking, 'Now what indications did we actually get? Just rapid vibrations in the aeroplane — smoke . . .'. His discussions with the first officer were then interrupted by ATC passing a new radar heading, further descent clearance to FL40 and instructions to change to East Midlands Approach Control. As soon as contact was established, the first officer began to read the one-engine inoperative descent and approach checklist. This activity was in turn interrupted by the approach controller asking for a test call to the aerodrome fire service, but a transmission by the commander elicited no response. The approach checklist was finally completed at 20.17:33hrs when the airliner was descending through 6,500ft and 15nm from touchdown. One minute later G-OBME was turned south of the extended runway centreline, and shortly afterwards Capt Hunt called for wing flaps to be selected to 1°. Throughout the descent there were further distractions from other aircraft using the same frequency as Midland 92.

Approaching 3,000ft the aircraft was turned starboard back towards the centreline, during which power was momentarily increased on No 1 engine to maintain height prior to G-OBME being cleared down to 2,000ft. The commander began a slow descent, calling successively for 2° and then 5° of flap. Gear was lowered after turning on to the centreline at 2,000ft, and on passing the outer marker 4.3nm from touchdown Capt Hunt called for 15° of flap. One minute later, when the 737 was 2.4nm from touchdown passing 900ft, No 1 engine suddenly stopped pushing out power. The commander immediately called for No 2 to be restarted and while the first officer strove to comply, Capt Hunt raised the aircraft's nose in an effort to reach the runway by 'stretching the glide'. Seventeen seconds after power loss, No 1 engine fire warning bell sounded, followed seven seconds later by the GPWS which operated with increasing frequency as G-OBME descended below the glideslope. The commander rescinded his order to carry out the fire drill, and at 20.24:33hrs he broadcast twice over the cabin address system, 'Prepare for crash landing'. Two seconds later, airspeed fell below 125kt. This being within some 7% of stalling speed, the stall warner automatically vibrated both control columns continuously until the airliner struck the ground at 20.24:43hrs.

Falling at 8.5ft/sec, G-OBME initially impacted at 113kt in a nose-high attitude in a level field at Molehill Farm just to the east of the M1 motorway near the Leicestershire village of Kegworth. Apart from losing the tail skid and APU door, and having both main landing gear legs dragged backwards, the airliner remained intact as it demolished a section of fencing on the eastern crest of the motorway. In the process of dropping 30ft across the motorway, it cut a swathe through trees growing on the embankment and lost 6ft of outboard left wing while fracturing a central lamp standard. As the central reservation barrier was being deformed by a now separated starboard undercarriage leg, the 737 finally collided with the base of the western embankment between 80-100kt. The fuselage was extensively shattered at this stage; the nose section travelled furthest up the embankment, the centre-section remained upright with wings attached and the tail-section buckled up almost inverted to the right. Although 39 passengers died in the accident, plus a further eight later from their injuries, the final toll could have been much worse had the crippled 737 not managed to avoid both the southern edge of Kegworth village and every vehicle on that busy motorway. Of the other 79 occupants on board Midland 92, 74 suffered serious injury including Capt Hunt. If only G-OBME's glide could have been stretched for another 3,000ft, it would have reached the safety of the Runway 27 threshold.

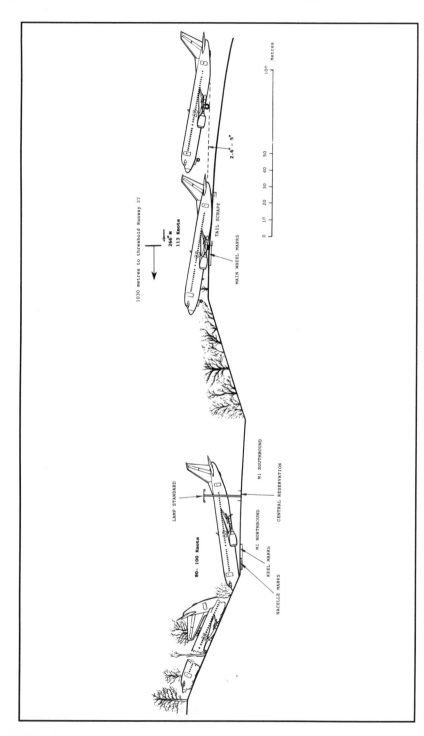

Midland 92's impact sequence at Kegworth on 8 January 1989.

After being notified of the accident, an AAIB investigating team began on-site work at Kegworth early next morning. In determining why so many lives had been lost, not to mention an airliner so new that British Midland had not yet given it a name, the flight recorders were to be of primary importance. G-OBME was fitted with a Sundstrand FDR, capable of recording 25hrs' worth of parameters and specific events on magnetic tape. It also carried a Fairchild CVR, an endless loop device of 30min duration which recorded pick-ups from the cabin address system, the flight deck and both pilots' microphones and headsets on four separate audio tracks.

Going back to the climb-out from Heathrow, the first sign of trouble came when the flight crew suddenly heard an unusual noise, accompanied by vibration, while passing FL283. Very soon afterwards there was a smell of fire and possibly some visible smoke in the cockpit. The pilots interpreted all this as evidence of a serious engine malfunction, which combined with the risk of associated fire, led them to act very quickly to contain what they perceived to be a potentially dangerous situation.

The CVR provided a confirmatory sound of 'rattling' and the FDR showed significant fluctuations in lateral and longitudinal accelerations. However, all FDR signs of severe vibration, rising exhaust gas temperature and fluctuating fan speed and fuel flow were confined to the left (No 1) engine.

Throughout the period of what must have been compressor surging on No 1, the FDR showed no problem with the other powerplant. Nevertheless, when asked by his commander which engine was causing the trouble, the first officer half-formed the word 'left' before saying 'right'. He was later to have no recollection of what caused him to make this assessment, though his hesitation may have arisen from genuine difficulty in interpreting engine instrument readings. Yet the AAIB believed that 'any uncertainty that he may initially have experienced appears to have been quickly resolved because, when the commander ordered him to 'Throttle it back' without specifying which engine was to be throttled back, the first officer closed No 2 throttle'.

This instruction was given some 19sec after the onset of vibration, during which time No 2 engine instruments maintained steady readings. Over the 11sec that elapsed since autopilot disengagement, the aircraft had rolled gently through 16° to the left, but the commander's failure to apply corrective aileron or rudder indicated to the AAIB that he did not detect from the aircraft's behaviour any loss of thrust from No 1 engine. Why did both pilots on Midland 92 become so mesmerised with the starboard engine when the evidence seemed to point strongly to the port? After the accident, Capt Hunt stated that he had judged No 2 engine to be at fault from his knowledge of the aircraft air conditioning system. He thought that as smoke and fumes seemed to be coming forward from the passenger cabin, and as the air for cabin conditioning came mostly from No 2 engine, the trouble must lie there. 'Whilst this reasoning might have applied fairly well to other aircraft he had flown,' stated the AAIB, 'it was flawed in this case because some of the conditioning air for the cabin of the Boeing 737-400 comes from No 1 engine.' This misjudgement possibly stemmed from the fact that despite Capt Hunt's wide experience, he had only flown 23hrs on 737-400 aircraft, but his assessment was further invalidated by the fact that it would be some time before the flight service manager confirmed that there had been smoke in the passenger cabin as well as the cockpit. The AAIB considered it to be more likely that, 'believing the first officer had seen positive indications on the engine instruments, (the commander) provisionally accepted the first officer's assessment'.

The abiding impression is that neither pilot was really sure which engine was at fault, but once each assumed that the other had seen something definite, they then fed off each other's misjudgement. It is easy to criticise with hindsight, but perhaps both pilots contributed to their chances of getting it wrong by being over-hasty in reaching a conclusion. The 737 Operations Manual was quite clear about the need for care in coping with non-normal happenings:

'Procedures that prescribe an engine shutdown must be evaluated by the Captain to ascertain if an actual shutdown or operation at reduced power is the safest course of action.

'This condition (engine fire, severe damage or separation) is recognised by . . . airframe vibration with abnormal engine indications with or without yaw. If the emergency is positively corrected, the Captain should evaluate the situation before proceeding with the next step.'

In the AAIB's opinion, the speed with which the pilots reached the wrong conclusion about which engine was at fault was contrary to both their training and operating instructions. If only they had taken more time to 'evaluate' the engine instruments (which subsequent tests showed to have been serviceable), it would have become apparent that No 2 was behaving normally and, from the large engine parameter variations that occurred when its compressor surged, that it was No 1 engine which was behaving erratically.

The provider of all this crucial information was the 737-400's Engine Instrument System (EIS), which combined what had been an array of individual electro-mechanical instruments on earlier 737 versions into two solid-state display units. One unit showed primary engine parameters such as exhaust gas temperature and fuel flow, while alongside were displayed secondary parameters for both engines such as oil pressure and vibration. Sensors fitted on each engine fed the vibration level dials displayed on the EIS scale. Criticisms would later be made of the dials' smallness — each was only the size of a 20p piece — plus their edge-lit symbology rather than old fashioned electro-mechanical pointers, but in AAIB's opinion '(the pilots') incorrect diagnosis of the problem must be attributed to their too rapid reaction and not to any failure of the engine instrument system to display the correct indications'.

Yet there would still have been time to redeem the situation had there not followed a fateful misimpression which appeared to confirm in the pilots' minds that the action they had taken in haste had in fact been correct. As soon as No 2 engine was throttled back, No 1 engine compressor surges and associated shuddering ceased. Although vibration continued to show on the FDR and be felt by many passengers, it was no longer perceived by the pilots and the burning smell seemed not to intensify. In spite of No 1 engine vibration indicator being at the top of its scale within two seconds of the onset of vibration, and remaining there for about three minutes (until after beginning the descent), both pilots were convinced that throttling back No 2 had cleared the problem. Evidence of this seemed to come 50sec later when the commander said, 'Seems to be running alright now'.

Although initial misidentification of the damaged engine set off the accident sequence, the decision to throttle back No 2 did not of itself lead directly to the crash. Indeed, the action could have been entirely appropriate if, in the absence of any positive guidance from the instruments, Capt Hunt had decided to throttle back each engine in turn to try and isolate the one causing vibration. Life only got tricky two minutes and seven seconds after the emergency began when No 2 engine, still in perfect working order, was shut down. The 737 'non-normal' checklist did not require engine shutdown in the case of severe vibration, provided there were no abnormal engine indications, nor if smoke or fumes were present in the cockpit. In closing down No 2 under the circumstances, the flight crew must have firmly believed that they were dealing with an engine fire.

Having shutdown No 2, Capt Hunt rightly decided to land at the nearest suitable airfield. He may have been influenced by the fact that Castle Donington was the company's main operating base, though it was more likely that he acted from a sense of urgency brought on by the 'fire', but in initiating a flight pattern designed to get down with minimum delay, he left himself little or no time to reconsider the nature of the emergency or to check that the actions taken up to then had been correct.

From the start of the descent, cockpit workload on G-OBME's pilots was high as they transmitted and received ATC directions, briefed British Midland Operations as well as their passengers, and completed descent and approach checks for a single-engined landing. As if that was not enough, the first officer attempted unsuccessfully to programme the flight management system for landing at a hitherto unspecified airfield, an unusual and rarely if ever practised activity, while his commander accepted a request to test call fire vehicles. Capt Hunt must have been confident that everything was in hand because he made no attempt to slow down the flight deck activity rate, re-engage the autopilot to reduce his own workload, ask ATC for a quiet frequency or resume his review of events after it had been interrupted by an ATC transmission. In the AAIB's opinion, 'there can be no doubt that the high workload in the cockpit contributed to the failure of the crew to notice the abnormally high reading on the No 1 engine vibration indicator that was evident for nearly four minutes after the initial vibration'.

It would still have been possible to restart No 2 engine in the descent, but when an increase in thrust was obtained from No 1 engine as the commander levelled momentarily at 3,000ft it must have reconfirmed to him that his previous actions had been correct. Although maximum vibration indications were again generated on the FDR, neither pilot appeared to notice anything untoward against the background of cockpit activity at the time. Four minutes later, No 1 engine lost power and the accident became inevitable. Some 50sec before the end, Capt Hunt instructed the first officer to 'Try lighting the other one up — there's nothing else you can do'. The CVR showed that the first officer tried to comply, and as the GPWS repeated its warning with increasing intensity, the commander twice said 'Try opening the other one up', but each time the first officer said 'She's not going'. Unfortunately, G-OBME was outside the envelope for a 'windmill' start, and the FDR showed no power becoming available from No 2 engine before impact.

Several passengers described heavy vibration immediately prior to the crash; one seated in the rear found it severe enough to open overhead lockers and shake out their contents. Ground witnesses under the final approach saw a fire-filled left engine intake together with flames, pulsating in union with 'thumping noises', streaming aft from the nacelle. It was this engine, together with its mate under the other wing, that would provide AAIB with the remaining pieces of the investigative jigsaw.

G-OBME was powered by two CFM 56-3C high bypass turbofan engines, each rated at 23,500lb thrust for take-off. Crash investigators found both engine nacelles to have been severely crushed and large forward sections to have become detached as the aircraft slid along the ground. Yet despite having sustained similar ground impact damage and distortion strains, No 2 engine bore no signs of the fire and significant fan blade leading edge damage that afflicted No 1.

After examination it was found that fan blade No 17 in No 1 engine had fractured following exposure to a vibratory stress level greater than that for which it had been designed. It all stemmed from a weakness which had not been detected during engine certification testing, and the net result was detachment of some 9in of outer blade which led to the series of compressor stalls. Although the detached piece of blade then lodged itself within the acoustic panels of the intake casing, its loss caused severe mechanical imbalance which allowed other blade tips to rub on abradable seals, causing smoke and burning smells to pass into the air conditioning system.

Compressor stalling on No 1 engine ceased once autothrottle was disengaged. When the left engine first lost power, the autothrottle would have tried to compensate by pumping extra fuel in. This forced the engine to stall and restart four times in 22sec, creating massive airflow distortions through the engine. Disengaging the automatics set a lower throttle lever angle than that required for a climb, allowing the engine to stabilise at a slightly lower running speed. Similarly during descent, the engine was not unduly troubled by being set to idle. However, opening up the throttle at 3,000ft on the approach must have shaken the detached piece of blade loose from its repository. Ingested into the core of the combustion chamber, it was then thrown around like a stone in a spin drier, causing 'cascading failure' of moving parts such that sections of fragmented fan blades would be found close to a piggery on the approach two miles short of the crash site.

Extensive secondary fan damage eventually brought about an abrupt loss of thrust, accompanied by compressor stalling, heavy buffeting and the emission of pulsating flames. No 1 engine fire warning, which intruded upon the flight deck 36sec before Midland 92 hit the ground, was initiated by a secondary fire on the outboard exterior of the engine fan casing. It was concluded that inlet damage caused by fan blade debris, combined with unions and seals loosened after prolonged running under conditions of excessive vibration, allowed ignition of atomised fuel or oil sprays by sparks generated by flailing fragmented blades. In contrast, No 2 engine was found to have been running normally when it was shut down, and detailed strip inspection showed that it remained fully serviceable up to ground impact.

The AAIB finally decided that the cause of the Kegworth accident 'was that the operating crew shut down No 2 engine after a fan blade had fractured in the No 1 engine. This engine subsequently suffered a major thrust loss due to secondary fan damage after power had been increased during the final approach to land'. In mitigation, the inquiry acknowledged that the combination of heavy engine vibration, noise, shuddering and an associated smell of fire were outside the pilots' training and experience, that the coincident cessation of noise and shuddering when No 2 engine was throttled back was very misleading, and that the flight crew were not informed of the flames emanating from No 1 engine which were observed by many on board including three cabin attendants.

Kegworth resurrected the old debate about the relative merits of rearward-facing passenger seats. Of the 79 people on board who lived, no fewer than 74 suffered serious injury, some grievously, as parts of the aircraft floor collapsed on impact and seats broke up. If G-OBME had been fitted with 25g rearward-facing seats similar to those on RAF transports such as the VC10, it is very likely that not only would many of the 47 fatalities have been saved but also the toll of head, neck and spinal injuries would have been significantly reduced. The airliner cabin of tomorrow should have aft-facing seats, which are much better at reducing impact injuries, plus lockers underneath rather than overhead to prevent 'death by falling booze'. But it all comes back to cost. A rearward-facing seat with effective restraint is a much heavier proposition than a forward-facer with simple lap strap, so airliners would be able to accommodate fewer people within their payload limits and fewer passengers per trip means higher ticket prices. You pays your money and takes your choice, or rather you pays less money and takes a bigger risk.

Including those improvements to seat design, 31 safety recommendations were to come out of the Kegworth investigation, but the most important lessons must be the human ones for which it is always difficult to legislate. To the world at large, Kegworth should never have happened. Here was a perfectly routine Belfast Shuttle that should have demanded nothing more from its pilots than safe pairs of hands, yet a perfectly functioning engine was shut down and the flight continued on a damaged one that was flown to destruction. The popular verdict was writ large in the media — pilot error.

Arguably the first misjudgement came when, as a problem became apparent in the climb, the commander took control away from the first pilot and disengaged the autopilot. Perhaps, having been a captain with British Midland for 14 years whereas the first officer had flown jet transports for only six months, Capt Hunt felt moved to transfer most of the responsibilities on to his very experienced shoulders. Whatever the reasoning, Capt Hunt took on too much. In trying to cope with all and sundry right down to check calls with fire engines, he denied himself the spare capacity to manage the situation effectively and dispassionately. As non-flying pilot, the commander had also been much more attuned to monitoring engine instruments in the climb than the first officer who had been primarily concerned with handling the aircraft. The AAIB felt that this rapid change of perceptual 'set' could have contributed to the first officer's identification of the wrong engine.

Thereafter an incident progressively turned into a crisis. Although the CVR showed the pilots working together as a team throughout the flight, with decisions being accepted jointly, no attempt seemed to be made to prioritise actions. For example, strict adherence to checklist actions may have averted disaster by highlighting the true engine situation — after all, that is what checklists are for — but such actions were started and suspended for lesser activities such as advising company operations of the situation.

It is undeniable that had there been three instead of two flight crew in the cockpit of Midland 92 — and in particular, a flight engineer with specific responsibility for monitoring the engines — the Kegworth accident would almost certainly not have happened. But while more people up front usually means safer, and more than two engines for them to look after is generally safer still, the loss of Midland 92 was not really brought on by too few aircrew being overstretched. The pilots were going into

Close-up of the wrecked Boeing 737-400 that was once Midland 92. The airliner managed to stagger across the busy motorway but when it finally came to rest at the base of the western embankment, the fuselage effectively shattered into three — the nose section which travelled furthest up the embankment, the centre-section, and the tail which buckled up almost inverted to the right.

their home airfield, an approach they probably knew better than any. Weather was fine and the crew seemed so on top of the situation that the LATCC supervisor believed his staff were dealing with nothing more than a straightforward diversion. However, while the pilots possibly lulled themselves into a false sense of security by making the facts fit their incorrect perception of what had gone wrong, they must have behaved differently had more information been forthcoming from down the back. Certainly the AAIB felt moved to state that if some initiative had been taken by one or more of the cabin crew who had seen the misbehaving left engine, 'this accident could have been prevented'. But prevailing airline training schedules did not cater for co-ordination between cabin and flight crew in such circumstances, and those attendants or passengers who noticed the commander's reference to the right engine may well have assumed that he had made a slip of the tongue, or that the problems they had seen with the left engine were in some way consequential to an important defect with the right, especially as the smell of smoke had dissipated by the time the commander made his announcement. 'I knew we had a problem,' admitted the flight service manager afterwards, 'but no emergency had been declared and the pilots were extremely busy. I thought they would have the information in front of them. It just seems incredible that they would not know which engine was on fire.' So although few down the back knew that 737 pilots could not see the engines from their cockpit, and anyway busy cabin staff rushing about stowing and reassuring could be excused for concentrating on their safety responsibilities rather than announcement details. It would also have taken a pretty confident traveller to stop a flight attendant in full flow to ask in effect, 'Excuse me, but does the pilot really know what he is doing?'

While Capt Hunt admits that 'we certainly made mistakes', he makes the very valid subsequent point, 'why did we make those mistakes?' Only a clear indication from the aircraft instruments would have shaken the pilots' confidence that, by luck and judgement, they had picked the correct engine to shut down. But they saw nothing to give them cause to reconsider what they had done.

To cope with such an ill-defined emergency as befell Midland 92, aircraft cockpit instrumentation needs to be of the best design possible. Certainly Boeing spared no effort in re-equipping their latest version of the world-beating 737, right down to fitting out a high tech cockpit with computer-driven devices in place of old dials with white needles. The only trouble was that no-one reprogrammed the traditional perceptions of old-fashioned pilots. Arguably, little yellow cursors one-third the length of old white needles were too small and discrete to warn effectively.

Furthermore, airliner vibration meters had a history of not being very reliable; on the DC-9, one of the nine aircraft on which Capt Hunt was rated, vibration meters had been so unreliable that pilots were allowed to fly with them disconnected. After Kegworth Capt Hunt was to discover that the latest generation of computer-driven vibration meters were extremely reliable. 'This is something,' he declared philosophically, 'we would have liked to have known at the time.'

Among AAIB's suggested improvements was an attention-getter whenever a vibration indicator reached maximum deflection. As later tests were to show that pilots made 60% more errors while reading 737-400 cockpit dials compared with earlier 737 versions, perhaps others besides Hunt and McClelland would have fallen foul of the apparent failure to align cockpit design theory with practical reality.

But the case for the defence does not end there. One of the 737-400's selling points was that it was merely a more sophisticated version of an old favourite on which airlines would not have to expend a disproportionate amount of crew conversion time. In fact Capt Hunt was to describe British Midland's pilot conversion course as 'nominal' — basically a 35mm slide lecture, with American voice-over, occupying a morning and part of an afternoon. Not much chance of absorbing all the nuances of cabin air conditioning here. Moreover, no simulator training was included for the very simple reason that there was no 400-series simulator available in the UK at the time. Far from Hunt and McClelland learning to cope with prospective -400 problems in safety, the first time they ever saw the problem that brought them down was when it was for real.

Yet there would have been no pilot error if there had been no engine failure in the first place. A more powerful engine having been needed to drive the larger 737-400, the natural solution was to upgrade the tried and tested CFM 56-3 fitted on 300-series aircraft. The only way to increase thrust in these circumstances is to increase the speed at which the engine rotates, but such a small percentage speed increase was needed to generate the requisite extra performance that the engine manufacturers contented themselves with factory test-bed trials. Had they proved the modified 56-3C engine in the air, across the whole range of speeds and environmental influences it would face in reality, they might well have discovered the catastrophic flutter that first manifested itself at Kegworth. Within six months two more 737s, one belonging to Dan Air and the other to British Midland, were to suffer almost identical engine faults. The offending engine version is no longer in production, having been completely redesigned, but the 'fix' came too late to save the lives and reputations lost on Midland 92.

The concluding word on pilot error is best left to Roger Green, one of the foremost experts in this field as Head of Psychology at the RAF's Institute of Aviation Medicine: 'Any pilot's performance is a product of the training he has had and the equipment he has been given to operate. But if you give him training that doesn't equip him to deal with a situation, are you going to call it pilot error if he gets it wrong? And equally, if you give him equipment which isn't as easy to use as it could have been, are you going to blame the pilot who maybe gets it wrong when he doesn't get time to sort it out?'

On top of suffering severe spinal injuries that confine him to a wheelchair, Capt Hunt was told in October 1990 that he was being compulsorily retired. At the same time, First Officer McClelland was told that British Midland was terminating his contract. Both pilots have paid a high price for what the AAIB termed the 'fatal misconception' of which G-OBME engine was good and which was not, though it must be said that 47 of their passengers paid an even higher one. However, if charges of human error are to be thrown around, should they be only levied on the pilots? What about those who designed the cockpit layout and engines, certified them as safe and reliable, and approved the conversion course on to type that did not include a single simulator ride?

At the Kegworth inquest Mr Charles Haddon-Cave, representing the bereaved and survivors, asked Mr Christopher Pollard, a senior AAIB inspector: 'Surely the best way of ensuring that an aircraft and engine are safe before letting it loose on the general public is to fly it around without 126 people on board, isn't it?'

Mr Pollard replied: 'That is a view.'

Replying to another question, Mr Pollard added: 'The manufacturers used a technique in which they had implicit faith which they had used in the past. The fallacy of that has now been exposed.'

Mr Haddon-Cave: 'At considerable cost.'

Mr Pollard: 'I cannot deny that.'

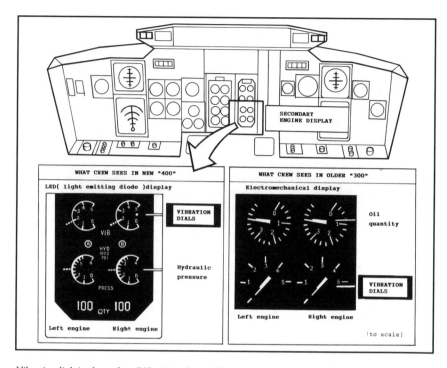

Vibration dials in the modern 737-400 cockpit (left) which relied on computer-driven LED pointers moving around the outside. Vibration levels fed from sensors fitted to each-400 engine are displayed up to a reading of 5 units; a normal reading was a little under 2 units. The older 737-300 used conventional needle pointers (right). Arguably more user-friendly, the -300 needles were certainly three times as long as the LED markers.

Given exchanges such as this, there is a disturbing feeling that Capt Hunt and First Officer McClelland, despite their admitted failings, were left to carry the can of pilot error because that was the cheap and easy option.

It is interesting that on three of the AAIB's more crucial recommendations — attention-getters on vibration instruments, the need for simulators during conversion training, and mandatory instrumented flight tests to demonstrate freedom from damaging vibratory stresses at all altitude conditions and powers which an engine will encounter in service — the CAA has reserved its position. The CAA has a duty to protect the travelling public but at the same time it has a duty to protect and regulate the interests of commercial aviation. Some survivors from Kegworth wonder if these two roles are compatible.

But when all is said and done, Kegworth re-emphasised that the more responsibility is given to machines, the more crews must be alert to inherently stupid devices screwing up. Whatever the computer-driven gizmos on board, engines in particular must always be treated with particular care because there is no going anywhere but down without them.

LOCKERBIE

Between 1946 and 1976, 41 aircraft are known to have been damaged or destroyed by the detonation of an explosive device placed within them. These 41 did not include known hijacking incidents, aircraft shot down in military or paramilitary fashion, unconfirmed cases or aircraft simply missing in suspicious circumstances. In other words, it is a very conservative estimate. Twenty-one of the aircraft were totally destroyed with 785 passengers and crew losing their lives. Around 20% of these fatalities occurred on British registered aircraft (including Hong Kong), but no automatic comfort was to be derived from flying 'Obscure Airlines Inc'. The affected aircraft comprised 21 different types, 16 were piston and 25 turbine engined, and they belonged to 26 airlines divided among 24 countries spread around the world.

Personal rather than political gain seems to have been the primary motive for aerial sabotage in the early days. A typical example was the Canadian Pacific Airlines DC-3 which left Quebec's L'ancienne Lorette airport at 10.25hrs on 9 September 1949. Commanded by Capt Pierre Laurin, one of Canada's younger airline pilots, the DC-3 carried 17 adult passengers, two infants and a crew of four northeast towards Baie Comeau, a small town near the mouth of the St Lawrence.

One routine position report was passed while over the wooded hills bordering the river but then, 40 miles out of Quebec and with the time registering 10.45hrs, a fisherman working the St Lawrence banks and a steamer captain two miles offshore heard a fearful explosion. On looking up they saw the DC-3 burst into flames and disintegrate. With pieces large and small spilling out of a large hole that emerged in its side, the airliner entered an uncontrollable left turn which only ended when it crashed some 500ft up the slope of Mount Torment. Men working a nearby sawmill and railway track raced to where the airliner lay scattered over the wooded mountain side, but it was obvious that they would find no survivors.

Canadian Department of Transport investigators soon agreed that no mechanical or electrical fault caused this accident. The DC-3 had in fact been brought down by an incredibly violent disruption centred on the forward luggage compartment behind the cockpit. Mail was stowed there that day, and further research confirmed that the explosion had been caused by a dynamite charge from a home-made bomb. This had probably been sent in a mailed package.

Investigations were made into the backgrounds of all the disaster victims. Three of the passengers had been senior mining executives, but the spotlight turned on less exalted fry a few days later when a woman named Marguerite Pitre tried to commit suicide in her Quebec flat. Subsequent detective work revealed that she was a friend of one Albert Guay, a Quebec jeweller, whose wife had died in the crash. Within a fortnight Guay was indicted on suspicion of having placed a bomb on the DC-3, and then the whole sorry story came out. Learning how to set off a small bomb from a pal whose job it was to dynamite trees, Guay got Marguerite's brother, a crippled clockmaker, to fabricate a timing device. He then made his wife a present of an airline ticket so she could visit relatives in Baie Comeau, though he probably omitted to mention that for an additional 50 cents he also took out a $10,000 policy on her life, payable to himself. Finally, he made Marguerite Pitre airmail the bomb on the same aircraft.

The only trouble was that once his wife was out of the way, Guay intended to marry a teenage waitress rather than Mrs Pitre. Consequently, two days after the crash Guay told Marguerite Pitre that the police were on to her. He persuaded her to sign a confession and gave her some pills to end her life, and such was Guay's hold over his erstwhile mistress that she almost succeeded in doing his bidding. But although Mrs Pitre lived to tell her tale, it did not do her much good because she eventually accompanied Guay and her brother to the gallows. With hindsight it is amazing that any of them thought they would get away with all this, but the mastermind was not the first to set great store by the maxim that the best place to hide a leaf is in a forest.

Others would follow Albert Guay's example, such as the son who blew up his mother and 43 other people aboard United Airlines Flt 629, out of Denver for Seattle, on the evening of 1 November 1955. Eleven minutes after the DC-6B left Stapleton Airport, an air traffic controller saw a tremendous flash and giant flare light up the sky. Having been pointed towards a detonation, the experts did not take long to find the residue of a dynamite explosion in No 4 baggage hold, or that a piece of luggage belonging to one passenger had been far more comprehensively blown to pieces than any other. In the end the culprit was convicted and executed, but 44 innocent people had died for $37,500 insurance money and an inherited share of a restaurant and house.

For as long as people murder their nearest but no longer dearest, the sabotaged airliner at the bottom of the sea must rival dumping in motorway foundations as among the most effective ways of disposing of a body. Moreover, as airliner cabins became jumbo sized, the work of suspicious investigators became all the more difficult as they faced trawling through the private lives of hundreds of passengers rather than a few dozen. But while modern high speed aircraft have grown in size and sensitivity, airport and airline security have developed apace. A modern Albert Guay will not only find it much harder to obtain explosive material in this terrorist-conscious age, but also he will have to beat the check-in body searches, sniffer dogs and x-ray machines that abound even at minor airports. Even if all that does not put him off, scanning electron microscopy and advanced chemical methods will ensure that his foul deed comes to light so long as the wreckage is recoverable. And with air traffic delays the way they are, not even an airline president can guarantee that any of his aircraft will be over a wide, deep ocean at a particular time. Consequently, it takes a team effort to sabotage an airliner today, and therefore the good news is that the lone murderer or insurance fraudster has been largely squeezed out of the airliner sabotage business over recent years. The bad news is that his or her place has tended to be taken by those who combine the organisational wherewithal with a fanatical desire to make the maximum impact — in other words, people willing to kill for a cause.

But when life was simpler, even political sabotage tended to be directed at specific individuals. Thus, on 11 April 1955, when an Air India Constellation suddenly dived into the South China Sea and fragments of wreckage indicated that an 'infernal device' had been placed in the starboard wheel well, the target appeared to be Chinese communist officials flying from Hong Kong to an Afro-Asian Conference in Bandung. Only in recent years has aerial sabotage been aimed at the general public to make a political statement. A classic case was the loss of Air India Flt 182 en route from Montreal to London on 23 June 1985. The 747 suddenly disintegrated while over the North Atlantic; there was not even time for a 'Mayday' call. The loss of all 329 passengers and crew on board was attributed to Sikh extremists, and the fact that events in the Indian sub-continent could have resulted in mass slaughter to the west of Eire was perhaps a supreme manifestation of how mankind now inhabits a global village.

The air travel business is certainly more complex than before. Just as railway branch lines brought travellers from the back of beyond to meet up with long-distance expresses, so comprehensive airline scheduling now involves short haul aircraft bringing passengers in to certain 'hub' airports for onward transmission far and wide. So it transpired on 21 December 1988 that 109 passengers intending to spend Christmas in the United States were ferried first on Pan Am Flt 103A — a Boeing 727 — from Frankfurt to their jumping off point at London/Heathrow. As the world's busiest international airport, Heathrow made a natural 'hub' and on arrival there, the 727 was taxied southeast of Terminal 3 into stand Kilo 16. Alongside on Kilo 14 was N739PA, a Pan American Boeing 747 christened *Maid of the Seas* which would fly the transatlantic leg. While their baggage was transferred to N739PA, the Frankfurt passengers joined people from other feeder flights waiting to board Flt 103 bound for New York/Kennedy. After six hours on the ground the 747, with Capt Jim MacQuarrie, his co-pilot, flight engineer, 13 flight attendants, 243 passengers and 20 tons of cargo including 43 bags of US mail on board, was pushed back from the stand. The time was 18.04hrs as Flt 103 was cleared to taxy to Runway 27R.

After an air traffic delay, N739PA took-off at 18.25hrs into heavy wintery evening cloud above London. Passing Bovingdon at 6,000ft, Flt 103 was cleared initially to FL120 and then to FL310, where it levelled off at 18.56hrs northwest of Pole Hill VOR. Two minutes later First Officer Ray Wagner established two-way radio contact with Shanwick Oceanic Area Control. Given that the Atlantic is too immense to be monitored by ground radar, all air traffic wishing to cross 'the pond' has to be allocated its own aerial corridor, staggered and separated in time, distance and height from any other, to minimise the risk of collision. Shanwick is the co-ordinating authority out to 30° west, and at 19.02:44hrs clearance delivery officer Tom Fraser passed, 'Clipper 103 is cleared from 59 north 10 west to Kennedy'. He did not receive any acknowledgement, nor did Capt MacQuarrie's crew make any subsequent transmission. Even as Fraser was speaking, Flt 103's secondary radar return disappeared from the radar screen. Multiple primary radar returns were then seen fanning out downwind for a considerable distance. Debris from the 747 was to be strewn along two trails, and as upper winds at the time were westerly at 115kt, lighter debris was eventually found out to the east coast of England some 130km away.

However, the main wreckage of Flt 103 fell on the town of Lockerbie in Dumfriesshire, Scotland. Situated 25 miles north of Carlisle this Annandale market town had a rich farming history dating back to Roman times, but it is not being unkind to say that up to 21 December 1988 Lockerbie had been notable for little more than its August lamb fair. That was all to change, beginning shortly after 19.00hrs as residents heard a rumbling noise like thunder which rapidly increased to deafening proportions. The noise, now resembling a jet engine under power, appeared to come from a meteor-like object trailing flame. It turned out to be N739PA's No 3 engine which finally embedded itself 15ft down in the middle of a street in the northeast part of Lockerbie.

Loading baggage containers into a Pan Am Boeing 747.

A larger delta-shaped object, resembling an aircraft wing (which is what it turned out to be) landed around the same time on the southern edge of town. The complete 196ft-span wing structure created a huge 30ft deep crater on impact, displacing not only Nos 13 and 16 Sherwood Crescent but also over 1,500 tonnes of earth and rock. Much of this fell on the adjacent A74 road between England and Scotland. PC Michael Stryjewski watched it all happen. 'The explosion was the equivalent really of a miniature atomic bomb. A mushroom of cloud and flames formed upwards.' This was not surprising given that inside the wing were tanks still filled with the 200,000lb of fuel necessary for the 3,000-mile Atlantic crossing, and that lot going up sent a fireball several hundred feet across high into the air. Although of relatively short duration, this caused fires up to 350m away, the worst being at Townfoot Garage. A ruptured gas main added to the chaos. It took until 02.22hrs the following day before the main seats of fire were extinguished. Seismic monitoring stations measured the crash at 1.6 on the Richter scale.

Just over 600m from the crater and across the railway tracks that bisected Lockerbie, the section of fuselage situated immediately aft of the wing fell on to Rosebank Crescent housing estate. It was accompanied by both body and the right wing landing gears. A number of palletised luggage containers and their contents showered over the long gardens that separated the two rows of council houses.

The flight deck and forward fuselage section, which remained as a single piece, landed approximately 4km east of Lockerbie. It was found in a field at Tundergarth, lying almost flat on its left side like some fish-head severed at the gills. The first people on the scene found the bodies of the flight crew still strapped in their seats.

The 747's flight deck and nose formed part of what was to be known as the southern wreckage trail. Although this line of debris stretched as far east as the North Sea, most of the significant items were to be found within 30km of the main impact crater. There was also a northern trail, marked at its western end by the lower rear fuselage on Rosebank Crescent and the grouping of Nos 1, 2 and 4 engines where they fell in Lockerbie. The rest of this trail contained mainly wreckage from the rear fuselage, fin and upper portions of both tailplanes, and numerous wing items such as flaps. Beyond 16km east, only items of low weight/high drag such as insulation or paper were found.

Graphic demonstration of the 8ft diameter Pratt & Whitney JT9D engine which powered Pan Am's 747 Clippers. Weighing 8,330lb each, it is amazing that four of these engines falling on Lockerbie did not cause more destruction than they did.

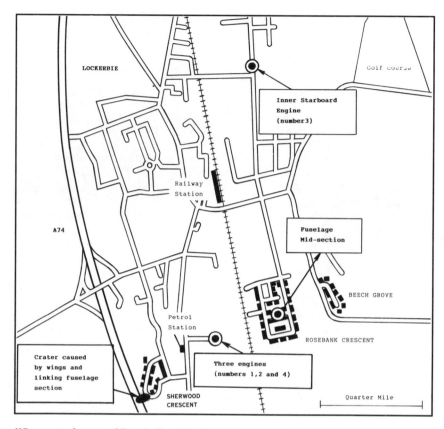

Where major fragments fell on the Scottish border town of Lockerbie.

But inert debris could be cleared away; it was the littering of Lockerbie town and the surrounding rolling countryside with bodies that would haunt searchers and rescuers for the rest of their lives. One news reporter, striding around near Sherwood Crescent in total darkness, found himself standing in what appeared to be a human stomach lying in a garden. Nearby, a woman's scalp hung from a hedge. There were other almost surreal sights, such as the body of a young man in a field, naked save for his underpants. His clothes must have been stripped off as he was sucked out of the disintegrating airliner but lying next to him, despite having fallen the same distance, was an unbroken bottle of Chivas Regal whisky.

In all, 32 nationalities, ranging from US servicemen through college students to honeymooners, died at Lockerbie that night. All 259 people on board Flt 103 perished plus 11 Lockerbie residents; another 5 were injured. Such was the scale of structural damage that 21 domestic properties eventually had to be demolished and an even larger number were to need substantial repairs.

Back at Heathrow, Pan Am executives requisitioned one of their 727s to fly up to the disaster scene. Numbers on board had to be restricted to 65 to land legally at Carlisle airport, and in amongst these favoured few was the AAIB team which started work straight away.

142

N739PA was a conventionally designed long range 'wide body' transport, differing from the majority of its 747 kin only in having more substantial floor beams and a large side loading door; these were US government-funded modifications to enable the aircraft to be quickly converted into a military freight carrier in time of national emergency. Although *Maid of the Seas* was 18 years old, having been the 15th 747 built, and had completed 72,464 flying hours and 16,497 flight cycles, AAIB investigators found its structure to have been in good condition with minimal areas of corrosion. In particular, examination of the torn skin edges of the biggest piece of intact evidence — the complete flight deck and forward fuselage lying in the field at Tundergarth — revealed no pre-existing structural or material defects which could have accounted for separation of this part of the airliner. Controls and switches on the flight deck showed the 747 to have been operating normally in cruising flight, with no signs that the crew had been reacting to rapid decompression, loss of control or any other emergency. In sum, there was no evidence of any aircraft fatigue, defect or malfunction having caused or contributed to the accident. Notwithstanding, it was clear from the beginning that *Maid of the Seas* had blown apart. Among the medical teams flown into Lockerbie on the fateful night was Dr Keith Little, senior consultant at Edinburgh Royal Infirmary's accident and emergency department. 'When I was in the Sherwood Crescent area,' he recounted later, 'the field behind the Crescent was scattered with pieces of human bodies. They were totally destroyed, reduced to 4-6in pieces. These pieces had fallen from a great height and actually had impacted into the ground so (the bodies) had not been destroyed on impact. They had been disintegrated into small pieces a long way up. In my limited experience of such matters, it looked as it there had been a major explosion high up and the pieces had just rained down.'

But while post mortem examination of the victims confirmed that the majority sustained multiple injuries consistent with in-flight disintegration and ground impact, there was no pathological indication of an in-flight fire or evidence that any of the victims had been injured by shrapnel from an explosion. There was also no evidence which unequivocally indicated that passengers or crew had been killed or injured by the effects of blast, nor were signs of explosive blast damage or sooting evident on any part of the structure or interior fittings in the front fuselage lying at Tundergarth.

As AAIB often found, the answer would come not as a bolt from the blue but only after painstaking sifting of all the evidence including careful analysis of data provided by the flight recorders. From the Sherwood Crescent crater out to a host of final resting places all points east, an estimated 4 million pieces of debris were recovered from across 845sq miles of southern Scotland and the borders. It was a magnificent effort which resulted in approximately 90% of N739PA's hull wreckage being taken to the Army Central Ammunition Depot Longtown, about 20 miles from Lockerbie. There it was identified and laid out on the floor in a two-dimensional grid plan reconstruction which revealed damage consistent with an explosion on the lower fuselage left side in the forward cargo bay area.

During wreckage recovery it was relatively straightforward to discriminate between forward and rear cargo hold containers; remains of the latter were almost entirely confined to the town, whereas forward hold contents were scattered along the southern wreckage trail. Out of the forward cargo remains two adjacent containers, one of metal construction and the other fibreglass, were found to exhibit damage likely to have been caused by an explosion. From this it was positively determined that the explosion had occurred within the metal container (serial

Flight deck and nose of Maid of the Seas *lying where they fell in a field at Tundergarth.*

number AVE 4041 PA), the direct effects of which were felt on the forward face of the adjacent fibreglass container and on the left side of the aircraft in the region of station 700.

While this work was in progress an AAIB inspector found, trapped within the folds of the buckled metal container skin, a tiny piece of printed-circuit board which forensic scientists subsequently identified as belonging to a Toshiba radio-cassette player. Inside an improvised explosive device (IED) had been built around the Czechoslovakian-made plastic explosive, Semtex. There was no evidence to indicate that more than one explosive charge had been placed on Flt 103; all other luggage containers only bore damage consistent with ejection into the high speed slipstream or from impact with the ground.

Two-dimensional reconstruction of the fuselage had established that there had been an explosion in the forward hold, and the location of the offending IED had been narrowed down to within a brown Samsonite suitcase loaded in the aft outboard quarter of a specific metal luggage container. Nevertheless, the means by which local explosive damage developed into complete structural break-up of the airliner including separation of its whole forward fuselage section could not be adequately determined without recourse to more elaborate examination. Consequently, wreckage forming a 65ft section of the fuselage (approximately 30ft either side of the explosion) was transported down to Farnborough where it was placed in a specially designed framework to form a fully three-dimensional reconstruction.

Alongside this work came examination of the FDR and CVR that were found close together just to the east of Lockerbie some 15 hours after the accident. All four CVR tracks were listened to for their full 30min duration, but there were no signs of any aircraft abnormalities or unusual crew behaviour. By synchronising air traffic and CVR tapes, it was possible to establish that Shanwick was transmitting Flt 103's trans-Atlantic clearance when, at 19.02:50hrs plus or minus a second, a sudden loud sound was heard on the cockpit area microphone. It was concluded that this sound was directly associated with detonation of the IED and signified the break-up of N739PA's structure. Recording stopped almost immediately afterwards, most likely when electrical power ceased to be available.

ATC tapes for the period 19.02hrs to 19.05hrs revealed no unexplained sounds that might have been attempted distress calls. Four radar sites were painting N739PA as it approached overhead Lockerbie, and it was possible to tell from the information they passed to the screen in front of Prestwick controller Alan Topp that Flt 103 progressed normally until secondary surveillance radar was lost. The last transponder return from the 747, timed at 19.02:46.9hrs, identified it at FL310: on the next sweep, when the aircraft would have been some 1nm further along track, the secondary response had been replaced by four primary returns. Experts concluded from this that the airliner was no longer intact and that items had been ejected at high speed, probably to both left and right.

Finally there was evidence from the engines. No 3 engine fell 1,100m north of the rest but all four struck Lockerbie with considerable force. No 2 engine, which fell closest to the crater, revealed blade deformity consistent with a major airflow disturbance whilst delivering power. Its air intake interior also bore paint smears and clear evidence of a strike by a length of cable similar in diameter and strand size to that attached to the closure curtain on a baggage container. This damage was readily explained by the fact that No 2 engine intake was positioned some 27ft aft and 30ft outboard of the explosion site. Given the position of the IED and the aircraft's groundspeed of 434kt, No 2 engine would have ingested significantly-sized debris within milli-seconds of the explosion.

All four engines revealed a greater degree of blade tip rubbing on the fan cases than noted by Pratt & Whitney specialists during any previous investigation. To account for this, *Maid of the Seas* must have undergone a marked nose-down pitch change combined with a roll to the left well within five seconds of the detonation. This would have inclined the axes of airflow sufficiently to produce tip rub damage while all four engines remained attached to the wings.

Co-ordination of the findings from all this evidence suggested the following 747 disintegration sequence. The detonation of an IED, containing 1Kg of Semtex and situated approximately 25in from the fuselage skin, generated a high intensity shock wave which expanded out of the baggage container downwards and rearwards. On reaching the inner surface of the aircraft skin, energy was partially absorbed by punching a 18-20in diameter 'starburst petalled' hole in the forward lower port fuselage structure and disrupting the cabin floor. Major cracks then propagated out following puncturing of the pressure cabin, but the IED's impact did not finish there. While much of its remaining energy would have carried on out into the atmosphere, more than enough was returned inside the fuselage as a reflected shock wave. There it joined with high temperature gases to travel along ducting and cavities to produce significant structural damage in areas remote from the explosion site. The combined effect of what might be termed direct and indirect explosive forces destroyed the structural integrity of the forward fuselage. 'Little more then remained between stations 560 and 760 than the window belts,' concluded the AAIB, 'although much of the cargo-hold floor structure appears to have remained briefly attached to the aircraft.'

Three-dimensional reconstruction of Boeing 747 N739PA in a Farnborough hangar.

Research carried out by the Cranfield Institute of Technology showed debris on the longer and straighter southern wreckage trail to have been released while N739PA was initially disintegrating but still in level flight. It then pitched down markedly and rolled left, probably as a result of inputs applied to the flying control cables by movement of the structure. This manoeuvre imparted torsional and bending loads such that the belt of 40 windows on the left of the aircraft 'popped'. The barely retained forward fuselage then deflected to the right about the starboard window belt before peeling away from the structure at station 800. Separation was complete within three seconds of the explosion, and as it fell away the lower nose section struck No 3 engine with sufficient force to detach it from its pylon. Pieces and contents of the front fuselage also struck the tail surfaces, substantially damaging them in the process. The separated fuselage structures continued to break apart in the descent.

Reaching the vertical around 19,000ft, the rapidly decomposing airliner then started to lose its tail fin, probably as a result of flutter. Most of the 747 disintegrated while descending nearly vertically from 19,000 to 9,000ft, the pieces falling straight down to final various impact points. It was during this phase that the northern wreckage trail came into existence; although narrower than its southern counterpart, it eventually grew to the stage where it could be described as 'almost like a carpet laid across the countryside'.

Once established in the vertical dive, the rest of the airliner's fin torque box came apart, possibly allowing the remainder of the aircraft to yaw sufficiently to cause side load separation of Nos 1, 2 and 4 engines with their pylons. Break-up of the rear fuselage occurred during this phase, again possibly due to yaw induced loads, allowing a section of cabin floor and baggage hold plus three landing gear units to

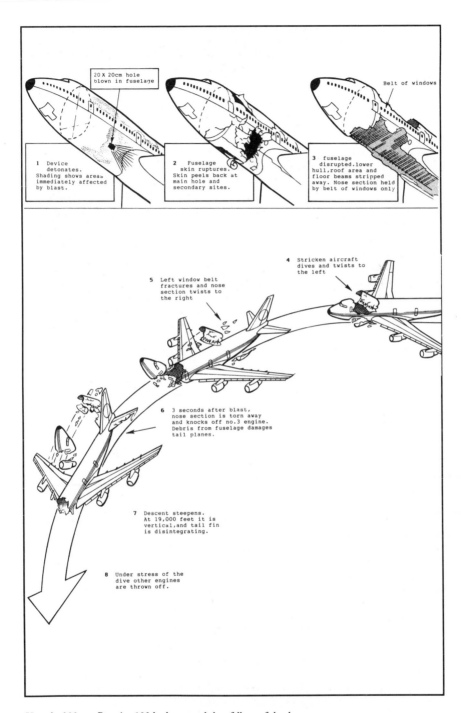

1 Device detonates. Shading shows areas immediately affected by blast.

20 X 20cm hole blown in fuselage

2 Fuselage skin ruptures. Skin peels back at main hole and secondary sites.

3 fuselage disrupted. lower hull, roof area and floor beams stripped away. Nose section held by belt of windows only

Belt of windows

4 Stricken aircraft dives and twists to the left

5 Left window belt fractures and nose section twists to the right

6 3 seconds after blast, nose section is torn away and knocks off no.3 engine. Debris from fuselage damages tail planes.

7 Descent steepens. At 19,000 feet it is vertical, and tail fin is disintegrating.

8 Under stress of the dive other engines are thrown off.

How the 300-ton Pan Am 103 broke-up and then fell out of the sky.

fall on Rosebank Terrace. Highest density items such as the 17,500lb nose section or the engines and pylons, each of which weighed about 13,500lb, fell closest to the town. The main wing structure, virtually the only major part left, now 'flew' on unencumbered until it hit Sherwood Crescent at a high yaw angle. A mere 94sec elapsed between the explosion and the first piece of wreckage landing on Lockerbie.

The investigators concluded that the detonation of an IED some seven minutes after Flt 103 reached cruising level led directly to the destruction of *Maid of the Seas* with the loss of 270 lives. Five remedial measures, described as 'suggestions intended to stimulate thought and discussion,' were offered by the AAIB. Four concerned flight data recorders, aimed at keeping them working during and after an explosion such that, for example, they did not dump data in the event of a power loss. The final recommendation was that manufacturers and airworthiness authorities undertook a systematic study with a view to identifying measures that might mitigate the effects of explosive devices and improve the tolerance of aircraft structures and systems to explosive damage. A first thought was that baggage container design be modified to be more energy absorbent and/or to release explosive energy directly towards a fuselage blow-out panel.

While half the AAIB's investigative strength, supported by 22 separate organisations around the world, inquired into the worst air disaster in British history, possibly the largest murder hunt the world has ever seen ran in parallel. No organisation has ever claimed responsibility for what the Sheriff Principal of South Strathclyde, Dumfries and Galloway described as a 'criminal act of murder', but after a thorough investigation, of which the Scottish dimension alone cost £8.5 million, some felt confident enough to make a pretty good guess as to the culprits.

It was undeniable that luggage pallet AVE 4041 PA, holding the bomb in the Samsonite suitcase, had been loaded at Heathrow, but Special Branch detectives established that none of the bags in it originated in London. Most had been transferred off feeder Flt 103A from Frankfurt, but there were seven or eight bags in the bottom layer which had come direct from other airports.

Responsibility for resolving the confusion fell to the forensic scientists of the Royal Armament Research and Development Establishment (RARDE). Based at Fort Halstead on the North Kentish Downs overlooking Sevenoaks, RARDE's expertise stretched back to 1605 when it was set up to investigate the gunpowder plot to blow up the Houses of Parliament. Two of Britain's foremost explosives experts and veteran investigators of many an IRA bombing, Alan Feraday and Thomas Hayes, took charge of the Lockerbie work. Weeks of detailed wreckage sifting was to yield a fragment of charred loudspeaker grill here, and a tiny screw melted into a suitcase there, which eventually combined the confirm the presence of the IED in the Toshiba radio-cassette recorder.

RARDE next had to establish the exact location of the lethal suitcase within luggage pallet AVE 4041 PA to determine where it had been loaded. After moulding varying amounts of Semtex into Toshiba radios, Alan Feraday built five bombs which were wrapped in clothes and packed into five Samsonite suitcases. Each suitcase was loaded in a pallet similar to AVE 4041 PA and the bombs blown up. 'Results clearly indicate', concluded the test report, 'that the case containing the IED was not in the bottom layer of passenger luggage.' This meant that the fatal Samsonite had come from Frankfurt.

Going back another stage, RARDE eventually concluded that this case 'probably arrived at Frankfurt on a flight or an airline other than Pan Am' and was then 'inter-lined' on to Pan Am Flt 103A to London. This had been a crucial stage in the plot because the switch between airlines was carried out without the suitcase being identified as unaccompanied. But in Frankfurt's defence, although luggage transferred on to Flt 103 at Heathrow was subject to x-ray screening, there was no reconciliation procedure there either to ensure that inter-line passengers and their baggage travelled on the same aircraft.

After more months of meticulous work on fibres fused into Samsonite fragments, RARDE was able to draw up a detailed list of clothing that had been with the bomb in the suitcase. A blue Babygro rompersuit provided the single most important lead — a label with the inscription 'Malta Trading Company'. This information was aligned with the computerised printout itemising the 111 bags which had been loaded on to Flt 103A from Frankfurt. The list showed that one bag had been transferred from Air Malta Flt KM180 which had flown in from Valletta that lunchtime, but no passenger who boarded Flt 103A had come from Malta.

On 30 August 1989, a Scottish detective flew to the Mediterranean to visit the Malta Trading Company and another clothing manufacturer located on an industrial estate in Birkirkara. It was his lucky day because a numbered trouser fragment from the Samsonite remains was found to match an order delivered to Messrs Gauci on 18 November 1988. The detective moved two miles downhill to the Gauci shop where the owners remembered a man buying a large amount of clothing, the details of which exactly matched the items Alan Feraday had identified as being inside the Samsonite suitcase right down to the blue Babygro. The man was described as Libyan, aged about 50, clean shaven and well dressed who bought the clothes 29 days before the bombing. It had been raining outside and as the 'Libyan' stepped towards the shop door, he had turned back and asked for an umbrella.

Five umbrellas were recovered from the Lockerbie crash, and once they were retrieved from the property store for re-examination, a black one appeared to show signs of blast damage. It was driven by police car to Fort Halstead where within hours RARDE discovered minute Babygro fibres embedded in its nylon surface. All the signs pointed to the bomb being placed inside the unaccompanied bag from Malta.

Abu Talb, a senior member of the Popular Front for the Liberation of Palestine-General Command (PFLP-GC), was in Malta at the crucial time. It was originally mooted that radicals in Iran hired the Damascus-based PFLP-GC to attack an American airliner in retaliation for the shooting down by the USS *Vincennes* of a commercial Iranian airbus over the Straits of Hormuz on 3 July 1988. It had all been a tragic mistake; the Airbus was mistaken for a potentially hostile Iranian F-14. Veiled apologies were of little avail. The loss of 290 Muslim passengers — 66 of whom were children — was especially inflammatory because they were pilgrims being ferried to Mecca for Id Al-Adha, the main religious festival of the year, in four days' time. 'To them,' said one authority, 'these dates and calendars are very important,' so it may not have been coincidental that Flt 103 was downed four days before Christmas Day. But on 14 November 1991, Britain and the US pronounced two Libyans responsible for bombing Pan Am Flt 103. Both were said to be members of Libya's intelligence service, and their probable motive was retaliation for the American bombing raid on Tripoli in 1986.

Much has been made of the apparent fact that the bombing of Flt 103 took place against the backdrop of warnings that trouble was brewing. Apart from the security bulletin describing the PFLP's Toshiba IED, on 5 December 1988 an anonymous telephone caller told the US Embassy in Helsinki that within the next fortnight a Finnish woman would carry a bomb aboard a Pan Am aircraft flying from Frankfurt to the US. Although this warning was publicised around US embassies in Europe, Finnish police quickly determined that the call was unreliable. Subsequent investigations by other governments also concluded that the call was in no way connected to Flt 103, and President Bush's Commission into the Lockerbie disaster found no evidence suggesting otherwise. As an aside, if airlines went public every time they received a potentially threatening call, at best they would soon stand accused of gratuitous scaremongering and at worst it would close down air traffic around the world.

Whatever the true story of Lockerbie, those of us not privy to the murky world of double bluff and political expediency are unlikely ever to hear it. But that should not invalidate the safety lessons, the first of which is that more stringent efforts to reconcile bags with passengers might have foiled the terrorist attack. When Flt 103 left Heathrow's Terminal 3, no-one knew that the 747 was carrying an extra bag that had been inter-lined through to Pan Am from elsewhere. Months before, Pan Am stopped reconciling or searching inter-line baggage in favour of simply x-raying it. Airline executives said that the FAA's Director of Aviation Security had given verbal authority for the change, but the official in question denied this.

To rely solely on x-raying of inter-line baggage was, in the judgement of the Sheriff Principal, a defect in the system which contributed to the 270 deaths at Lockerbie. 'However,' he continued, 'I do not think any finding that a general laxity in security on the part of Pan Am was relevant to the circumstances of the deaths would be justified in the absence of any evidence as to how their performance compared with that of other airlines.' Not that they did not pay; Pan Am's Chairman, Thomas Plaskett, was to put the cost to his airline of the Lockerbie bombing at almost $250 million and was to play a part in the airline's ultimate financial collapse in December 1991.

Arguably, the best deterrent would be to convince all future bombers that no matter who they are or whence they flee, world revulsion combined with international police co-operation will ensure that they are caught and dealt with severely. But that day is a long way off. The sad fact remains that none of the killers of the 270 people who died at Lockerbie have yet been arraigned in court, and even if they ever are, convicted terrorists do not seem to stay in prison for long before they are exchanged or released on some pretext or other. Even capital punishment holds little terror for the suicide bomber or prospective martyr. Those clever enough to hide the evidence of their villainy are even harder to bring to justice: if Flt 103 had blown up while over the sea, the AAIB thought it 'very probable that the relatively few small items of structure, luggage and clothing showing positive evidence of the detonation of an explosive device would not have been recovered'. Sadly, as with all aspects of flight safety, rhetoric is no substitute for effective action. Defence against the airline bomber, like a suit of chain mail, must come from various interlocking parts.

The first step is to build more protection into and around the vitals of every airliner. This is not easy; even though *Maid of the Sea*s had a beefed-up main deck floor as part of its military modifications, the strengthened beams did not save her over Lockerbie. The recent survival of a Thai Airways Airbus Industrie A300, after a grenade exploded in a lavatory near the rear pressure-cabin bulkhead, shows that the latest generation of airliners are proving stronger than their predecessors. But it is impossible to aim for a completely armoured airliner; it would probably be too heavy to get off the ground for a start. If enough Semtex gets on board, there is very little that you can do, so the next link in the armour is to do everything to stop explosives getting on board in the first place.

A large container holding baggage awaiting loading on to Flt 103 was left open and unattended at Heathrow for half an hour. The eradication of unthinking weaknesses such as this is just as crucial to the fight against terrorism as the scattering of high tech around every airport. For example many hopes rest on thermal neutron analysis (TNA) to detect plastic explosives. It has been estimated that to install TNA machines at 40 international airports would cost $175 million; the only trouble is, the bomb that destroyed Flt 103 is believed to have weighed half or less than the amount of Semtex a TNA machine would reliably detect under normal working conditions. Human vigilance, in the form of passengers never letting luggage out of their sight or accepting apparently intrusive questioning and examination of bag contents with a good grace, is just as much the key to survival as reliance on magic machines.

Good security makes demands. Work is being done on a vapour detection system for checking for people with explosives. Tests are promising, but the time it takes to check each passenger — 30sec — has been deemed too long. Once again we return to the old question about how much individuals should be willing to contribute towards their own safety. Too much expensive security risks adding unacceptable sums to airline tickets, but on top of that too much time spent hanging around airports waiting for often desultory and brusquely administered security checks are just as likely to put prospective travellers off.

Pan Am's senior Vice President, Tony Mule, highlighted a related problem that airlines face once the memory of the latest disaster fades from the public memory:

'It has been proved time and time again that a passenger's first real measure of airline performance is whether his or her flight departs when the schedule says it is going to depart...All they know is they plan to be on time and expect Pan Am to keep them on time. When departure time comes and goes, and the plane is still at the gate, their concern becomes a black mark on Pan Am's record for the public to see.'

Perhaps, when all is said and done, it might forestall a lot of nugatory expense and attempts to change human nature if the travelling public refuses to have anything to do with Mao Tse Tung's aphorism, 'Kill one, scare a thousand'. By all means apply common sense precautions, but there can come a time when a civilised travel system can do no more. The threat must always be kept in perspective, and the best way to do that is to temper the shock/horror headlines with the fact that more people die every year in Britain from inhaling other people's cigarette smoke (over 300) than were killed at Lockerbie. As pioneer aviator Wilbur Wright said way back in 1908, 'If you are looking for perfect safety, you will do well to sit on the fence and watch the birds'.

AFTERTHOUGHT

Notwithstandlng everything written so far, the last 40 years have witnessed a quantum jump in airline reliability and safety. It is not so long ago that a pilot flying the latest Boeing Stratocruiser could just about cross the Atlantic in 16hr given a good tail wind. Even then he might have to land at night in fog-bound Europe with nothing more sophisticated than paraffin flares to mark runways. Everything on board, from the prone-to-fail piston engines to the black boxes which provided the navigator with only groundspeed and drift, were crude and rudimentary. Little wonder that in 1950 there were just under 18 deaths per million passengers carried.

Jet airliners such as the Boeing 707, which could transport more than double the 'Strat's' complement almost twice as fast at levels well above the worst of the weather, revolutionised air travel. Yet though reliability conferred by the emerging jet age halved the number of passenger deaths per million by the early-1960s, it was only the start. Technology has got better and better. For example autopilots combined with autothrottle can now fly a whole profile from take-off to landing, while electronic 'glass' cockpits enable much more data of far greater accuracy to be presented to pilots. Not content with ushering in a brave new world, technology has also improved the old; the aero engines of 1990 are 10 times more reliable than those of even a decade ago.

But although science and technology have done us proud, improvements can have drawbacks. On 4 January 1990 a Northwest Airlines Boeing 727 landed safely at Tampa Airport, Florida, having diverted there after the starboard engine fell off. Modern mountings are designed such that if an engine seizes up, compressor/turbine rotational energy is allowed to break the engine away rather than risk damage to the airframe. In pre-empting one potential risk, a new one could emerge in the shape of a 3,400lb engine dropping 35,000ft on to an unsuspecting world below.

Although airline deaths are now under one per million passengers carried, 1989 was the decade's second worst flight safety year with 1,764 deaths from 55 accidents. Even after deducting those involving sabotage or other unlawful interference, over 1,000 of the remaining 1,450 fatalities resulted from aircrew error. Research by the International Air Transport Association confirms that some 70% of take-off and landing accidents stem from the same cause. Human failing remains aviation safety's last great frontier.

On 25 January 1990, Avianca Flt 052 left Medellin, Colombia en route for John F. Kennedy International Airport, New York. While working New York Air Route Traffic Control Center, the 707 crew briefed that they were low on fuel and could not make their Boston alternate. 'I think we need priority (into Kennedy)', a flight crew member said.

As Avianca Flt 052 was being vectored for an instrument landing on Kennedy's Runway 22 Left, Flight Engineer Moyano reviewed the procedure for executing a missed approach with low fuel. He told Capt Cavledes, who was flying the 707, that 'the power must be applied slowly and to avoid rapid accelerations and to have a minimum nose-up attitude'. The time was about 21.04hrs.

Kennedy Tower cleared Flt 052 to land at 21.20:01hrs. It is unclear from the CVR whether the captain was wearing his radio headset, so there was confusion as to what he heard and what not. Thus at 21.20:21hrs he is heard to ask, 'Are we cleared to land, no?'

'Yes sir', replied his co-pilot, First Officer Clotz, who was definitely using his headset, 'we are cleared to land.'

Several times on the approach, Tower asked Flt 052 to increase speed to 150kt. Eventually ATC had to take the airliner behind, TWA Flt 801, out of the approach sequence because it was gaining on Flt 052. Terminal Radar Approach Control (TRACON) had advised the Avianca crew of a 10kt wind shear on the approach between 1,500 and 500ft, and at 21.22:57 the co-pilot said, 'This is the wind shear'. The 707 had repeatedly dropped below the glideslope and shortly afterwards the GPWS sounded. 'Where is the runway?' cried the captain, followed three seconds later by, 'I don't see, I don't see it. Give me the landing gear up, smooth with the nose'.

'Smooth with the nose, smooth with the nose, smooth with the nose,' enjoined the flight engineer.

'We don't have fuel,' the captain said.

The crew executed a missed approach, climbing to 2,000ft and turning south. At 21.24:06hrs the captain said to the co-pilot, 'Digale que estamos en emergencia (tell them we are in emergency)'.

'That's right on to one eight zero on the heading', was all the co-pilot said in response to the Tower's instruction two seconds later. 'Advise him we are emergency', repeated the captain at 21.24:22. Two seconds later he asked, 'Did you tell him?'

'Yes sir . . . I already advised him.'

Forty five seconds later the captain said, 'Advise him we don't have fuel'. The co-pilot contacted TRACON and informed them of the missed approach. Fifteen seconds later, after acknowledging an instruction to climb and maintain 3,000ft, the co-pilot said, 'Ah, we're running out of fuel sir'.

At 21.26:35hrs TRACON said, 'Avianca zero five two, ah, I'm gonna bring you about 15 miles northeast and then turn you back on to the approach . . . Is that fine with you and your fuel?'

'I guess so,' the co-pilot responded, 'thank you very much.'

'What did he say?' the captain asked.

'The guy is angry,' replied the flight engineer.

'Fifteen miles in order to get back to the localiser,' said the co-pilot.

About four minutes later the co-pilot misunderstood an instruction to turn on to finals meant for TWA Flt 801. Seventeen seconds passed before TRACON corrected the mistake by turning the 707 north. At 21.31:02hrs, Avianca Flt 052 became No 2 in the pattern.

One minute 28 sec later Flt 052's No 4 engine flamed out, followed almost immediately by the flight engineer saying, 'Flame out on number three, essential on number two, on number one'.

'Show me the runway,' called the captain.

'Avianca zero five two, turn left heading two five zero intercept the localiser.'

The sound of an engine spooling down was heard before the CVR ceased business less than half a minute later. The 707 crashed into a hill on Long Island at about 21.35hrs, killing 73 people including the flight crew.

Nothing was found to be wrong with the aircraft, nor was its fuel contaminated. In other words, without human error this accident would not have happened. Moreover, the loss of Avianca Flt 052 contained some classic human error symptoms. First, the crew was aware that fuel was low long before they carried out the missed approach, so the basic problem hardly crept up unannounced. Yet having appreciated the problem, they did next to nothing to counter it. Despite being repeatedly urged to declare a fuel emergency to ATC, the co-pilot never did so. The captain never appreciated this because he did not appear to know what was, and more importantly what was not, being broadcast. Not content with that oversight, the captain then flew pretty inadequately under the circumstances. He knew that he had only enough certain fuel for one approach yet he stayed consistently low and slow, added no wind shear factor, and flew such an inaccurate ILS that he was unable to find the runway when he needed it most.

Most probably the failure to declare a fuel emergency stemmed from one of the greatest causes of human error — pride. It takes courage to admit publicly to having fouled up, but there can come a time in a crisis when not to cry for help is about as useful as throwing a drowning man both ends of the rope.

Yet before the cry goes up for more legislation to prevent this sort of occurrence, it is vital that pilots are left with a large measure of flexibility and responsibility so that they do not become mere monitors in whom we risk not being able to rely when we need them most. Additionally, aviation options are rarely clear cut enough to sit comfortably in a legislative straight-jacket.

In March 1990 a Qantas Boeing 747-400 with 360 passengers and 21 crew on board approached western Europe after fighting headwinds for 13hrs all the way from Singapore. Having used an excess of fuel in the process, the captain had to decide whether he could still make it to Heathrow or would need to top-up in Amsterdam or Copenhagen. After being advised by Belgian and British ATC that the weather was good over southeast England and that there were no traffic delays, he elected to continue on into Heathrow.

Approaching Clacton on the Essex coast, the captain received clearance for a straight-in approach to land. But while descending over Ongar, he was suddenly told to stack for up to 20min over Lambourne beacon. With insufficient fuel to comply, he promptly declared an emergency. The 747 was given priority across London, landing with a mere four tons of fuel slopping around in the tanks.

This was nothing like a near-disaster, but it could have been if the captain had complied with ATC stacking instructions without thinking through their implications. The incident typifies the problems faced by everyone involved with airline operations day in and day out. The weather can never be trusted to behave, air traffickers can never predict with certainty when their kit may go on the blink or some other unforeseen circumstance ruin their day, and if the captain had taken the ultra-safe option and diverted into Amsterdam, he risked 360 raspberries from down the back.

Which harks back to the contradiction that often exists between the real world and perfect safety. Operators want to run safe services, but their prime aim is to make a profit. Airport authorities and aerospace manufacturers could expend enormous sums without necessarily producing a meaningful safety improvement. As for the travelling public, they want to travel safely but they do not want to turn up three hours early to run the gauntlet of increased security measures; they do not want to miss out on duty frees; they chafe at the limit of one small piece of cabin baggage per person and they certainly do not relish being reminded about potential risks during preflight briefings.

But such difficulties should not be used to excuse inaction. There is much that can be done to cut down human error, especially as sins of error or omission are not confined to the air. Dozy individuals still drive fuel tankers or other airfield vehicles into parked aircraft far too often for us to have any great faith in man having become more reliable over the years. Aircraft designers must take account of this. For example, Boeing is producing a new 777 airliner for first delivery in 1995. Among its optional extras this 360-seat jet will have folding wingtips to enable it to operate from cramped terminals. As sure as anything, somewhere, sometime a Boeing 777 will taxy out with a wing not properly locked and secure for flight after having been folded. Whether this results from trying too hard to meet a departure time or from somebody being lax is relatively unimportant; the incident will happen and the time to build in a guarantee that this novel feature never endangers a 777 is during the design stage rather than much more frantically and expensively after the event.

Although it will have little appeal to those seeking headline-grabbing quick fixes, most human error accidents result from mundane causes rather than from people being at full stretch. Frustration and boredom are particular reasons why humans are the weakest links in the safety chain. After being held for half an hour awaiting air traffic clearance to fly from Frankfurt to Madrid, a flight crew gets frustrated. Pressure mounts to claw back time, some potentially dangerous corner is cut, and an incident occurs for which the pilot carries the can. But the delay, which generated the frustration in the first place, came about because that short flight had to be cleared through 10 air traffic zones. Given that a flight of the same duration across the US might involve just two, should not a system which keeps European skies stifled in the grip of 42 ATC control zones operated by 22 different countries not also be arraigned as an accessory in the safety dock?

When it comes to boredom, the simplest sorties are the ones to watch because flowing adrenalin keeps pilots on their toes. It may be churlish to say so but technology seems to have converted nearly every airline trip into a relatively simple operation. Arousal levels are becoming too low and even when striding half way round the globe, it is easy to forget that you are in an aircraft hurtling through space.

In other words, most pilots are finding lack of challenge built into the chic new flight deck technology. But where to go from here? Another brain on the Kegworth flight deck may well have prevented the accident, and many would argue that airlines should revert to three-crew operations in an effort to reduce the chances of human error. But would the extra manpower costs, which would be enormous, really bring a measurable benefit? In the automated 'glass' cockpit of the future, three bored crew might be actually worse than two.

There is a good case for redressing the balance back from hardware to humans. If a pilot rarely handles an aircraft because its flight systems have been made to do everything better, he could become dangerous if and when those magical systems fail and he is faced with a non-standard situation. Rather than spend money on more flight crew, perhaps airlines should concentrate their limited financial resources on providing 'hack' aircraft on which current staff could fly manually every month minus passengers. Only 'hands-on' time in the air confers the physical and mental ability to control and navigate with confidence and competence.

Flight safety is a bit like virtue; everybody is in favour but only so as long as it does not make too many tedious demands. But if flight safety's true worth, as *Flight* magazine would have it, is observed only in its absence, then it is too intangible to be sold as anything other than a cause. And it is too late to become a true believer only when a crisis crops up.

There is no common link apparent in recent fatal airline accidents. However, growth in air travel during the late-1980s drained experienced pilots from regional airlines. Given that the traditional excess of pilots from the military seems, at least in the US, to be drying up, some experts express concern about pilot inexperience. 'We're starting to see evidence,' said a senior FAA official in 1989, 'of what I would call the operational accident where perhaps more experience in the cockpit would have made the difference.' In an ideal world, pilot pairing in the cockpit should always ensure that two inexperienced pilots are not assigned to the same flight, but life is no longer that straightforward. Some airlines now have more than 7,000 pilots, so it is even more crucial that individuals rather than some large organisation assume personal responsibility for safety.

This process must start with education because there are no new accidents, only new pilots. Given that 'experience', in the words of Dean Inge, 'is a good teacher but her fees are very high', the wise pilot learns not so much from his own mistakes as from those of others. It is much more cost effective to 'think' flight safety regularly — debating 'what if?' with other flight crew members, and possibly learning something new about your aircraft's foibles at the same time — than to take the crash course.

Flowing from knowledge and aircraft handling ability comes the confidence to make the right decisions. Combine this with the wise words of Mark Twain — 'it is better to be careful a hundred times than to get killed once' — and you acquire a 'gut' instinct about what is right and wrong that stems from knowing what the hell you are doing. All of which finally confers the strength of character to stand fast in the face of unpopular decisions that just happen to be right. It is a virtuous circle, but it does not come without effort. Irrespective of natural ability, everybody has to work at operating aeroplanes. Whichever way you look at it, flight safety is no accident.

SELECT BIBLIOGRAPHY

Ralph Barker, *Great Mysteries of the Air* (Chatto & Windus, 1966)
Stephen Barlay, *Aircrash Detective* (Hamish Hamilton, 1969)
David Beatty, *Stranger Encounters* (Methuen, 1982)
Alan Bramson, *Master Airman* (Airlife, 1985)
Andrew Brookes, *Crash!* (Ian Allan Ltd, 1991)
J. G. Chandler, *Fire and Rain* (Texas Monthly Press, 1986)
S. T. Deane, *Fire in the Cabin* (1988)
Len Deighton and Arnold Schwartzman, *Airshipwreck* (Jonathan Cape,1978)
Harold Dick with Douglas H. Robinson, *Graf Zeppelin and Hindenburg* (Smithsonian Institution Press, 1985)
A. J. Jackson, *Avro Aircraft Since 1908* (Putnam, 1965)
David Johnston, *Lockerbie* (Bloomsbury, 1989)
Fred Jones, *Air Crash* (Robert Hale, 1985)
Clayton and K. S. Knight, *Plane Crash* (Greenberg, 1958)
Fred McClement, *Anvil of the Gods* (J. B. Lippincott, 1964)
Fred McClement, *It Doesn't Matter Where You Sit* (Cassell, 1970)
Michael M. Mooney, *The Hindenburg* (Hart-Davis, MacGibbon, 1972)
Harold Penrose, *Architect of Wings* (Airlife, 1985)
Douglas H. Robinson, *Giants in the Sky* (G. T. Foulis, 1973)
Oliver Stewart, *Danger in the Air* (Routledge & Kegan Paul, 1958)
Stanley Stewart, *Air Disasters* (Ian Allan Ltd, 1986)
Dale M. Titler, *Wings of Mystery* (Dodd, Mead & Co, 1966)
Betty Tootell, *All Four Engines Have Failed* (Andre Deutsch, 1985)
Arthur Weingarten, *The Sky is Falling* (Hodder and Stoughton, 1977)

Finally, *Disaster in the Air* could not have been written without access to the detailed investigations and conclusions contained within MCAP, AAIB, Dept of Commerce and NTSB Accident Reports. I am eternally grateful to the men and women who painstakingly compiled them and if any false conclusions are drawn from their labours, the errors are mine alone.

INDEX